Legacies of
World War II
in South and East Asia

The **Institute of Southeast Asian Studies (ISEAS)** was established as an autonomous organization in 1968. It is a regional centre dedicated to the study of socio-political, security and economic trends and developments in Southeast Asia and its wider geostrategic and economic environment.

The Institute's research programmes are the Regional Economic Studies (RES, including ASEAN and APEC), Regional Strategic and Political Studies (RSPS), and Regional Social and Cultural Studies (RSCS).

ISEAS Publishing, an established academic press, has issued almost 2,000 books and journals. It is the largest scholarly publisher of research about Southeast Asia from within the region. ISEAS Publishing works with many other academic and trade publishers and distributors to disseminate important research and analyses from and about Southeast Asia to the rest of the world.

Legacies of
World War II
in South and East Asia

edited by
David Koh Wee Hock

ISEAS

Institute of Southeast Asian Studies
Singapore

First published in Singapore in 2007 by ISEAS Publishing
Institute of Southeast Asian Studies
30 Heng Mui Keng Terrace
Pasir Panjang
Singapore 119614

E-mail: publish@iseas.edu.sg
Website: <http://bookshop.iseas.edu.sg>

The responsibility for facts and opinions in this publication rests exclusively with the authors and their interpretations do not necessarily reflect the views or the policy of the publisher or its supporters.

ISEAS Library Cataloguing-in-Publication Data

Legacies of World War II in South and East Asia / edited by David Koh.
    Papers originally presented at a Conference on World War II : Transient and Enduring Legacies for East and Southeast Asia 60 Years On, organized by ISEAS, Singapore on 4 August 2005.
    1. World War, 1939–1945—East Asia—Congresses.
    2. World War, 1939–1945—Southeast Asia—Congresses.
    I. Koh W. H., David (Wee Hock, David)
    II. Institute of Southeast Asian Studies.
    III. Conference on World War II : Transient and Enduring Legacies for East and Southeast Asia 60 Years On (2005 : Singapore)
    IV. Title: Legacies of World War Two in South and East Asia
D767 L49   2007

ISBN: 978-981-230-328-8 (soft cover)
ISBN: 978-981-230-468-1 (hard cover)
ISBN: 978-981-230-457-5 (PDF)

Cover photo: Memorial to the civilian victims of the Japanese Occupation 1942–45, Singapore. This memorial is dedicated to civilians of Singapore's four major races — Chinese, Malays, Indians and Eurasians — who suffered during the Japanese Occupation; thus the memorial has four main pillars.
Back cover photo: The epitaph inside the Memorial.

Typeset by Superskill Graphics Pte Ltd
Printed in Singapore by Photoplates Pte Ltd

Contents

Preface

Sixty years after the end of World War II, are memories of the war fading away or are the issues it generated still real? To find an answer to this question, the Institute of Southeast Asian Studies organized an international conference in 2005. It brought together a diverse group of scholars who examined different aspects of the war's legacy. Their general conclusion was that the political and social fallout from the war is alive and divisive.

Two examples present themselves readily. One example is how former Japanese Prime Minister Junichiro Koizumi's visit to the Yasukuni Shrine prevented China, Japan and South Korea from sitting down together to talk about Northeast Asian integration, and wider Asian integration. Only the presence of ASEAN in the driver's seat of the East Asian Summit process made any kind of dialogue on the issue possible. The other example is the question of comfort women. Japanese Prime Minister Shinzo Abe's statement — that there is no evidence that Japan's government or army forced women to work in military brothels during the war — appeared to go back on a 1993 apology for the comfort women. His stance has upset many Asian countries and the United States.

The above and other unresolved issues such as the improvement of relations among and between the states in Northeast Asia, with implications for the rest of the international community, will be areas for study in the decade ahead.

Ambassador K. Kesavapany
Director
Institute of Southeast Asian Studies, Singapore

Foreword

The year 1945 saw the end of the greatest and most devastating conflict mankind has ever known. World War II was waged as a total war: a global conflict fought without restraints. In the upshot, the human and economic costs of almost six years of fighting were staggering: the war was believed to have cost over US$2 trillion; an estimated 50 million people (roughly 35 million civilians and 15 million soldiers) were killed; cities and industries completely demolished and laid waste; and millions of people uprooted by massive population movements.

The changes that came in the wake of the war were as dramatic. The European continent underwent a major transformation in the aftermath of the war. The end of war in Europe was quickly followed by the Cold War, which in very profound ways provided the framework of the economic and political reconstruction following the dismantling of the German New Order. The Cold War was to influence international politics for more than forty years.

The end of the war triggered the beginning of the end of the European empires in Asia and Africa. Political independence and the departure of the erstwhile colonial powers marked for the new sovereign states of Asia the first successful stage of nationalism. What followed were the more formidable tasks of constructing the post-colonial state and meeting the related challenges of economic and social development. In many ways, the post-war history of the new states of Asia were chronicles of the strategies and methods adopted by these new states to cope with the problems they had inherited from their individual colonial past and wartime experiences. For many individuals and states across Asia, "deeply layered" memories of the war continue to dwell in their current consciousness. Some are orchestrated, but many are spontaneous and even cathartic. National memorialization of war and occupation, textbook controversies, relations between Japan and its Northeast Asian neighbours, "blood debts", and "comfort women" are some of the present-day realities that consistently elicit strong emotions across generations, young and old. Tim Harper reminds us that while the events of 1945 "may now be slipping out of the memory of the living", these "ubiquitous" memories may continue to speak differently to new generations.

While Asad-ul Iqbal Latif may be right that "World War II has gone missing in action from the politics of contemporary Singapore", it has certainly not stopped taxing the minds of academics and scholars in the country. The universities in the country, National University of Singapore and Nanyang Technological University, have separately organized conferences commemorating the sixtieth anniversary of the fall of Singapore (2002) and of the end of the war (2005). It was on the latter occasion that the Institute of Southeast Asian Studies brought together an illustrious gathering of scholars to reflect on what the war has continued to mean for Asia, some sixty years after the event. While the debate about which legacy is enduring and which is transient may have been grist to the mill of a good academic debate, the insightful essays that are contained in this volume, the outcome of that meeting at the Institute, are thoughtful reminders that in many tangible ways, the war continues to cast its long shadows over many aspects of public and personal life in Asia. The chapters in this volume provide deep and often introspective accounts and analyses of the continued impact of the war in the countries of Southeast Asia, East and South Asia, and by spreading the discussion and analyses across a wider spectrum of states and societies that were involved in the war, the contributors to this volume have collectively provided richer and more nuanced accounts of the varied meanings and memories of the war in different parts of Asia. In sum, the chapters in this volume have provided a better understanding of how the long-term effects of the war are not only felt in the political arena and in international relations, but in schools, education, textbooks, languages and popular culture as well. The stories they tell are not unlike a great epic with a continuously unfolding plot, often with unexpected twists. World War II might have ended sixty years ago, but it is not a forgotten war. Cheah Boon Kheng's assertion that "exorcising the ghosts of World War II will take a long time" is applicable to Malaysia, as it surely must be for the rest of Asia.

I trust readers will find the essays in this volume thought-provoking and engaging.

Tan Tai Yong
Associate Professor of History and Dean
Faculty of Arts and Social Sciences
National University of Singapore

About the Contributors

David CHANDLER has degrees from Harvard College, Yale University and the University of Michigan. He taught Southeast Asian History at Monash University from 1972 to 1997, and is now an Emeritus Professor there, and also a Fellow of the Monash Asia Institute. He has also held visiting appointments at the University of Michigan, Cornell University, Georgetown University, the University of Wisconsin, and the University of Paris. His books include *A History of Cambodia* (4th edition, 2007), *The Tragedy of Cambodian History* (1991), *Facing the Cambodian Past: Selected Essays* (1996) and *Brother Number One: A Political Biography of Pol Pot* (2nd edition, 1999). He is also a co-author in *The Emergence of Modern Southeast Asia*, edited by N. Owen et al. (2005) and co-editor with Christopher Goscha, of *L'espace d'un regard l'Asie de: Paul Mus 1902–1969* (2006).

CHEAH Boon Kheng retired in 1994 as Professor of History at the Universiti Sains Malaysia in Penang, Malaysia. Since his retirement he has held visiting fellowships in Singapore, Canberra and Malaysia. He was Visiting Professor at the School of Humanities, Universiti Sains Malaysia during June 2004–June 2005. He has written extensively on Malaysian social and political history and is the author of the following books: *The Masked Comrades* (1979), *Red Star Over Malaya: Resistance and Social Conflict During and After the Japanese Occupation, 1941–1946* (1983); and *Malaysia: The Making of a Nation* (2002).

Sunanda K. DATTA-RAY has practised and taught journalism in Britain, India, the United States and Singapore for nearly fifty years, always seeking to set contemporary events in the context of historical evolution. This interest in the past is reflected in his two main books, *Smash and Grab: Annexation of Sikkim*, and *Waiting for America: India and the US in the*

New Millennium. Now Visiting Senior Research Fellow at Singapore's Institute of Southeast Asian Studies (ISEAS), he was educated in India (La Martiniere, Calcutta) and England (University of Manchester) and worked on British newspapers before joining *The Statesman*, a leading Indian daily newspaper published from Calcutta and Delhi, of which he became Editor in 1985. Since leaving India at the end of 1991, he has been Editor-in-Residence at the East-West Center, Honolulu; Editorial Consultant, *The Straits Times*, Singapore; Visiting Fellow, Corpus Christi College, Oxford; and Senior Fellow, Wee Kim Wee School of Communication and Information, Nanyang Technological University. He is now a columnist in several publications in India and abroad, including the *International Herald Tribune*, and essayist in *Time* magazine. He is currently engaged at the ISEAS in researching Minister Mentor Lee Kuan Yew's role in Singapore's relations with India.

Tim HARPER is University Senior Lecturer in History at Cambridge University and a fellow of Magdalene College, Cambridge. His first book, *The End of Empire and the Making of Malaya* (1999), came out of his doctoral work on war, communist insurgency and the achievement of independence in Malaya and Singapore. Since then, he has published widely on Southeast Asian and World History. He is a contributor to *Globalization in World History*, edited by A.G. Hopkins (2002). His most recent works, co-written with Christopher Bayly, are *Forgotten Armies: Britain's Asian Empire and the War with Japan* (2004) and *Forgotten Wars: the End of Britain's Asian Empire* (2007). He continues to spend a lot of time travelling and researching in Southeast Asia. He has held visiting positions in Malaysia, Singapore, France and the United States, and is a Fellow of the Royal Historical Society.

Andrew HORVAT is Visiting Professor at Tokyo Keizai University where he is also scholar in residence at the International Center for the Study of Historical Reconciliation. Between 1999 and 2005, as Japan representative of The Asia Foundation, Horvat convened symposiums on topics related to historical reconciliation in Northeast Asia. In 2001 Horvat co-hosted a conference comparing the treatment of negative aspects of the past in the teaching of history in the high schools of seven nations. The papers and proceedings of the conference appeared in multilingual format as *Sharing the Burden of the Past: World War II Legacies in Europe, Asia and America*, co-edited with Gebhard Hielscher (Tokyo: Asia Foundation and Friedrich

Ebert Stiftung, 2003). He has also taken an active role in the hosting of symposiums on World War II slave labour (2002), restitution of cultural property looted during wars and periods of colonial rule (2004), and the role of civil society in historical reconciliation in Europe and East Asia (2006). Prior to joining The Asia Foundation, Horvat was a Tokyo-based journalist covering Japan and the Asia-Pacific region for the *Associated Press*, *Southam News* of Canada, the *Los Angeles Times*, the *Independent* of London and Public Radio International's "Marketplace" business programme. He received a citation for excellence in business broadcasting from the Overseas Press Club of America in 1994, and was awarded a Shintaro Abe fellowship the following year. He is author and translator of nine books and numerous articles.

HUANG Jianli is Associate Professor with the History Department of the National University of Singapore. His primary area of research interest is on the history of Republican China from the 1920s to 1940s. He has published a book on the Kuomintang's attempt in depoliticizing student movements from 1927 to 1949. He is now working on the topic of local governance in the Chinese city of Chongqing during the wartime years from 1937 to 1945. His secondary field of research is on the history of the Chinese community in Singapore, especially during the post-war period and with emphasis on its relationship with China. He has written research pieces on the Sun Yat Sen Nanyang Memorial Hall, Tiger Balm Gardens, Chinese business elite, Chinese-educated activists, and student movements in postwar Singapore.

Reynaldo C. ILETO is Professor in the Southeast Asian Studies Programme of the National University of Singapore. He was Associate Professor at the University of the Philippines and Australian National University, where he remains Adjunct Professor. He has held the Burns Chair in History at the University of Hawaii, and fellowships at Kyoto University, and Tokyo University of Foreign Studies. His first book, *Magindanao 1860–1888: The Career of Datu Utto of Buayan,* was revised and reissued in 2007. His *Pasyon and Revolution: Popular Movements in the Philippines*, won the Benda Prize in Southeast Asian Studies as well as the Ohira Memorial Prize, and has been translated into Catalan, Vietnamese, and Japanese. His third major work, *Filipinos and their Revolution: Event, Discourse and Historiography*, took first prize in the Philippine National Book Awards. He also wrote the section on "Religion and Anticolonial Movements" in the *Cambridge History of Southeast Asia*. In 2003, he was awarded the Fukuoka Asian Culture Prize for academic excellence. His new volume of essays, *Knowledge and Pacification: Essays on the U.S. Conquest and the Writing of Philippine History*, will be launched in late 2007. He is currently completing a book for ISEAS on *History and Nation-building in the Philippines*.

Takashi INOGUCHI obtained his Ph.D. in 1974 from the Massachusetts Institute of Technology. From 1977 to 2005 he was a Professor of Political Science, Institute of Oriental Culture, University of Tokyo. Since April 2005, he has been a Professor of Political Science, Faculty of Law, Chuo University and Professor Emeritus, University of Tokyo. From 1995 to 1997, he was an Assistant Secretary-General of the United Nations assigned to The United Nations University Headquarters in charge of Programmatic Activities. He is a Member of the Legislative Council and the Science Council of Japan. He is also Executive Editor, *Japanese Journal of Political Science* (Cambridge University Press), and Chairman, Executive Committee of the Asian Consortium for Political Research. His latest publications include: *American Democracy Promotion* (2000), *Japanese Foreign Policy Today* (2000), *Values and Life Styles in Urban Asia* (2005), *Japanese Politics* (2005), *Governance and Democracy in Asia* (2006), *Political Cultures in Asia and Europe* (2006), and *The Uses of Institutions* (2007).

Asad-ul Iqbal LATIF is Visiting Research Fellow at the Institute of Southeast Asian Studies. He was a Fulbright Visiting Scholar at Harvard University's Weatherhead Center for International Affairs. His areas of research include Singapore's political and strategic relations with China, India and the United States. He graduated with Honours in English from Presidency College, Calcutta, and received his Master of Letters in History at Cambridge University, where he was Raffles (Chevening) and S. Rajaratnam Scholar. He was a member of the president's committee of the Cambridge Union Society, the university debating club, and a member of the editorial committee of the *Cambridge Review of International Affairs*. A journalist for twenty-five years before joining ISEAS, he worked at *The Statesman* in Calcutta, *Asiaweek* in Hongkong, and the *Business Times* and the *Straits Times* in Singapore. He was a Jefferson Fellow at the East-West Center in Hawaii in Spring 2001.

Richard Z. LEIRISSA is Professor of History at the Department of History, Faculty of Humanities, Universitas Indonesia, Jakarta. He received his Bachelor of Arts from Universitas Indonesia 1965, his Master of Arts from University of Hawaii, USA in 1974, and his Ph.D. from Universitas Indonesia in 1990. He has taught courses on History of Southeast Asia, Early Modern History of Indonesia, and Methodology.

Thitinan PONGSUDHIRAK is Director of the Institute of Security and International Studies (ISIS) and Assistant Professor of International Political Economy at the Faculty of Political Science, Chulalongkorn University. He has authored a host of articles and book chapters on Thailand's politics, political economy, foreign policy, and the role of the media in democratization, as well as ASEAN and East Asian security and economic cooperation. He is frequently quoted and his op-eds have regularly appeared in international and local media outlets. He has worked for *The Nation* newspaper, *The BBC World Service*, the Economist Intelligence Unit (EIU), and Independent Economic Analysis (IDEA) as well as occasional consulting projects related to Thailand's macroeconomy and politics. He received his B.A. from the University of California at Santa Barbara, M.A. from the Johns Hopkins School of Advanced International Studies, and Ph.D. from the London School of Economics. His current projects include book and journal chapters on the emerging regional order in East Asia, Thai foreign policy under Thaksin, the violence in southern Thailand, Thailand's elusive democratic consolidation, Thailand's political crisis of 2006, and the politics of bilateral free trade areas. He is working on a book focusing on the connection and continuity between Thailand's economic crisis of 1997 and its political crisis of 2006.

TAN Tai Yong is Associate Professor of History and Dean, Faculty of Arts and Social Sciences, National University of Singapore (NUS). He has written extensively on Sikh and Punjabi history, as well as on Southeast Asia and Singapore. His recent publications include *The Garrison State* (2005), *The Aftermath of Partition in South Asia* (co-authored, 2000) and *The Transformation of Southeast Asia: International Perspectives on De-colonisation* (co-edited, 2003). He was Head of the History Department at the NUS from 2000 to 2003, and is currently Acting Director of the Institute of South Asian Studies at NUS.

Robert H. TAYLOR, a leading scholar on Myanmar, received his Ph.D. from Cornell in 1974. He conducted extensive research at Rangoon University in 1978 and 1982 and has visited Burma/Myanmar frequently since 1975. After teaching at Wilberforce University in Ohio and the University of Sydney, he taught at the School of Oriental and African Studies (SOAS), becoming Professor of Politics in the University of London and Pro-Director. He was subsequently Vice-Chancellor of Buckingham University. He is a Professorial Research Associate at SOAS and, from December 2003, an Associate Senior Fellow of the Institute of Southeast Asian Studies, Singapore. He lives in London and provides consultancy services on Myanmar and Southeast Asian affairs. He has authored *The State in Burma* (1987) and contributed to *The Emergence of Modern Southeast Asia: A New History* (2005). He has edited *Handbooks of the Modern World: Asia and the Pacific* (1991), *Burma: Political Economy Under Military Rule* (2001) and *The Idea of Freedom in Asia and Africa* (2002). His other publications include *The Foreign and Domestic Consequences of the KMT Intervention in Burma* (1972) and contributions to *In Search of Southeast Asia* (2nd ed., 1985).

WANG Gungwu is Director of the East Asian Institute and Faculty Professor in the Faculty of Arts and Social Sciences, National University of Singapore and Emeritus Professor of the Australian National University. His books include *The Nanhai Trade* (1958, 1998); *The Structure of Power in North China during the Five Dynasties* (1963, 1967); *China and the World since 1949* (1977); *Community and Nation* (1981, 1992); *China and the Chinese Overseas* (1991); *The Chineseness of China* (1991); *The Chinese Way: China's Position in International Relations* (1995); *The Chinese Overseas: From Earthbound China to the Quest for Autonomy* (2000); *Don't Leave Home: Migration and the Chinese* (2001); *Anglo-Chinese Encounters since 1800: War, trade, science and governance* (2003*)*; *Diasporic Chinese Ventures* (2004). He is Fellow and former President of the Australian Academy of Humanities; Foreign Member of the American Academy of Arts and Science; Member of Academia Sinica; Honorary Member of the Chinese Academy of Social Science. He was awarded the International Academic Prize, Fukuoka Asian Cultural Prizes. In Singapore, he is Chairman, Institute of Southeast Asian Studies; and Lee Kuan Yew School of Public Policy. He received his B.A. and M.A. degrees from the University of Malaya in Singapore, and Ph.D. from the

University of London (1957). He taught at the University of Malaya (Professor of History, 1963–68). At Australian National University (1968–86), he was Professor and Head, Department of Far Eastern History and Director, Research School of Pacific Studies. From 1986 to 1995, he was Vice-Chancellor (President) of the University of Hong Kong.

Part One

Overview

Chapter One
Opening Remarks[1]

Wang Gungwu

On behalf of the Institute of Southeast Asian Studies let me welcome all of you to this very interesting conference, for us to reflect on sixty years of change since the end of World War II.

ISEAS is one of my favourite institutes because it is one of those institutes that has a memory and we historians like that. I recalled that about ten years ago ISEAS had a conference on "War and Memory" to commemorate the fiftieth anniversary of the end of the war in Southeast Asia. I was at that conference and I remember how memorable and interesting it was — it stimulated us to think about the past but also to relate it to the present. This conference is an even more conscious effort to relate it to the present, about the impact on us today.

Let me say that there are two very important different aspects of this conference compared to the previous one. This one talks about World War II, while the previous one was really more about war and memory in Malaysia and Singapore. Second, this is about World War II in a much larger region. Both are very large concepts. World War II was a global war, and East and Southeast Asia put together is a much larger area than our previous conference topic. By broadening it, this larger perspective can help us think through some of our more local concerns as well.

World War II, of course, is understood quite differently in a number of places. I was struck by that long time ago. But for most people, World War II represented the war that was fought largely in Europe to begin with, and then enlarged to cover the rest of the world. For our region, it is a little bit less clear. There had been a war that had started earlier between China and Japan. For Japan there was the Pacific War that really started with Pearl Harbour. Thus, neither of these two views quite matches the more commonly understood meaning of World War II, which was measured by wars in Europe. I am struck by the fact that if we use different periods and different dates we may have a somewhat different perspective on what is enduring and transient.

When we talk about legacies, what is enduring and what is transient, I really don't know how to define enduring and transient. Enduring in what sense? The enduring ones, at least on the surface, looks like those that keep on being talked about year after year, and nobody is ever ready to forget. Is that what we mean by enduring? I am not sure but I am just speculating on how we understand the word.

What is transient? Is anything really transient if we can remember it? Does transient mean that those things that we quite easily forget or want to forget? Again I am not sure that we all use the words in the same way. I shall make a simple attempt to define it. Enduring means those that do affect us constantly, and actually has some meaning for us every now and again. I find that on the whole what endures has been those matters that are taken up politically. "Politically" is defined broadly to include matters of security, of defence, and of political relationships between countries. At that level, much is enduring about wars and World War II is no exception, naturally.

But then what is transient in some areas may not be as transient elsewhere. In areas like in commercial relationships, economic developments, and the kind of cultural interactions that continue, all of them may well be permeated by memories of a war, particularly a war that was so spectacular and dramatic in its time. They actually may permeate and be pervasive all the way. But is it enduring? How does one define it? It is transient in the sense that it is not recalled all the time. We do not constantly refer to World War II in our commercial, economic developments, in our cultural interactions, or the social relationships among people between communities, and so on. But it may well be there; there may be an underlying impact on all our thinking and all our connections and linkages. It is a matter of what one emphasizes. But clearly the political ones are the ones that are usually brought up every time we talk about what is enduring in our memories about the war. If we take that definition and I find it quite useful, or at least simpler, to do so, then it seems to me that the enduring aspects of World War II are very clear. Here are a number of things clear to me.

One of them is that World War II brought an end to empires, at least to the traditional empires where strong conquest polities seek to rule the territories they conquered as their colonies. We may have different kinds of informal and other virtual empires, but the traditional empire basically came to an end. I do not think anybody in the world today would accept anybody, any country trying to create and establish an empire today. To me that is pretty enduring. Before that, for centuries and centuries all over the world, people had to live with empires, one kind or another, some bigger, some smaller. There was always the prospect of some kingdom or some ruler trying to create an empire. I feel that after 1945 the world was sick and tired of empires and pretty well wanted to see their end. If I am right, then at least this legacy has endured sixty years. I hope it will endure even longer than that and we can call it the end of the age of empires.

The second thing is probably a little less enduring because there were some uncertainties, for people in this region anyway, in the creation of Southeast Asia. Before 1945, the term "Southeast Asia" was never widely accepted or used. It was created for a specific purpose. From a geographical concept it began to take on political, historical, cultural and other connotations. People in the region are building up this idea of Southeast Asia as something that should or deserve to endure, to last. This has gone on for the last fifty, sixty years. It is still uncertain because all these talk about East Asian Community with the various ideas of ASEAN+1, +3, +5, +6, and so on, may dilute the concept of Southeast Asia. These concepts may not endure quite as long as the end of empires that I spoke of. Nevertheless, I feel reasonably confident that whatever may happen in the future, the core group of Southeast Asian countries would have a good chance to endure, provided they play their game well (the rules of the game now are becoming more and more transparent) in their relationship with their neighbouring regions and sub-regions, like East Asia or South Asia, and the Pacific. And provided they play this role together as a united institution under the umbrella of ASEAN or something like it, that could continually remind the smaller countries of Southeast Asia of their potential force as a unified political community, or economic community. If they can retain that sense of community, then they have a chance of allowing this concept of Southeast Asia to endure for a long, long time. As I said, there are uncertainties but I have some hope that this is the second enduring legacy of World War II.

Finally I just want to talk about different perceptions of what is World War II. I am very struck by how the two different regions of East Asia and Southeast Asia that we are talking about today look at World War II differently. Quite clearly for Southeast Asia, World War II was primarily the war from 1941 to 1945 when the Japanese started the war in this part of the world. But for countries like Japan, Korea and China, there was another war that had been going on off and on since the beginning of the twentieth century on the Korean Peninsula, in Manchuria, in different provinces in China. The contentions of Northeast Asian countries like Japan, Korea and China had been going on much longer than that. It did not start just in 1937; I would date it from the end of the Russo-Japanese War when the Japanese were confident enough to actually take a position on the Korean Peninsula and then moved into Northeast Asia, into Manchuria. For those three countries, World War II had a much longer history and you can argue about exactly when it began. It probably did not begin in any specific time but there was a deep sense of struggle and war that had pursued these three countries for a much longer period. The end of World War II did bring that particular conflict to an end. But because it took a longer time, it lasted longer in the memories of people. For Southeast Asia, three-and-a-half years or four years, it is probably easier to forget. But for those three countries, Japan, Korea and China, forty years or at least forty years, forgetting will take longer an will probably be harder. This helps to explain the enduring pains and memories, painful memories that still persist in East Asia and that seem so much more stark and dramatic than for those people in Southeast Asia. This time span may be relevant. I am not suggesting that it explains everything, but I put it to you that it is a major factor why that memory in Northeast Asia is so much more enduring than the memories of World War II in Southeast Asia.

NOTE

1. The text is transcribed from the opening speech given by Professor Wang to the ISEAS conference, "World War II: Transient and Enduring Legacies for East and Southeast Asia 60 Years On".

Chapter Two
A Long View on the Great Asian War

Tim Harper*

On 15 August 1945, as rumours of the Japanese surrender filtered through to the people of Asia, the coerced collaborator and Malay nationalist, Mustapha Hussain, wept bitterly: the collapse of Japan had forestalled the declaration of independence for Malaya by just forty-eight hours. At a stroke, the political promise that the war had seemed to bring was swept away. Yet, a little later, he was to reflect that "although the Japanese Occupation was described as one of severe hardship and brutality, it left something positive, a sweet fruit to be plucked and enjoyed only after the surrender." The rest of Mustapha's life would be consumed by his need to reconcile himself to these events; by a regret for the lost opportunity and the vindication of his own role.[1] This kind of debate would be played out, privately and publicly, across the region for a generation or more. It largely dictated the terms of historical writing, which has evolved as a pursuit of some kind of balance sheet, or moral reckoning.[2] For example, the dilemma between resistance and collaboration has been presented most often in stark terms, and the question still troubles national historical memory two generations on. Above all, writing has focused on the immediate issue of war: the extent to which the war acted as a defining watershed of modern

Asian history.[3] Historians are too easily seduced by idea of watersheds, and ought to be suspicious of them. It is only more recently that historians have begun to view these epochal events through a longer lens, and this has allowed new themes to emerge: of slower, more ambiguous shifts in society, state and region, in the making of identity and memory. It is the aim of this collection to explore these continuing, substantive legacies, and this essay attempts to suggest some areas in which they might lie. It begins with a brief synopsis of the war within the longer duration of Asian history, and then moves to survey its more ephemeral and enduring legacies.

THE GREAT ASIAN WAR IN WORLD HISTORY

The sixtieth commemoration of the end of World War II was probably the last of its kind. There are few veterans left to parade at cenotaphs; in 2005, the average age of *hibakusha* — the survivors of Hiroshima — was seventy-two years.[4] From the perspective of the former colonial powers, the anniversary is an occasion to remember the "forgotten armies" that fought in what is still seen as a relatively minor theatre of a larger European war.[5] This perspective must now be reversed. The Great Asian War was longer and ultimately bloodier than Europe's war. It claimed around 24 million lives in occupied Asia, the lives of three million Japanese, and three and a half million more in India through war-related famine. Of the victims, the European, American, Australasian casualties numbered perhaps one per cent of the total. The Asian war had its several holocausts in the slaying of civilians, the coercion of slave labour, and in mass rape. The first skirmishes began 1931 and for much of Asia, 15 August 1945 was merely a brief hiatus in the fighting. Many of the definitive political events of the war — the declarations of independence in Vietnam and Indonesia — occurred in the interregnum after the fall of Japan. So too did some of the most horrific internal violence, the memory of which has been formative to individual nation states such as Myanmar and Malaysia.

The impact was all the more dreadful for the fact that these were societies that did not know war; still less the full ferocity of modern, mechanized conflict. The Great Asian War was the most general conflict in the region since the Mongol invasions of the thirteenth century, and the most intense since the great struggles for primacy on mainland Asia in the early modern era. Apart from the cultivation of minority groups for specific martial roles — as policemen and auxiliaries for small colonial wars — one of the defining features of Western rule in Southeast Asia was its largely successful attempt to demilitarize local society. During this period martial traditions never died; they were kept alive by the vivid memories of anti-colonial resistance. But their sudden reassertion — in the emotive blood rituals of the Burmese *thakin*; in the regimental discipline of the Japanese-sponsored militias — was, nevertheless, a dramatic event. It fired the political militancy of the day. It conferred significant political legitimacy on men in uniform, and fostered a "parade-ground nationalism".[6] In China, the war must be seen in the context of a decades-long cycle of military violence that "unmade" the nation and extorted a horrendous toll on its people.[7]

There is another adjustment of historical vision to be made. The war must be seen within a broader sweep of Japan's commercial and political engagement with the region.[8] Japan was a cultural presence in Asia long before it became a military one. Japanese intellectuals built up a formidable storehouse of knowledge of Southeast Asia. As a stimulus to trade, bringing a distinctive vision of modernity, Japan acted as a vital link in the modern economic emergence of Southeast Asia. Meiji models of self-strengthening made an impact both in the Islamic archipelago and on the Buddhist mainland.[9] When, by 1918, the barbarity of World War I seemed to challenge the universality of Western models of civilization, a pan-Asian response began to develop, in which Japan played a crucial role.[10] Southeast Asian views of Japan were never without ambivalence and reserve, but Japan's background presence gave later notions of "co-prosperity" a degree of resonance in the minds of Asian elites, despite its perversion in the hands of militarists. Moreover, the logic of Japanese interests drew it back into the region at a very early stage after the war, and in the same strategic areas — Malayan iron mining, for example — in which it had such a pronounced investment before 1941. The Japanese expatriate community began to return as "advisers", in Indonesia for example, exploiting their wartime connections.[11] By 1972, Southeast Asian countries purchased nearly 12 per cent of total Japanese exports and supplied 16 per cent of total imports. Indonesia led the way by 1979, with 35.4 per cent of Japan's total manufacturing investment and 43 per cent of investment in mining in Southeast Asia.[12] "Even after the war", one Japanese historian has observed, "many Japanese business and entrepreneurs still thought of Indonesia as a sort of second Manchuria."[13]

But at a more fundamental level, the war marked the passing of an era of globalization in Asia. Under the sway of large poly-ethnic empires, the great arc of Eurasia from the Middle East to Japan had been connected as never before in its history. The Indian Ocean had been a cosmopolitan arena, a place of great social mobility.[14] By the inter-war years, faced with the growing policing of movement and the hardening of territorial boundaries, the massive flows of people that had dominated Asian history for a century or more began to ebb. But it was the Great Asian War that made this process irreversible. By the end of the war, transport had ground to a halt, and borders were battle fronts. During the Japanese Occupation, the largest migrations were either forced, as in conscription for the railway projects, or the flight of refugees from troubled areas, as in the mass exodus of Indians from Burma and Chinese from the towns and mines of Malaya. At the war's end travel, trade and remittance had resumed, and migrant communities raced to restore ties with their homelands. But in the longer term, the great political upheavals in India and China gave these journeys a new finality.

Whereas before the war much of the politics of Asia was conducted in long-distance, transnational terms, the conflict was a final display of the political muscle of the diasporic networks of the age of empires. The National Salvation Movement was the largest political undertaking of the Overseas Chinese. Attempts to revive it after the war, for example in Tan Kah Kee's patronage of the China Democratic League in Singapore and Malaya, lacked credibility and collapsed in the face of Kuomintang-Chinese Communist Party factionalism, and the growing pressure to root Chinese politics in the Nanyang. When the communist armies entered the port cities of China, the seaboard would close to migration for two generations; Tan Kah Kee himself returned to China in 1949. The Indian Independence League, with its centres in Japan, Thailand and Singapore, was similarly the highest expression of overseas Indian nationalism. After 1942, with the congress high command in jail, Subhas Chandra Bose claimed the moral leadership of the nation, and the right to take up arms against the Raj. Yet the Indian National Army too collapsed in 1945, its civilian leadership broken by British witch-hunts. Many post-war journeys from Southeast Asia, South Asia and China were passages into banishment or exile. Dying empires and new nations guarded their frontiers jealously. Much was lost in the process. The dream of a greater Malay nation floundered against the Dutch blockade of the Indonesian Republic. Once prosperous ports — Rangoon, Penang, Surabaya — became backwaters, and their cosmopolitan-minded minorities: Baghdadi Jews, Hadrami Arabs, Peranakan Indians and Straits Chinese went into decline. More enclosed state structures were being erected that placed more importance on internal identity politics, the local defence of status and nationality, than the pursuit of global sympathies.

Wherever these new "national" boundaries were drawn, they broke up older communities that had transcended them, and left behind "orphans of empire".[15] The war forced the pace of internal consolidation within these new modern nation states. After the fall of the colonial cities in 1941 and 1942, the focus of the fighting shifted to previously isolated borderlands and forest frontiers. The resistance armies and their allies in South East Asia Command mobilized hill peoples and "tribals" into clandestine armies, and drew them, often for the first time, and sometimes reluctantly, into wider political currents. Nagas, Kachins, Karens, Lushai, Shans and the Orang Asli of the Malay Peninsula acquired arms and leadership along with a heightened sense of identity. Some of these communities now saw themselves as small "nations". Under Japanese rule, various regional movements sensed an opportunity to bid for greater autonomy. But after 1945, their myriad aspirations were confronted with big states, governed by dominant lowland communities; militant small nations collided by equally determined majority ethnicities, whether Hindu Indian, Buddhist Burman, or Muslim Malay.[16] Many of these struggles, in one form or another, are still with us.

As old geographical connections were broken, the very idea of the region was reshaped. The Japanese had sought to create a new Asian entity, with Japan as its political and spiritual epicentre. Imperial armies unified the littoral from Singapore, through Thailand to the borders of Assam by armed invasion, and created a massive chain of influence right across Asia. But the region that emerged most strongly from the war was to be smaller than this. The idea of "Southeast Asia" as a region was itself a product of formation of a separate South East Asia Command in 1943.[17] What was diminished was its Indian Ocean connections. The British hoped to keep this alive: it was the resources of the Indian Sub-continent that propelled General Slim's armies back into Southeast Asia by 1944. For many months from 1944 to 1946, Allied South East Asia Command ruled a large part of the whole area from the borders of Bengal and Assam to Singapore and on to the seas north of Australia. Its writ even temporarily penetrated into southern Indochina and Indonesia: the first time in history that the region was forged into a political unit. The cost of this ultimately destroyed the Raj: this was its last imperial adventure; the use of Indian expeditionary forces to occupy Japan, Indonesia and Vietnam, its last martial act. Nehru acknowledged the importance of the region in his triumphal progress through Burma and Malaya in the spring of 1946. The Asian Relations Conference in New Delhi in 1947 voiced Asia's manifest destiny. But there was no echo of Japan's wartime rhetoric of "Asia for the Asiatics"; memories of the suffering of war were too tender. New nations, and nations fighting to be born, focused on the struggles within their own borders. India's later sponsorship of the Afro-Asian movement was an expression of internationalism between states, not a foretaste of a more organic order to come. Sukarno had attended the Tokyo Greater East Asian Conference in November 1943; twelve years later, at Bandung, he made no mention of it; the Japanese delegate — a former official from Manchukuo — kept a very low profile. The rhetoric of "Asia for the Asians" had become the heritage of all: part of the internationalism of the left — such as Tan Malaka's "Aslia" — and in the idea of ECAFE (1947) as an "economic parliament of Asia".[18] For a generation, Japan, having lost an empire, had yet to find a role. Post-war Japanese initiatives, such as the Ministerial Conference for the Economic Development of Southeast Asia (SEAMCED) in 1966 were soon overshadowed by ASEAN. As the new regional body developed its "ASEAN Way" it turned for inspiration to generalized Islamic-Indic notions of *musyawarah*, and the practical lessons of regional autonomy and non-interference.[19] For all its evocative beginnings, the Japanese ideal of a new Asian order had no direct inheritance. The dire conditions and oppression of the end of the war killed it off. The post-war years were a time of narrowing vision. The writing of history has followed this trend; it has dissolved into smaller, regional and national fragments. It is the task of volumes such as the present one to try and recombine some of these fragments to make more sense of passing and enduring legacies of the Great Asian War.

PASSING LEGACIES

The immediate legacy of the Japanese conquest of Southeast Asia was the abject humiliation of the Western powers. In Mustapha Hussain's words again: "When the British returned to rule Malaya in 1945, they no longer faced Malays of the pre war mould. They were confronted instead by a Malay community whose souls and spirits were no longer static and no longer accepting." This is recurring motif of memoirs of the occupation. It is, in retrospect, difficult to see how the mystique of European power in Asia survived for as long as it did. Military defeat exposed the fragility of European rule, the bankruptcy of its racial policies, the shallowness of its bureaucratic reach. Through a long lens, we can trace back the new kinds of politicization, the richness of experiment in attitudes and ideas, for a long period before the occupation. Yet what the memoirs capture, and historians often miss, is an euphoria; a sense of historical possibility that was dramatic and new. What was the source of this novelty? In part, it came from the rhetoric of "co-prosperity" and from Japanese cultural policy.[20] But all imperialisms make cultural claims and employ cultural power, and the Japanese empire, like all empires, wore a Janus face. It saw its destiny in cosmoplastic terms: a faith in its capacity to redraw maps and boundaries, as it understood them, and to reshape identities.[21] But, like its European predecessors, it was also crippled by the contradictions between its universal pretensions and the stark realities of its exploitation. The claims of the Japanese regime represented a break with the past in one crucial sense: the idea that a state should seek active demonstrations of allegiance from its subjects; the idea of the state as a consciousness-raising force. This was a claim European power had never made, nor sought. This idea would lie at the heart of post-war political communication and post-colonial nation-building.

Ultimately, what was significant about all this was not what it achieved for the Japanese empire as to what it allowed others to achieve for themselves. The significance of the Japanese victories lay not solely in the shattering of the cultural power of the West — it had never been wholly credible — but in the forging of new methods by which national culture could be asserted and validated. The uniforms, the marching, the drilling and the flag-waving of wartime indelibly imprinted themselves on the mind of the people of the region. In the past colonial peoples had at best been led by lawyers, exploiting the niceties of European constitutional traditions to lever their way into largely impotent municipal bodies and legislative councils. Now all these nations had martial leaders who embodied a reinvigorated and redefined form of militant patriotism. Japanese state-building revealed new tools for state-building, fresh pageantry in the repertoire of rule. This was driven by technology, or at least by the idea of it, and by its conviction in its ability to inculcate a new thought process. At the heart of this was language itself. In Indonesia, as is well known, the occupation gave impetus to *bahasa Indonesia* but it was the idea of language as a mind-shaping force, the sense that language was "the soul of the nation" that had a more general currency in the region. This broader shift was more important than specific policies. It marked not only the immediate generation who lived through it — the people who could remember the songs, primers and parades — but longer and more subliminally in state practice and political vocabulary.[22]

These new innovations were eagerly embraced by the young. War is always a time for youth. It overturns patriarchal structures and the discipline of schoolyard; for a time, it confers power and independence on adolescent fighters: the *pemuda*, the *thakins*, the Chinese middle school students in arms in the Malayan jungle. This could not have been a sharper contrast with the hierarchical obsessions of the pre-war elites. Their rarefied bureaucratic finesse was, at a stroke, obsolete. Overnight, the rituals of power had changed. As the old order lost ground in the early stages of the war, the actions of youth acquired a new legitimacy.[23] Taken out of the hands of Japanese administrators, this generated a new popular culture. Across the region, theatre, dance, cartoon art flourished; much of these mediums built on the modernity that had arisen in the inter-war years, and in which the Japanese — not least as pedlars of technology — had been so visible. Even where Japanese cultural policy had little appeal, in the Philippines, for example, where it was received with great cynicism, the methods by which a new Asian idiom was developed was influential later at the time of the Laurel government.[24] Where we see resistance to the Japanese — in China, in the guerrilla wars in Malaya and Vietnam — similar mediums arose.[25] This was a new style: it was chic, in ways that aided the recruitment of guerrilla armies right across the region. As Rudolf Mrazek has described the scene in Indonesia: "dressing gaily and behaving bohemian, the apocalypse of standard and uniform, made even the billiard generation appear, for awhile at least and to some extent, serious and meaningful".[26]

The legacy of all this was, however, in many ways transient and uneven. The position of women exposes many of the contradictions at work. Women provided much of the backbone of nationalist movements, but failed to reap the full benefits of their participation. Women found new opportunities, new employment, new images for conduct and style; for example in Indonesia, *sanggul ikut emancipasi*, the new hairstyles that came with work in factories. But women also bore some of the worst of the hardship and felt some of the most brutal violence of the long Asian war. Often the propaganda directed at them re-enforced old stereotypes and gender roles.[27] There was reaction to this new mood of emancipation across the region. A major preoccupation of post-war regimes, often led by older elites, would be in clawing back some of the influence that had been ceded to youth generally, and to women, to finding ways of neutralizing this legacy of the war. The anarchic *élan* of youth clashed with the puritanism of Communism or religious revival. This even extended to language itself; in Malaya, for example, as elite nationalists emerged and began to reclaim leadership of the community from what they saw as young, pernicious, ill-formed upstarts, they appropriated the new terminologies of politics but stripped them of any "dangerous" meanings.[28] These kind of conflicts lay the heart of the "Asian spring" of the interregnum: the hiatus after the Japanese surrender when the new-won freedoms contended with the establishment of more conservative, patriarchal forms of regime. The closing of this new popular space was contested at every step. This was a defining moment for national politics, and a source of memory and counter-memory in its own right. To some it stands for a series of missed political possibilities, a nation not fully realized. To others, the period is seen as a dark valley, and the memory of it is invoked to set and to justify the setting of limits to those possibilities.

ENDURING THEMES

If the some of the most vivid legacies of the war lay in the space it created for dramatic new political initiatives, a more enduring, if more prosaic legacy was form of the state itself. The large literature on state formation in Southeast Asia pays scant attention to the Japanese legacy. But in some ways it had a crucial influence. The military government operated more directly than most colonial administrations. From the early part of the war, the state became a palpable presence in the lives of many Asians for the first time. Japanese power did not fall uniformly, but in general the state's ambitions to intervene in production and to organize labour grew dramatically, and with tragic results. The Japanese administration attempted to make contact with the people in ways that had never before been attempted: quite literally through the impress of registration of population. The state trespassed into areas of neighbourhood, even family life, that the Europeans had veered away from. This soon generated deep resentments, particularly in the field of faith. The day the Japanese ordered people to bend in prayer to the Imperial Palace in Tokyo was, as Hamka termed it: "the day of the severest trial for Muslims".[29] Japanese state-building was driven by what one Japanese historian has called a "ideological, fanatical romanticism".[30] Its credibility was fatally eroded by the needs of the war machine; by incomprehension and inefficiency, punctuated by arbitrary and terrible violence.

However, this brief, flawed state-building would be a benchmark for subsequent regimes. It signalled a deep shift in the way government and politics was regarded. It swept away economic *laissez faire* and unleashed the possibilities of centralized planning and state intervention. Everywhere, a new generation of Asian politicians — across the political spectrum — looked to the state for the transformation of society. An understaffed, inexperienced and monoglot Japanese administration was more dependent on local knowledge than the Europeans had been. Japan sought to train new Asian cadres for the Greater East Asian Co-prosperity Sphere. The Japanese emphasis on technical education supplied new opportunities for advancement.[31] The steam soon went out of these efforts, nevertheless in these years Asian managers began to take over the state.

They inherited damaged goods, however. The modern state in Southeast Asia was an external, colonial imposition, and was never strong; its bureaucratic norms, the integrity of its institutions were for better or for worse, severely compromised during the war. Whilst Japanese legal reforms in Indonesia, for example, abolished some of the ethnic categories of the old colonial order, the Japanese also weakened key institutions such as the judiciary.[32] The state also was shaped by the militancy of the time, above by militarization, and the bureaucracy's growing obsession with its own security. The times had conferred legitimacy on fighting men, and had created — in Indonesia, Malaya, Burma and elsewhere — institutions with a dual civilian and policing or military role. Supporting associations were built around this. It is important not to draw too linear a connection with the post-colonial era — much would happen in the meantime — but in Indonesia at least, by the 1970s, commentators still felt they were witnessing the physical and psychological distortions of war. A soldier's spirit lay at the heart of state: "this harsh philosophy took root in the soul of Japanese-trained Indonesians who later became officers in the Indonesian army after independence".[33]

The state was compromised in another way. If state-formation became more indigenized in this period, it did so in familiar, familial terms; in forms in which scholars have seen as possessing a long continuity in Southeast Asian history.[34] As the war drew on, well-placed Asian administrators positioned themselves as protectors of local communities. The widespread strategies of avoidance of the Japanese regime strengthened the operation of patronage. This forged new linkages, reciprocal services, and also corruption. There were winners and losers in this process, but generally, it created new linkages between Asian elites, their family and extended networks and political and commercial power.[35] These links often had violent edges. The proliferation of corruption had its roots in the preference given in the purchase of goods to Japanese individuals and *kumais*, groupings of companies in certain fields; this gave rise to new business partnerships with local entrepreneurs. So too did the competition to supply the *butais*, the garrison forces. But it also created a chain of local traders and agents who advised and supplied the Japanese; "armchair brokers" and "field-brokers", with their runners who ferreted out supplies to order.[36] Again, it is important to note that this was the elaboration of a pre-war trend: corruption was rife within the colonial administrations of the 1930s and the Allied military occupations after 1946 were riddled with systematic graft. But in the war, the foundation were extended of a system that Japanese scholars would later identify right across Asia as "*ersatz*" or "crony" capitalism.[37]

The ways these newer deeper concerns emerge tells us much about the changing role of historical memory. It is clear that memories are deeply layered. Much of the terrain of memory is largely unmapped. In this some of the more enduring legacies of the war are yet to be fully explored: in gender relations, in attitudes to authority; in the very acts of memorializing, and the way people in the region think about history; or, at a more mundane level, in dress codes, in ceremonial, in play, in food habits and bodily practices. It is also clear that memory has changed over time; that different themes come to the fore at different periods. This reflects the way the society seeks to fashion its public history or a generational mood of nostalgia. But perhaps above all, historical memory speaks to contemporary anxieties.[38] Recent narratives of the conflict have tended to highlight its hidden costs. They include the stories of the vast "armies" of Asian workers who laboured and died in the terrible wartime conditions prevailing across British Asia.[39] They place at their centre some 100,000 women and girls who were pressed into service as sexual slaves, by direct compulsion, as "comfort women".[40] The surviving victims still struggle for recognition and reparation. This may yet be one of the most enduring legacies of the Great Asian War. Even in the 1950s to 1970s, when memories were immediate, debates over "blood debt" and Japanese neo-colonialism carried with it anger at the culpability of colonial and post-colonial government in their treatment of the issues as well as at the government of Japan. In the same way, anger over the "comfort women" issue has been shaped by the reticence of governments in pursuing the issue: this deepens its universal consequence. It is because these issues remain of universal concern that memory, at such a distant remove, and even amongst today's young, can be so intense.[41] These issues of the veracity of the historical record, of atonement and accountability, remain vitally important because they speak to a society's desire for confrontation with their past, and the dangers of ignoring this. The events of 1945 are now slipping out of the memory of the living. Their memory remains ubiquitous, but it can perhaps speak rather differently to a new generation.

NOTES

*   This article develops ideas that emerge from my collaborative work with Christopher Bayly, *Forgotten Armies: Britain's Asian Empire and the War with Japan* (2004) and *Forgotten Wars: The End of Britain's Asian Empire* (2007). I am greatly indebted to him.

1. Insun Mustapha, trans., and Jomo K.S., ed., *Malay Nationalism before Umno: The Memoirs of Mustapha Hussain* (Kuala Lumpur, 2005), p. 313.

2. For a thoughtful discussion of one case, Cheah Boon Kheng, "Memory as History and Moral Judgement: Oral and Written Accounts of the Japanese Occupation of Malaya", in *War and Memory in Malaysia and Singapore*, edited by Patricia Lim Pui Huen and Diana Wong (Singapore, 2000), pp. 23–51. This was a path-breaking collection.

3. The standard exposition of the debates is W.A. McCoy, ed., *Southeast Asia under Japanese Occupation* (New Haven, 1980). For a more recent summary, Nicholas Tarling, *A Sudden Rampage: The Japanese Occupation of Southeast Asia, 1941–45* (Singapore, 2001).

4. Chris Hogg, "Hiroshima Survivors Keep Memories Alive", <http://news.bbc. co.uk/2/hi/asia-pacific/4735163.stm>.

5. Most recently, Jon Latimer, *Burma: The Forgotten War* (London, 2004); Brian MacArthur, *Surviving the Sword: Prisoners of the Japanese 1942–45* (London, 2005). See also Jan A. Krancher, ed., *The Defining Years of the Dutch East Indies, 1942–1949: Survivors' Accounts of Japanese Invasion and Enslavement of Europeans and the Revolution that Created Free Indonesia* (London, 1996).

6. I owe this phase to John Lonsdale, "Globalization, Ethnicity and Democracy: A View from 'the Hopeless Continent' ", in *Globalization in World History*, edited by A.G. Hopkins (London, 2001), p. 198.

7. Hans van de Ven, *War and Nationalism in China, 1925–1945* (London, 2003).

8. Shimizu Hiroshi and Hirakawa Hitoshi, *Japan and Singapore in the World Economy: Japan's Economic Advance into Singapore 1870–1965* (London, 2002).

9. For example, Barbara Watson Andaya, "From Rum to Tokyo: The Search for Anti-colonial Allies by the Rulers of Riau, 1899–1914", *Indonesia* 24 (1977): 123–56.

10. Prasenjit Duara, "The Discourse of Civilization and Pan-Asianism", *Journal of World History* 12 (2001): 99–130.
11. Junko Tomaru, *The Postwar Rapprochement of Malaya and Japan, 1945–61: The Roles of Britain and Japan in South-east Asia* (Houndmills, 2000), pp. 115–21.
12. Shoko Tanaka, *Post-war Japanese Resource Policies and Strategies: The Case of Southeast Asia* (Ithaca, 1986), ch. 3.
13. Masashi Nishihara, *The Japanese and Sukarno's Indonesia: Tokyo-Jakarta Relations, 1951–1966* (Kyoto, 1976), pp. 211–12; Hikita Yasuyuki, "Japanese Companies Inroads into Indonesia under Japanese Military Administration", in *Japan, Indonesia and the War: Myths and Realities*, edited by Peter Post and Elly Touwen-Bouwsma (Leiden, 1997), p. 152.
14. For this, see Sugata Bose, *A Hundred Horizons: The Indian Ocean in the Age of Global Empire* (Cambridge Mass, 2006).
15. Robert Cribb and Lea Narangoa, "Orphans of Empire: Divided Peoples, Dilemmas of Identity, and Old Imperial Borders in East and Southeast Asia", *Comparative Studies in Society and History* 46, no. 1 (2004): 164–87.
16. For a useful comparative account, Clive J. Christie, *A Modern History of Southeast Asia: Decolonisation, Nationalism and Separatism* (London, 1996).
17. Donald K. Emmerson, " 'Southeast Asia': What's in a Name?", *Journal of Southeast Asian Studies* 15, no. 1 (1984): 1–21. See also Craig J. Reynolds, "A New Look at Old Southeast Asia", *Journal of Asian Studies* 54 (1995): 419–46.
18. Michael Haas, *The Asian Way to Peace: A Story of Regional Co-operation* (New York, 1989).
19. Amitav Acharya, *Constructing a Security Community in Southeast Asia: ASEAN and the Problems of Regional Order* (London, 2001), ch. 2.
20. Grant K. Goodman, ed., *Japanese Cultural Policies in Southeast Asia during World War II* (New York, 1991).
21. For this emphasis see the interesting studies in *Imperial Japan and National Identities in Asia, 1895–1945*, edited by Li Narangoa and Robert Cribb (London, 2003).
22. Yoji Akashi, "The Koa Kunrenjo and Nampo Tokubetsu Ryugakusei: A Study of Cultural Propagation and Conflict in Japanese Occupied Malaya (1942–45)", *Shakai Kagaku Tokyu* XXIII, no. 3 (1978): 39–66; Aiko Kurasawa, "Propaganda Media on Java under the Japanese 1942–45", *Indonesia* 44 (October 1987): 59–116.
23. For a classic statement, see Benedict Anderson, *Java in a Time of Revolution: Occupation and Resistance, 1944–46* (Ithaca and London, 1972).
24. Ricardo T. Jose, "Accord and Discord: Japanese Cultural Policy and Philippine National Identity during the Japanese Occupation (1942–45)", in *Imperial Japan and National Identities*, edited by Narangoa and Cribb, pp. 249–69.
25. For instance, Chang-Tai Hung, *War and Popular Culture: Resistance in Modern*

China, 1937–1945 (Berkeley, 1994); Greg Lockhart, *Nation in Arms: The Origins of the People's Army of Vietnam* (Sydney, 1989).

26. Rudolf Mrazek, *Engineers of Happy Land: Technology and Nationalism in a Colony* (Princeton, N.J., 2003).

27. Anton Lucas, "Images of the Indonesian Woman during the Japanese Occupation 1942–45", in *Women Creating Indonesia*, edited by Jean Gelman Taylor (1997), pp. 52–90.

28. Donna Amoroso, "Dangerous Politics and the Malay Nationalist Movement, 1945–47", *South East Asia Research* 6, no. 3 (1998): 253–80.

29. Harry J. Benda, *The Crescent and the Rising Sun: Indonesian Islam under Japanese Occupation, 1942–1945* (The Hague, 1958); Abu Talib Ahmad, *The Malay Muslims, Islam and the Rising Sun, 1941–45* (Kuala Lumpur, 2004).

30. Goto Ken'ichi, "Modern Japan and Indonesia: The Dynamics and Legacy of Wartime Rule", in *Japan, Indonesia and the War: Myths and Realities*, edited by Peter Post and Elly Touwen-Bouwsma (Leiden, 1997), pp. 14–30.

31. Harold E. Wilson, *Educational Policy and Performance in Singapore 1942–1945*, ISEAS, Occasional paper no. 16, Singapore, 1973.

32. Bas Pompe, "The Effects of the Japanese Administration on the Judiciary in Indonesia", in Peter Post and Elly Touwen-Bouwsma, eds., *Japan, Indonesia and the War: Myths and Realities* (Leiden, 1997), pp. 51–63.

33. Mochtar Lubis, "Lingering Suspicions", in *Southeast Asian Perceptions of Japan*, edited by Renato Constantino (Manila, 1991), p. 6.

34. For the state of play on these debates, see Tony Day, *Fluid Iron: State Formation in Southeast Asia* (Honolulu, 2002).

35. For example, see Robert Elson, *Suharto: A Political Biography* (Cambridge, 2002).

36. Chin Kee Onn, *Malaya upside Down* (Singapore, 1945), pp. 40–43.

37. For an early statement, Yoshihara Kunio, *The Rise of Ersatz Capitalism in South-East Asia* (Oxford, 1988).

38. William H. Frederick, "Reflections in a Moving Stream: Indonesia Memories of the War and the Japanese", in *Representing the Japanese Occupation of Indonesia: Personal Testimonies and Public Image in Indonesia, Japan and the Netherlands*, edited by Remco Raben (Amsterdam, 1999), pp. 16–35.

39. Michiko, Nakahara, "Labour Recruitment in Malaya under the Japanese Occupation: The Case of the Burma Siam Railway", in *Rethinking Malaysia*, edited by Jomo K.S. (Kuala Lumpur, 1997), pp. 215–45; Paul H. Kratoska, ed., *Asian Labour in the Wartime Japanese History: Unknown Histories* (Armonk, 2005).

40. Yuki Tanaka, *Japan's Comfort Women: Sexual Slavery and Prostitution during World War II and the US Occupation* (London, 2002).

41. For summaries, see Peter Li, ed., *Japanese War Crimes: The Search for Justice* (2002); Yoshimi Yoshiaki, *Comfort Women: Sexual Slavery in the Japanese Military During World War II* (New York, 2001).

Part Two

Southeast Asia

Chapter Three
Legacies of World War II in Indochina

David Chandler[1]

> *"It's going to be awfully hard straightening out Asia, what with China and Thailand and Indochina. I'd like to get into that."*

– U.S. President Franklin Roosevelt, talking to his wife, March 1945[2]

The components of French Indochina (Cambodia, the protected kingdoms that constituted Laos, and France's three possessions in Vietnam — Tonkin, Annam and Cochin-China) shared an anomalous experience in World War II, and for this reason the impact of the war was different there from elsewhere in the region.

To highlight the anomalies: no Indochinese soldiers (or very few) fought the Japanese in World War II. France, unlike the Netherlands, Great Britain, China and the United States, was never at war with Japan. Japanese troops came into Indochina in September 1940 with French permission and stayed on until the end of the war, while the French continued to administer the region right up to the Japanese *coup de force* of 9 March 1945, as discussed below. Finally, although Indochinese shipping suffered from Allied attacks, and some Allied bombardments of Indochinese cities occurred in 1945, Indochina emerged from the war with its population

— except for massive deaths in northern Vietnam due to famine in the summer of 1945, discussed below — and landscape relatively unscathed.

The Japanese behaved differently in French Indochina during the war from the way they did in other colonized parts of Southeast Asia. They made little or no effort to arm and empower Indochinese youth. They recruited no labour forces and bankrolled no nationalist figures. Indochina's large ethnic Chinese minority, protected by France, suffered none of the indignities that their counterparts experienced elsewhere in Southeast Asia. In Indochina, World War II produced no resistance heroes, no collaborators with the Japanese and no outright villains. There are no World War II museums or memorials in Indochina, no dominant narratives for school texts, no problems connected with collective memory and no bestsellers dealing with the war.

Although World War II had less dramatic effects on Indochina than it did on Indonesia, Myanmar, Singapore and Malaysia, three events that occurred in 1945 — and which needed the war to take place — altered the course of Indochinese history, and produced outcomes that can be observed today. The events led directly to the psychological weakening of French control, the independence of Vietnam (and its corollary, the end of "Indochina" as a concept), the subsequent communist domination of Vietnam and Laos, Ho Chi Minh's elevated status as the father of his country, Norodom Sihanouk's long years in power in Cambodia and perhaps most importantly to a tradition of multilateral foreign intervention in the region that persisted well into the 1990s.

The first of these events was the so-called Japanese *coup de force*. On 9 March 1945, Japanese troops in French Indochina, which had been garrisoned there since August 1940, abruptly placed all French military personnel under arrest and sequestered most European civilians. The *coup de force*, code-named Operation Bright Moon by the Japanese[3] should have been code-named Operation Lightning Bolt. It took the French almost completely by surprise. Within twenty-four hours, although some French military units resisted and others escaped on foot to China, France had lost control of its richest colonial possession. Looking back years later, the French diplomat Jean Sainteny wrote bitterly that the *coup,* more than anything else, "wrecked a colonial enterprise that had been in existence for eighty years".[4]

Without the *coup de force*, two other crucial events in 1945 that had long-term impacts later on would not have taken place. These are Ho Chi Minh's declaration of Vietnamese independence in Hanoi in September[5] and the influx of military contingents from Great Britain, China, France and the United States in the closing months of the year. These incursions, in turn, need to be seen as flowing indirectly from the *coup de force* and from the power vacuum that ensued — as far as outside powers were concerned — in Indochina in the closing months of 1945.

Ho's declaration of independence and the months of agitation by the Indochina Communist Party (ICP) that preceded it galvanized Vietnamese public opinion and, at least in the north, set in motion a genuinely independent and widely supported regime. Ho adroitly took advantage of the power vacuum that followed Japan's surrender and preceded the arrival of foreign troops in Indochina. Because of France's unwillingness to accept the possibility of independence for Vietnam, his declaration also triggered the First Indochina War (1946–54) and arguably, because Ho was a communist, set in train the Second Indochina War (c.1960–75) as well.

Ho's declaration brought France's colonial enterprise in Vietnam to a close, and by splitting Vietnam from Cambodia and Laos, temporarily ended the dubious validity of "Indochina" as a geopolitical concept.[6] In its thrust and its timing, the text resembled Indonesia's declaration of independence from the Netherlands, which had been promulgated a couple of weeks before. "Vietnam" and "Indonesia", indeed, were both enduring geographical concepts that were created in World War II. The main difference between the two texts as far as the future was concerned, was that communists had written one document and non-communists the other. Thus the United States pressed the Netherlands to grant independence to Indonesia on the one hand, and became allied with France to prevent the communists from gaining power in Indochina on the other.

The third event of 1945 that can be seen as producing legacies of World War II in Indochina was the influx of foreign troops into the region in 1945–46. The arrival of these troops marked a long-lasting alteration in Indochinese affairs. For over thirty years thereafter, powers in addition to France felt that they had every right to involve themselves in Indochina on a scale unmatched elsewhere in contemporary Southeast Asia, although there are some parallels to the Malaysian experience, and British intervention, between 1945 and 1957. The 1945–46 incursions provided a precedent for the subsequent ones, and although it would be an exaggeration to suggest that World War II brought Indochina into the world, the last few months of 1945 clearly brought the world irrevocably into Indochina.

Each of these events needed the catalyst of World War II, and sprang from France's ambiguously "neutral" record in the region in 1940–45. Perhaps the most crucial of the three was the *coup de force*. The French scholar Paul Mus, who was in Hanoi on 9 March and escaped from the city on foot, argued persuasively as early as August 1945 that French colonialism was "blown out of history" by the *coup*.[7] The idea that France was a civilizing, protective force became meaningless when its officials were put under lock and key. Mus has argued that the French mandate ended when, like the Dutch and other colonial powers, they failed to provide protection and their police became inoperative.

Like the Dutch in the Netherlands East Indies, but unlike the British and the Americans elsewhere in the region, the French expected to remain indefinitely in Indochina. Events in the closing months of 1945 forced them to alter their position temporarily for tactical reasons, but they never developed a coherent exit strategy from Indochina.

Shortly after the *coup,* Japanese authorities informed the French-installed "rulers" of Cambodia, Laos, and Annam-Tonkin (King Norodom Sihanouk of Cambodia, King Sisavong Vong of Laos and Emperor Bao Dai, who ruled over Annam and Tonkin) that they now were the rulers of independent states. In April, Emperor Bao Dai's quasi-constitutional regime in Hue, administered by the scholar-official Tran Trong Kim, proclaimed itself the government of "Vietnam", resurrecting a powerful term that had fallen out of favour in the nineteenth century and had been forbidden by the French.[8] In theory, the government claimed authority over the French colony of Cochin-China, reuniting it with the protectorates of Annam and Tonkin, although the Japanese remained in control of Cochin-China until August 1945. "Vietnam" was thus united for the first time since the French had taken over parts if it in the 1860s and 1880s. The Indochina Communist Party (ICP), whose inclusive name had been imposed on its founders by their mentors in Moscow, had already resurrected the term "Vietnam" secretly in 1941, and when Ho Chi Minh declared Vietnam's independence in September 1945, he capitalized on the word's deep resonance with the Vietnamese people. The revival of Vietnamese national identity, inside inclusive "Vietnamese" borders that erased the internal ones that had been drawn by the French between Tonkin, Annam and Cochin-China, was a crucial legacy of the war, flowing indirectly from the *coup de force*.[9]

The quasi-independent governments that the Japanese sponsored throughout Indochina in the summer of 1945 suffered from inexperience and poor communications. They had no revenues to speak of. The best organized of them, Tran Trong Kim's in Hue, was hampered by a devastating famine in the north brought on by drought, Japanese expropriations of rice, and Allied bombing of coastal shipping between Cochin-China and the north. The Viet Minh, no longer fearful of the French army or police, took advantage of the famine which may well have caused the deaths of half a million people, to whip up anti-French and anti-Japanese feeling, to disrupt local patronage patterns, and to enrol supporters.[10]

Had France retained control of Indochina up to the Japanese surrender, Ho's declaration would never have occurred, nor would foreign troops have poured into the region in 1945 and the process of decolonization might have been very different. The *coup de force*, in other words, was a hinge on which the subsequent history of Indochina can be said to have swung.

At another level, the father of Vietnamese independence, Ho Chi Minh (1890–1969) owes his prominence largely to the fact that he was able to coordinate the so-called August Revolution, taking advantage of the power vacuum that followed Japan's surrender to the Allies. Without the *coup* French police and military forces would probably have been able to hold Ho and his followers in check. The ICP and its military wing, the Viet Minh, would not have been able to spearhead the independence movement. To close off these speculations, the First Indochina War might have been delayed for several years, non-communist nationalists in Vietnam and elsewhere might have made greater headway, and Ho himself might never have become the undisputed father of Vietnamese independence or the unassailable icon that he is today. As usual, the "what ifs" and "if onlys" of history highlight the contingencies, rather than the alleged inevitability of events.

On a smaller scale, King Norodom Sihanouk (1922–), like Ne Win, Ho Chi Minh and Sukarno, was to a large extent a creature of World War II. The French chose him in 1941, when he was a month shy of his nineteenth birthday, as a pliable instrument of colonial policies. In fact, as his memoirs assert, the young king gained the sense, between 1941 and 1945, of his inherent popularity and of the possibilities of absolute rule once the French had been persuaded, almost painlessly, to relinquish their control. From another angle, Sihanouk is a legacy of World War II, for without the Japanese presence in Indochina, France might well have chosen someone more experienced to assume the Cambodian throne.

FOREIGN MILITARY INTERVENTIONS IN INDOCHINA, 1940–41

Foreign military intervention in Indochina began in September 1940, when 6,000 Japanese troops entered Tonkin to prevent supplies reaching their enemies in southwestern China. The Japanese came in with French permission but they were unprepared to take power in Indochina. French officials acceded to further Japanese demands in 1941, when 30,000 more troops came into the region. The commanders of the colonial troops in Indochina — less than a quarter of whom were European — also agreed to cooperate with Japan against foreign incursions, which, after Japan's expansion into Southeast Asia in December 1941, could only have come from Allied forces.

The second foreign incursion occurred at the end of 1940, when the Thai regime of Pibul Songkram, sensing French weakness, attacked Laos and Cambodia. The Thai gained some victories on the ground but their naval units were severely damaged by French aircraft. In a Japanese-brokered peace agreement, France was forced to relinquish parts of Laos and large portions of northwestern Cambodia — 65,000 square kilometres in all — to the Thai.[11] The French administration reacted to these losses by shoring up the royal regimes they had set in place in Cambodia and Laos.

For the next fifty years, relations between Thailand and Cambodia were perennially lacking in trust, and while the uneasiness had its roots in earlier times when the Thai had invaded Cambodia and annexed Cambodian land, relations were particularly strained by the annexations that occurred in World War II. Later on, relations deteriorated further. Cambodian ill feelings flared up most recently in the anti-Thai riots in Phnom Penh in January 2004.

In the closing months of 1945, what David Marr has called "a bewildering variety of [foreign] armed forces"[12] entered French Indochina from Great Britain, France, and China. Small U.S. units had entered the region before the end of the war. These incursions had the cumulative effect of internationalizing Indochina.

None of the intervening powers (except France, to be sure) sought to colonize Indochina or to gain long-term access to its resources. American forces were seeking intelligence. Those of Great Britain and China, for their part, were following policies set at the Potsdam conference where it was decided that following the surrender of Japan, Chinese troops would temporarily occupy northern Vietnam, release prisoners of war, disarm the Japanese and accept their surrender. British troops were to perform similar tasks south of the Sixteenth Parallel — that is in Cochin-China, southern Annam, and Cambodia. No clear arrangements were made concerning Laos — a situation that favoured the peaceful resumption of French control.

French activities were more open-ended. A small French military contingent reached Saigon in early October while British and Indian troops were still there. Communist resistance there, never as well organized as in the north, was quickly put down, and French administration in Cochin-China and southern Annam was re-established. British troops, in the meantime, had disarmed Japanese forces in Cambodia and released Allied prisoners there, ending the kingdom's six months of semi-independence.[13]

The Chinese occupation of Tonkin and northern Annam lacked the pro-colonial bias of the British forces. Although Chinese troops released French prisoners of the Japanese, they kept French officials from attending the formal surrender ceremonies celebrated in September 1945. They warned local people about the "enemies of Vietnam", meaning the French, and did nothing to encourage the re-imposition of French control.[14]

American intervention, which occurred earlier, was on a much smaller scale. It consisted of limited military action by units of the Office of Strategic Services (OSS) — code-named the Deer Mission — which entered Tonkin to gather intelligence about the Japanese. These young, low-ranking Americans established rapport with Ho Chi Minh's guerrilla forces, known as the Viet Minh, who provided them with helpful information.[15] The Deer Mission would never have been allowed into Indochina before 9 March 1945. Their anti-colonial bias and friendship with Ho Chi Minh angered the French and impeded French negotiations with Ho that began in October 1945. Ho Chi Minh needed allies in his struggle, and his friendly gestures toward the Americans appear to have been genuine and anxious as well as manipulative.

The anti-colonialism of the OSS personnel echoed Franklin Roosevelt's hostility to Charles de Gaulle and his abhorrence to continuing French control of Indochina, which was an *idée fixe* in the closing years of his life.[16] Stein Tonnesson has suggested that Roosevelt's antipathy had serious consequences in France and Vietnam in 1945,[17] but the quasi-policy was shelved after the President's death. By 1947, U.S. policy-makers agreed that an alliance with France was more important than driving the French from Indochina. Ho's communist affiliations, which he never concealed, also soon became a crucial factor in America's backing away from supporting the independence of a Vietnam in which Ho was certain to play a crucial role.[18]

The military interventions by Great Britain, China and France had a far greater impact on the subsequent politics of Indochina than the brief sojourn of OSS operatives ever did. The British and Chinese interventions had unforeseen results. Peter Worthing and others have argued that the Chinese occupation of northern Vietnam aided the consolidation of Ho Chi Minh's regime. In Worthing's words, "By first allowing the fledgling Vietnamese government to remain intact ... and then by forcing the French and the Vietnamese to come to a peaceful agreement in March 1946, the Chinese made a substantial contribution to the Vietnamese revolution."[19] The British intervention probably saved Cochin-China for France, accelerated the re-imposition of French control in Cambodia and led indirectly to French officials hiving off Cochin-China as an "independent state" in 1946.[20] Between them, the British and Chinese interventions broke (or more accurately, postponed) the fragile unity of "Vietnam" that had been hoped for by Ho Chi Minh and his colleagues and declared by Bao Dai's government in March 1945. In the nineteenth century, French colonialists had broken the Vietnamese empire into three parts. The interventions by China and Great Britain in 1945 (combined, in the north, with the establishment of Ho's regime) broke the country into two — a condition that hardened into reality after 1954 and endured, at enormous cost, until the end of the Second Indochina War in April 1975.

In contrast, the sincere but ephemeral friendship that a handful of young Americans had with Ho Chi Minh and with Vietnamese nationalists in the south made little difference to policies that developed in America or Vietnam in the post-war era. Had the Americans been more sensitive to French concerns, it is conceivable but unlikely that France and Ho Chi Minh might have made some progress in their early mistrustful negotiations. On the other hand, had the Chinese been harsher toward Ho's regime, or had the British been more sensitive to Vietnamese (and perhaps to Khmer) nationalist aspirations, the first Indochina war might not have taken the same form and Indochina's post-war history might have been very different. Finally, as this chapter has suggested, the Japanese *coup de force* and the sudden extinction of French control had foreshadowed most of Indochina's political history after 1945.

CONCLUSION

Alfred McCoy has argued that while World War II "represented little more than a transition period for most of Southeast Asia, it did indeed transform European attitudes and capabilities within the region".[21]

In fact, and sadly, very few French attitudes toward Indochina were transformed by the war or by the tumultuous events of 1945, although they should have been, especially because as I have argued, following Paul Mus, events in the closing months of the war sharply diminished French capabilities to control or "possess" the region. American anti-colonial attitudes, on the other hand, which formed the basis of U.S. policies in World War II toward Indochina, soon wilted in the face of Cold War exigencies and the importance of retaining France as an ally in Europe.

The principal legacy of World War II in Indochina was, to use a French phrase, the *fait accompli* of Vietnamese independence under the leadership of Ho Chi Minh that France stubbornly refused to acknowledge. With Ho's declaration of independence, the independence of Laos and Cambodia (and therefore the end of "Indochina") became only a matter of time. Ho himself, as I have suggested, was a creature of World War II, in the sense that he would probably never have gained so much power so quickly without the anomolous conditions imposed by the Japanese *coup de force* and the sudden end of World War II.

Because of Ho Chi Minh's communist affiliations, his declaration of independence (unlike the similar document in Indonesia) carried in its wake almost thirty years of war, fought to determine the dimensions of "Vietnam" as a territory and a nation. Cambodia and Laos were inexorably drawn into this conflict, which soon became an Indochinese war. The Lao and the Khmer gained little from the fighting and suffered enormous losses. Larger powers led by the United States and China were drawn into the region by the pressures of the Cold War, just as the power vacuum produced by the Japanese *coup de force* had drawn them to the region in 1945.

Finally, the fact that so many larger powers felt themselves fully entitled to be in Indochina and entitled to "straighten it out" in Roosevelt's playful words, is also a legacy of the war. The prolonged American involvement in Vietnam is the most striking example of this entitlement, which in the 1950s and 1960s spilled over into U.S. policies toward Laos and Cambodia.

World War II also internationalized French Indochina and thrust it
back into a world from which the French had purposely isolated it for
eighty years. This internationalization meant that Thailand felt itself entitled,
when France was weak, to revive its territorial ambitions in Indochina, and
to pursue policies aimed at subverting the governments of Cambodia and
Laos after World War II. It pursued these policies toward Laos and Cambodia
after these countries gained their independence.

Thus, although the experiences, collective memories and the physical
impact of World War II were in themselves less significant in Indochina
than in other parts of Southeast Asia, events that took place during the
closing phases of the war, and in fact needed the war in order to take place,
have altered and shaped the political history and the political alignments
of the region significantly ever since.

NOTES

1. I am grateful to Susan Chandler, Christopher Goscha and David Koh for
their helpful comments on an earlier version of this chapter.
2. Cited by Stein Tonnesson, The *Vietnamese Revolution of 1945: Roosevelt, Ho
Chi Minh, de Gaulle and a World at War* (Oslo, 1991).
3. See Ralph Smith, "The Japanese Period in Indochina and the Coup of
9 March 1945", *Journal of Southeast Asian Studies* IX (1978), pp. 268–301
and Tonnesson, *The Vietnamese Revolution*, pp. 238–54. On the aftermath of
the coup in Cambodia, see David Chandler, "The Kingdom of Kampuchea,
March–October 1945: Japanese-Sponsored Independence in Cambodia in
World War II" *Journal of Southeast Asian Studies* XVII/I (March 1986): 80–
93. On Laos, see Grant Evans, *A Short History of Laos* (Sydney, 2003), 76ff.,
and Martin Stuart-Fox, *Buddhist Kingdom, Marxist State: The Making of
Modern Laos* (Bangkok, 1996), pp. 35–36.
4. Jean Sainteny, *Ho Chi Minh and Vietnam* (Chicago, 1972), and p. 67. See
also Sainteny, *Histoire d'une paix manquée* (Paris, 1967).
5. David Marr, "Ho Chi Minh's Declaration of Independence" in *Essays into
Vietnamese Pasts*, edited by Keith Taylor and John Whitmore (Ithaca, NY,
1995), p. 232 cites a contemporary French assessment of the document of
declaration as "a borrowed concoction of bookish internationalism and
chauvinistic patriotism, an mélange of intellectual Marxism and primitive
social demands". If the adjectives are removed, the description is reasonably
accurate.
6. The Vietnamese revived the concept of Indochina in the early 1950s when
they established subordinate communist parties in Cambodia and Laos. The
linear descendants of these parties now govern Laos and Cambodia. While
the current Cambodian party has abandoned Marxism-Leninism, it still

claims to have been founded in 1951, the year in which its predecessor party was established by Vietnam. The Lao Party retains a Marxist-Leninist orientation.

7. Paul Mus, *Le Vietnam chez lui* (Paris, 1946), p. 17. Mus trekked for 400 kilometres over the next ten days to join up with French units in northwestern Tonkin. See David Chandler and Christopher Goscha, eds., *L'espace d'un regard: L'Asie de Paul Mus (1902–1969)* (Paris, 2006).

8. The kingdom called itself *Viet Nam De Quoc* (Imperial Vietnam); Tonnesson, *The Vietnamese Revolution*, p. 284ff. In the same period, Cambodia used "Kampuchea" as the spelling of the country's name in Western languages, a policy revived by Democratic Kampuchea (DK) in 1975–79.

9. Similarly, Prince Phetsarath of Laos, in October 1945, before the French resumed full control declared that all the components of Laos now constituted a unified kingdom. The French were forced to concur. "Laos" and "Vietnam", in other words, can be seen, territorially, as legacies of World War II. See Grant Evans, *A Short History of Laos* (Sydney, 2002), p. 76.

10. On the famine, see Tonnesson, *The Vietnamese Revolution*, pp. 292–95 and Huynh Kim Khanh, "The Vietnamese August Revolution Reinterpreted", *Journal of Asian Studies* XXX/4 (August 1971): 761–82. See also Pierre Brocheux, "L'occasion Favorable 1940–1945: Les Forces Politiques Vietnamiennes Pendant la Seconde Guerre Mondiale", in *L'Indochine Francaise 1940–1945*, edited by P. Isoart (Paris, 1982), pp. 131–67.

11. For a discussion of the Franco-Thai war, see John Tully, *France on the Mekong* (Lanham, MD, 2003), pp. 333–39. The territories were returned to French control in 1946. Few visitors to Bangkok realize that the so-called "Victory Monument" there commemorates the Franco-Thai war. In 1961 I met a Frenchman in Cambodia who had been captured by the Thai during the fighting. He was displayed in a cage in the Bangkok zoo, and verbally harassed by onlookers for several days before being released.

12. David Marr, *Vietnam 1945: The Quest for Power* (Berkeley, 1995), pp. 67–68. The French were purposely not invited to the Potsdam conference.

13. On events in Cambodia in October 1945, see David Chandler, *The Tragedy of Cambodian History* (New Haven, 1991), pp. 25–27.

14. See King C. Chen, *Vietnam and China, 1938–1954* (Princeton, NJ: 1969); and Peter Worthing, *Occupation and Revolution: China and the Vietnamese Revolution of 1945* (Berkeley, 2001).

15. See Archimedes Patti, *Why Vietnam? Prelude to America's Albatross* (Berkeley, 1980) and the testimony of former OSS operative Frank White in United States Senate. Committee on Foreign Relations, *Causes, Origins and Lessons of the Vietnam War* (Washington, D.C., 1972), pp. 145–60. A colleague of Frank White, George Wickes, a retired professor at the University of Oregon, has written that the entire OSS delegation in Cochin-China was vehemently anti-colonial (Wickes, letter to author, 18 July 2004).

16. See Gary Hess, *The United States' Emergence as a Southeast Asian Power, 1940–1950* (New York, 1987); Tonnesson, *The Vietnamese Revolution*, pp. 126–35 and Gary Hess, "Franklin Roosevelt and Indochina", *Journal of American History* 59 (September 1972): 353–68.
17. Tonnesson, *The Vietnamese Revolution*, p. 412.
18. Hess' *United States' Emergence* astutely compares evolving U.S. policy toward Indochina and policies toward other colonial entities in Southeast Asia.
19. Peter Worthing, *Occupation and Revolution*, p. 173.
20. On the British incursion, see "On the French re-entry into Laos in 1946"; see Evans, *Short History*, pp. 80–83. On Cochin-China as an "independent state" — a decision taken by French officials there in June 1946 — see Gary Hess, *United States' Emergence*, p. 199.
21. A.W. McCoy, *Southeast Asia under the Japanese Occupation* (New Haven, 1977), p. 11.

REFERENCES

Brocheux, Pierre. "L'occasion favourable 1940–1945: Les Forces Politiques Vietnamiennes Pendant la Seconde Guerre Mondiale". In *L'Indochine Francaise 1940–1945*, edited by P. Isoart. Paris: PUF, 1982, pp. 131–67.

Chandler, David. "The Kingdom of Kampuchea, March–October 1945: Japanese-Sponsored Independence in Cambodia in World War II". *Journal of Southeast Asian Studies* XVII/I (March 1986): 165–88.

———. *The Tragedy of Cambodian History: Politics, War and Revolution since 1945*. New Haven: Yale University Press, 1991.

Chandler, David and Christopher Goscha, eds. *L'espace d'un regard: l'Asie de Paul Mus (1902–1969)*. Paris: Les Indes Savantes, 2006.

Chen, King C. *China and Vietnam and China, 1938–1954*. Princeton, NJ: Princeton University Press, 1969.

Dunn, Peter. *The First Indochina War*. London: Hurst, 1988.

Evans, Grant. *A Short History of Laos*. Sydney: Allen and Unwin, 2002.

Hess, Gary. *The United States' Emergence as a Southeast Asian Power, 1940–1950*. New York: Columbia University Press, 1987.

———. "Franklin Roosevelt and Indochina". *Journal of American History* 59 (September 1972): 353–68.

Huynh, Kim Khanh. "The Vietnamese August Revolution Reinterpreted". *Journal of Asian Studies* XXX/4 (August 1971): 761–82.

Marr, David. "Ho Chi Minh's Declaration of Independence". In *Essays into Vietnamese Pasts*, edited by Keith Taylor and John Whitmore. Ithaca, NY: Cornell University SEAP, 1995.

———. *Vietnam 1945: The Quest for Power*. Berkeley: University of California Press, 1995.

McCoy, A.W. *Southeast Asia under the Japanese Occupation.* New Haven: Yale University Southeast Asian Monograh Series, 1977.

Mus, Paul. *Le Vietnam chez lui.* Paris: Hartmann, 1946.

Patti, Archimedes. *Why Vietnam? Prelude to America's Albatross.* Berkeley: University of California Press, 1980.

Rosey, George. *The British in Vietnam.* London: Panther Books 1970.

Sainteny, Jean. *Ho Chi Minh and Vietnam.* Chicago: Cowles, 1972.

———. *Histoire d'une paix manquee.* Paris: Fayard, 1967.

Smith, Ralph. "The Japanese Period in Indochina and the Coup of 9 March 1945". *Journal of Southeast Asian Studies* IX (1978): 268–301.

Stuart-Fox, Martin. *Buddhist Kingdom, Marxist State: The Making of Modern Laos.* Bangkok: White Lotus, 1997.

Tonnesson, Stein. *The Vietnamese Revolution of 1945: Roosevelt, Ho Chi Minh, de Gaulle and a World at War.* Oslo: International Peace Research Institute, 1991.

United States Senate, Committee on Foreign Relations. *Causes, Origins and Lessons of the Vietnam War.* Washington, D.C.: Government Printing Office, 1972.

Tully, John. *France on the Mekong.* Lanham, MD: University Press of America, 2003.

Worthing, Peter. *Occupation and Revolution: China and the Vietnamese Revolution of 1945.* Berkeley, University of California Press, 2001.

Chapter Four

Transient and Enduring Legacies of World War II: The Case of Indonesia

Richard Z. Leirissa

The Indonesian islands were overrun by the Japanese military forces in March 1942. The defence of the Netherlands of Indonesia Army was very poor since it was not prepared for an international war. Its commander-in-chief immediately capitulated, the governor-general detained and later sent to a concentration camp in Manchuria. Almost all Dutch government officials were detained and placed in various concentration camps.[1] Only a few of them succeeded in escaping to Australia. The Japanese divided Netherlands Indonesia into three administrative units. Java and Madura were placed under the control of the 16th Army and Sumatra under the 25th Army, and Kalimantan and Eastern Indonesia under the Second South Seas Fleet.

In one stroke the economic and political institutions of Netherlands Indonesia, built step-by-step in about 300 years, were wiped out. Supervised by Japanese military and government officials, the second and third echelons in those institutions consisting mostly of Indonesians were given opportunities to replace their former Dutch bosses. One of the main objectives of the Japanese occupational forces was to prepare the Indonesians in facing an invasion by the Allies forces. Their main strategy to accomplish this was by systematically eliminating every Western element in Indonesian society and culture.

The existence of widespread Western elements was the reason Netherlands Indonesia was known by some scholars as "a dual society".[2] Some of the main characteristics of the dual society are as follows. The inhabitants of Indonesia were legally divided into "Europeans" with a higher social status and indigenous (inlanders) with a lower status. "Inlanders" with certain characteristics could obtain the legal status of "European". Especially since the beginning of the twentieth century a dual school system was created, one for the majority of Indonesians and another for the "Europeans". The occupational and the remuneration systems were also mainly dualistic, increasing the gap in social status between the two races. The Japanese eliminated the "Europeans" school system, the Dutch language, and the Dutch salary system.

Indonesia is one of the countries in Southeast Asia where the imprints of the Japanese Occupation is still a reality. I will try to make this clear by commenting on various aspect of present life in Indonesia, like education, foreign language proficiency, the salary system, the intrusion of religion into politics, a strong refusal to appreciate modern norms and values, and the foreign policy. The Indonesian elementary and secondary school system followed the second rate school system built by the Dutch. Since the early twentieth century, the Dutch government followed a pluralistic system of education by distinguishing between systems of elementary and secondary schools — one for "Europeans" and another for indigenous people living in the cities and the countryside.[3] Dutch ("European") children went to the Europese Lagere School (ELS) or European Elementary School, where Dutch was used in every grade. Indonesian children whose parents were government officials were also allowed to go to ELS. Beside that, indigenous children living in the cities went to the Hollands Inlandse School (HIS) or Dutch Indigenous School where Dutch was also the official language but the standard of the teaching materials were lower then in the ELS. In the countryside, elementary schools of even lower standards were built for children of the peasants who had to attend school only for two years and where the official language was the local language. At the high school level, a five-year Hollands Burger School (HBS), or Dutch Citizens School, was built for Dutch citizens. Indonesians were provided with a six-year secondary school system divided into two levels, the three-year Meer Uitgebreid Lagere Onderwijs (MULO) or the extension of elementary, followed by another three years of Algemene Middelbare School (AMS) or general secondary school. The difference in intellectual gap between the two systems was very great, especially since the HBS provided a broad understanding of Western culture and proficiency in foreign languages. The school systems were in fact meant to keep every section of society in its place with minimum possibility for social climbing.

During the Japanese Occupation all the Dutch schools (ELS and HBS) were abolished. The HIS and AMS became models for Indonesian schools — the Sekolah Rakyat (elementary school) and the Sekolah Menengah Pertama (first level high school) and Menengah Atas (second level high school). The schools used only the Indonesian language and abolished everything that had a Western flavour, such as the Dutch language, and all other Western languages, songs, geography and history. This school system established during the Japanese Occupation is still in use today with various minor alterations.

The present elementary and secondary school system as a continuation of the Japanese system is one of the causes of intellectual degradation among schoolchildren of today. First of all the lack of training in foreign languages makes it very difficult for university students today to read and understand foreign textbooks which, in many cases, are the only textbooks available. This is very different from countries where the colonial school system is more or less in use, and foreign languages like English is still intensively taught at the secondary level. This situation of course made the matter of the education of Indonesians no worse off than the situation under the Dutch.

Textbooks written for elementary and secondary school levels also lack this intellectual depth. One case in point is history textbooks. In spite of the efforts of the government to write a much more representative history of Indonesia to be used in schools, most text books of Indonesian history is in fact a rewriting, with a specific twist, of colonial textbooks published before World War II. The authorities, however, commissioned these original texts during the Japanese period. The first book written in Indonesian by an Indonesian during the Japanese period was given the title *Sejarah Indonesia* [Indonesian history], written by a novelist and first published in 1944–45. The method and moral used by Sanusi Pane, the writer of the book commissioned by the Japanese, became the guiding principles for history textbooks until the 1970s. In those textbooks, written by non-historians, Indonesian figures were presented in Dutch colonial textbooks as villains had their images reversed to become national heroes. Only this revision was new in those history textbooks. The storylines were not much different from those in the colonial textbooks. This is due to a lack of research by the textbook writers. At present there is a conscious effort at the university level to avoid this odd way of writing history. In the 1970s the government published a six-volume history of Indonesia meant to be the standard book on Indonesian history.[4] But this project turned out to be a failure because of differences in approach used by university historians in writing the six volumes as a continuing story of Indonesia from prehistoric times until the present.

Since everything "European" had to go during the Japanese Occupation, it is not surprising that this also happened in the system of remuneration. During the colonial period a dualistic system also existed in the salary of the government officials, with the salary system of the Dutch personnel following the system used in the Netherlands, while Indonesian personnel received much lower pay due to their supposedly lower living standards. Nationalistic sentiments, or rather xenophobia, caused this lower pay system to be upheld, since the spirit at that time was that everything Dutch had to go, without a revision of payscales to reflect ever-increasing costs of living.

As a consequence the present salary system of Indonesian government officials does not meet even basic needs. Many officials, especially the lower echelons, complain that the monthly salary lasts only for several weeks. It is thus not surprising that corruption exists everywhere from the bottom level to the highest level, from the stealing of office stationery to be sold in the market by the lower echelons, to the embezzlement of government and public projects funds. The large scale corruption can mostly be found in government-owned business organizations. The government has announced its intention to bring to justice every single offender in those business organizations, but since even law enforcement is sometimes determined by politics, there is no certainty whether the policy will be implemented to the letter. Limited government revenue is certainly a major handicap for the revision of the salary system of the government officials. But since so much of the government funds are lost through illegal means, is it not much better if this lost part of the official budget were allocated legally to the salaries of the government officials? It is certainly worth a try.

With the increasing social change in Indonesian society, demands for education have also increased. But since the content and system of the elementary and secondary schools still continue with the old ways as described earlier, would this bring a change in outlook of the masses, especially in its global sentiments? The present educational law (issued in 2003) that among others, enforced the obligation of students of elementary and secondary schools to follow their own religion as part of the curriculum is indeed a setback. Its demand that every school provides teachers for every official religion certainly adds to the burden of schools budgets. This policy could also result in an increased sense of difference among the students. Since certain religions are principally against modernization, this would also increase the dislike among the young people of values and norms built in the modernization process. The respect for man-made law and the judicial process, which is characteristic of certain religions, would implant a negative outlook on modern society among the young students, and could grow later into a feeling of hatred especially towards the West where most of the impetus of modernization originates.

Although modernization has been part of the main trend of Indonesian society since the late colonial period, there are strong indications that a great segment of society shows little appreciation for this trend. Among this segment there is a refusal to accept the fact that normal ways of life at present is only possible if Western norms and values, which is the main impetus to modernization, are integrated into the main local cultures. For many the West is an antithesis to the proper ways of living. This is especially true among the masses who have only elementary or even secondary education. To them, present-day ways of living are frustrating, and are viewed as a strong and continuous threat to the traditional ways of life in past societies as rendered by their own past or in some other past described in holy scriptures.

One instance is the marriage law issued in 1974. It is stated in this law that "Marriage partners must hold the same religion, otherwise one partner must make a written declaration of change of religion". The change of religion based only on the needs of a marriage ceremony is certainly psychologically unhealthy because there is always the possibility that one of the married partners was reluctant to convert. Besides, the law requiring marriage based on religious affiliations could also enlarge the cleavages in Indonesian society. Surely there must be other more effective means to increase the religiosity among Indonesia citizens then through schools or marriages.

The continuation of this trend of conservatism is certainly damaging in two ways — first, domestically, and second, in Indonesia's foreign relations. Domestically it increases tensions among those segments of population, between the desire to enjoy the benefits of modernization and the refusal to accept the values that made modernization possible in the first place. This can be seen as a legacy of the Japanese military occupation, with its strongly imposed measures to reject and even hate the Allies (West), and an even more strongly propagated ideology of co-prosperity with the Japanese, as though the prosperity of Japan was not the fruits of the same trend of Westernized modernization. These ideas were implanted into every segment of society using propaganda techniques and sometimes physical pressures, creating a strong anti-West mindset especially among those lacking in education. At present the idea of "Japanese co-prosperity" is easily replaced by a supposedly better way of the past as described in certain religious texts.

The anti-West conservatism goes hand-in-hand with a hatred of the reality of city living, with its modern buildings occupied by prosperous working and occupational groups. This situation is easily blamed on the West, which is pictured as an "inhuman" and "corrupted" society. To prevent Indonesians from suffering this "social illness", a number of grass-roots organizations recommended the implementation of Islamic laws according to the Quran. The implication of the implementation of Quranic laws is dualism in the judicial system, since it is required that all Muslims be tried according to the religious laws.

At the grass-roots level there were also radical groups aimed at implementing the "Jakarta Charter". The document was the product of a compromise between the secularists and the Islamic clerics to incorporate Islamic law within the basic principles and foundation of the constitution of 1945. The political move failed and instead only "*Pancasila*" was made the basic principles of the national state.[5] But the wish to implement the "Jakarta Charter" never died. This was demonstrated during the sessions of the MPR (Majelis Permusyawaratan Rakyat) or Peoples Consultative Assembly in 2003 to revise the 1945 Constitution. In the end the secularist and the moderate Muslims won the day and prevented the inclusion of the "Jakarta Charter" as the foundation of the constitution.

Indeed, at the elite level the wish to implement Islamic law has been lately rather weak.[6] But the tendency to use religion as a means in politics is still strong among the elites of the Islamic parties. Religion was used as a political means during the Japanese military occupation, whereas during the colonial period, especially in the first half of the twentieth century, the official Dutch policy was to prevent this. The Japanese military succeeded in uniting conflicting Islamic political parties during the colonial period into one organization, Masyumi, to use it as a propaganda tool against the Allies.

It should be clear that among Muslim intellectuals today, there is a tendency to prevent the use of religion as a means in politics. Since there are so many nuances among Islamic political parties, it is better to speak of a spectrum of political Islam in Indonesia. At the extreme end there are Islamic parties that aim to implement Islamic law, while at the other end there are those that have minimal requirement for membership, such as being just a Muslim.

Among the Islamic parties, Partai Bulan Bintang (PBB) for example, has a political agenda that, among others, include a declared aim of implementing the Islamic law. During the general elections of 2004, PBB lost heavily and consequently has no representatives in the elected parliament (Dewan Perwakilan Rakyat or DPR). Partai Keadilan dan Kesejahteraan (PKS), during the campaigning for the 1999 elections announced outright that its aim was the establishment of Islamic law. It turned out that PKS also lost heavily at the elections of 1999. But anticipating the elections of 2004, the party corrected itself by omitting the implementation of Islamic law as its aim, and emerged as one of the largest parties in parliament. Whereas during the campaigning for the 2004 elections Partai Amanat Nasional (PAN) added Islamic law to their political platform and lost heavily in the parliamentary elections. A different pattern was found among the traditional Islamic scholars (*ulama*) who were mostly united under the Nahdatul Ulama (NU). The official policy of NU is non-participation in politics as an organization, but individually its members were free to enter politics. Since a strong tendency exists among members of NU to enter politics, a party was created for them, Partai Kesejahteraan Bangsa (PKB). It did rather well in the parliamentary elections, but lost totally in the elections for president. This must have been due, in part, to the fact that the chairman of NU was also the chair of the party (PKB).

Thus while at the grass-roots level, groups and peoples existed with a strong wish for the implementation of Islamic law, among the Muslim elite, especially among the leaders of most of the Islamic political parties, there is caution and in fact refusal to do so. But it is undeniable that a mass of support with radical Islamic political sentiments is certainly an asset to the political parties campaigning against secularist parties like the Golkar, Partai Demokrat, or Partai Nasional Indonesia Perjuangan (PDI-P). The Islamic parties in a way depend on those radical elements and, except perhaps for NU and PKB, would never confront them directly when those radicals turn to violence and unlawful actions. There is also always the possibility that certain Islamic political parties would resume the fight for the implementation of Islamic law if the situation is conducive. They only need the emergence of a strong pro-Islam climate like the situation before and immediately after the 9/11 bombings in New York and Washington, D.C. in 2001.

In fact violent conflicts connected to Islam already started in 1996, among others the burning of Chinese churches and schools in Situbondo (East Java) and the violent riots in Sukabumi (West Java), Jakarta and Medan (North Sumatra). Robert Hefner, who studied Islam in Asia and in Indonesia, is of the opinion that these violent events were connected with the efforts of a number of army generals ("green generals") to influence the situation so that President Suharto would be re-elected in the 1999 elections.[7] But no less because of their covert activities, Suharto had to step down in 1997.

But it seems that the community conflict starting in 1998 (following the fall of Suharto and the emergence of *"Reformasi"*) must have other causes, although the involvement of the military in one way or another must also not be omitted.[8] A fight between a Christian and a Muslim youth in Poso (Central Sulawesi) in December 1998 developed into a community conflict that continued sporadically until 2001. In January 1999 community conflicts (between Muslims and Christians) started in Ambon and its surrounding islands and even spread to Northern Maluku. In the first four days of the conflict alone, 54 people were reported dead and about 20,000 more had to find refuge at military installations. The conflict in Maluku continued violently until 2003 with thousands of people killed; even more were injured and lost their homes.[9] In February 1999 a similar pattern of conflict broke out in Singkawang, Central Kalimantan. In the following month the conflict spread to the surrounding area, killing about 60 and causing about 1,500 to settle elsewhere, and forced Muslim Madurese (migrants from Madura) to flee the area.[10] The conflict in Kalimantan also went on for several years.

After the 9/11 attack on the United States, violence and terrorism increased in several places in Indonesia. In September hundreds of radical youth began "sweeping" the streets for foreigners, especially U.S. citizens, and demanded that they leave the country immediately. In November documents were found indicating that the al-Qaeda leader of Spain was responsible for the terrorist training camp in Poso, Central Sulawesi. In the same month Laskar Jihad, a Muslim military organization, began attacking Christian villages in Poso.

Beginning in the year 2000 bombs began to explode in important buildings in Jakarta. On Christmas Eve 2001 churches in the capital also became the target, followed by renewed bombings in 2002. In September 2003 the Jakarta Bourse was bombed. Since the year 2000 expatriates became the new target of suicide bombings. The Bali bombings on 12 October 2002 was the most devastating, killing 202 lives including 89 Australians, among others. The JW Marriot Hotel in Jakarta was bombed on August 2004, followed by very destructive bombings outside the Australian Embassy in September 2004. Recently, in May 2005, a bomb exploded in the marketplace in Tentena, Central Sulawesi, killing 22 innocent people. Also in May 2005, preceded by gunshots at a karaoke club in Ambon (Maluku), a number of policemen were shot at close range at Loki on the island of Seram, also in Maluku. It turned out that young men trained at the al-Qaeda training camp in southern Philippines were the perpetrators.

At the start of the violence in 1999 it was not yet clear who was behind those killings and bombings, but by 2002 it became clear that two Islamic clerics, Umar Thalib, the leader of Laskar Jihad and Abu Bakar Ba'asyir, had connections with international terrorism. Umar Thalib was a cleric from a Muslim boarding school in Yogyakarta (Central Java) where he recruited his fighters to be sent to Poso and Ambon. He denied having any connection to Osama bin Laden, but he might have had financial backing from other sources in the Middle East. Abu Bakar Ba'asyir was the leader of a Muslim boarding school in Surakata and seemed to be the covert leader of Jamaah Islamiah, the Southeast Asia branch of al-Qaeda.[11] It was strongly suspected that Jamaah Islamiyah was behind the bombings, although Indonesian courts were not able to find evidence to prove it.

Although the bombings continued with expatriates as targets, since 2003 the intensity of community conflicts in Indonesia began to decline, especially in Maluku and Poso. International pressures, especially from the positive actions by the United States, Europe and Australia against terrorists around the world might have influenced the Indonesian military to take strong action against the terrorists in Indonesia.

Consequently, foreign policy towards the West of the Indonesian government depends very much on the ups and downs of the mood of the Islamic political parties and the radical organizations. During the reign of President Suharto, with tight control over politics and the minimization of democratic rule, the foreign policy of Indonesia was rather moderate. Only the East Timor issue soured its relationship with some European countries. But with the end of Suharto's rule in 1997 there began a strong anti-Western climate not unlike that in the Sukarno period (1950–68). Henceforth the relationship with the West had to be carried out very cautiously without causing too much strong reactions from the radicals. Although the situation improved somewhat with the strong measures against terrorism, the underlying roots of revivalism, and thus anti-Western feelings, cannot be eliminated in Indonesia without economic development and the realization of economic prosperity among the people, a new concept of school education and a realistic salary system for government officials.

NOTES

1. L. de Jong, *The Collapse of a Colonial Society: The Dutch in Indonesia During the Second World War* (Leiden: KITLV (Koninklijk Instituut voor Taal-, Land- en Volkenkunde) Press, 2002).

2. J.J.P. de Jong, *De Waaier van het Fortuin. De Nederlanders in Azie en de Indonesische Archipel, 1595–1950* (Den Haag: Sdu Uitgeverij, 1998), pp. 365–72.

3. Ibid., pp. 373–76.

4. Nugroho Notosusanto and Marwati Djoened Poesponegoro, *Sejarah Nasional Indonesia* (Jakarta: Balai Pustaka, 1975) (six volumes).

5. Sekretariat Negara RI, *Risalah Sidang Badan Penyelidik Usaha-usaha Persiapan Kemerdekaan Indonesia (BPUPKI), Panitia Persiapan Kemetrdekaan Indonesia (PPKI)*, Jakarta 1995, pp. 385, 412–40.

6. Among the elites one should in fact differentiate between "reformists" and "revivalists". See Yousef M. Choueiri, *Islamic Fundamentalism* (London: Printer Publisher, 1990). Translated into Indonesian, the two concepts became Islam reformist and Islam Radikal: see for instance, Tarmizi Taher, "Anatomi Radikalisme Keagamaan dalam Islam", in *Radikalisme Agama*, edited by Bachtiar Effendi and Hendro Prasetyi (Jakarta: PPIM-IAIM), pp. 1–40.

7. Robert Hefner, *Civil Islam: Muslims and Democracy in Indonesia* (Princeton: Princeton University Press, 2000).

8. "Peace for Poso: Highlighting the State's Role may Stop the Poso Conflict", <http://insideindonesia.org/edit/72/politics/>.

9. In May 2005 sporadic violence broke out again, but this time the target was a police post and a karaoke club. According to official reports the perpetrators were trained in an al-Qaeda camp in Southern Philippines. Hundreds of guns

and ammunition were also discovered at the campus of STAIN (State Institution for Islamic Studies) in Ambon.

10. *History of Indonesia: Reformasi, 1998 till Today.* <http://www/indonesia photo.com/content/view/103/46/>.

11. Ibid.

Chapter Five

The 'Black-out' Syndrome and the Ghosts of World War II: The War as a 'Divisive Issue' in Malaysia

Cheah Boon Kheng

INTRODUCTION

In Malaysia there is no let-up in the people's interest on the World War II. The ghosts (read: memories) of the war are very much alive. Suffering, hardships, resistance, torture, horror and terror — these are the evergreen memories that the war calls up in the public imagination. But this is in sharp contrast to the official view, which emphasizes remembering only the positive rather than the negative aspects of the war. In fact, the Malaysian government is determined to exorcise the ghosts of the war, especially the dark and ugly aspects within the public consciousness relating to the anti-Japanese movement, the inter-racial clashes and the massacres and atrocities committed by Japanese troops during the Japanese Occupation. One Malay historian has detected what he calls a "black-out" syndrome relating to the war.[1] This chapter examines the psychological dimensions of the war. This is important to the understanding of why the war has still left such deep psychological scars in the public mind, after having ended sixty years ago.

While every ethnic community in Malaysia suffered during the war, none would deny that the war was Japan's greatest hour. It militarily defeated a European imperial power, Britain, conquered and occupied Britain's colonial territories of Malaya, Sarawak and Sabah for three-and-a-half years. In its immediate impact, the war triggered off a series of events and changes. It represented an important turning point in Malaysia's post-war social and political history. It exacerbated inter-ethnic tensions and conflicts, awakened the peoples' national consciousness, and expedited their struggle and march towards self-government and national independence.

OFFICIAL POLICY TOWARDS THE WAR

Local views on the war within popular culture differ, however, from that of the official history of the war, which is tied up with Malaysia's internal and international politics. The Malaysian government's present policy of "Looking East" is to be friendly with Japan and with other East Asian countries like China, Taiwan and North and South Korea. It has, therefore, tended to adopt a "forgive and forget" attitude towards Japan's wartime role. But local feelings against atrocities that Japanese troops committed towards the people in wartime Malaya, Sarawak and Sabah are still strong. Yet, despite this, the government tends to gloss over or close an eye toward much of the occasional outcry that arises. It has tended to look more positively than negatively at Japan's contribution, particularly to its support for and awakening of wartime Malay nationalism. While the Malaysian government remains non-committal on the recent Chinese and South Korean protests with regard to the Japanese history textbooks on the war and on Japanese Prime Minister Junichiro Koizumi's visits to the Yasukuni memorial shrine for the war dead, local Chinese newspapers have sided with the Chinese and Korean stand on the issues. There has also been a revival of Malaysian Chinese claims for further "blood debt" from Japan.

As far as the Malaysian government is concerned, the issue of Japanese military atrocities and the "blood debt" claims to the Japanese government is now closed. The blood debt issue was officially settled in 1966, when Japan agreed to make a gift of RM25 million to Malaysia for the purpose of purchasing two ocean-going vessels from Japan. After protracted negotiations, Malaysia's then prime minister, Tunku Abdul Rahman, accepted the gift as the final and complete settlement of the unpleasant events of World War II. Earlier, the Japanese government had rejected the claims for war reparations in Malaya, arguing that these had been settled with Britain, the imperial power in Malaya, immediately after the war.

In 1995 on the fiftieth anniversary of the war, some observers attributed the low-key mood of the event to the attitude of the then Malaysian prime minister, Dr Mahathir Mohamad. Although he did not lay down any official policy on the issue, Dr Mahathir in early 1994 had told the visiting Japanese Prime Minister Tomiichi Muruyama that he felt there was no need for Japan to keep apologizing over its conduct in the war.[2] This was seen as being sympathetic to Japan with whom Malaysia has enjoyed a warm diplomatic and economic friendship. At ceremonies marking the fiftieth anniversary, Malaysian government officials acknowledged that while Malaysians of all races had fallen victim to Japanese troops, yet the Japanese had inspired the people with an anti-colonial spirit and awakened Malay nationalism.[3] The current Malaysian Prime Minister Abdullah Ahmad Badawi is also intent on prolonging the good existing ties with Japan whom he regards as one of Malaysia's important trade and business partners. However, on 25 May 2005, on a visit to Tokyo, he urged Japan and China to settle their differences, adding, "If ever there was a time for outstanding historic statesmanship in East Asia, it is now", otherwise they would take a wrong turn and "skid down the slippery slope to oblivion and the dark ages".[4]

THE WAR IN MALAYSIAN HISTORY TEXTBOOKS

School history textbooks before and after Malaya's independence in 1957, and even after the formation of Malaysia in 1963, had given a fuller account of the war, and tended to look favourably at the victorious Western Allied Powers and also at the local anti-Japanese resistance forces, especially the predominantly Chinese guerrilla force, the Malayan People's Anti-Japanese Army (MPAJA). Consequently, they provided fuller details of the Japanese Occupation and of Japanese military atrocities. But recently the emphasis has changed. Take the case of Malaysian history book for 1990, and for 1992 for Form Three. While they discuss the form of Japanese military administration, its educational and economic policies, and the social hardships suffered during the occupation, they present only a brief account of the reactions of the different ethnic communities. The commissioned writers, mostly historians from local universities, toned down Japan's "acts of aggression" and de-emphasized Chinese anti-Japanese activities while playing up the more positive aspects of the occupation, such as how it inspired the anti-colonial spirit and Malay nationalism. A pandering to Malay nationalism is noticeable with more coverage given to the courage and heroism of Malay members of the anti-Japanese resistance units, *Wataniah* [For the Fatherland], and *Askar Melayu Setia* [Loyal Malay Soldiers]. The British formed both these groups belatedly in 1944–45, unlike the MPAJA, also a British-sponsored force, which had been formed at the outbreak of the war in 1941. In the new version the MPAJA is mentioned only in a single line.[5]

It is possible that the textbook writers had been asked to play down the communist-dominated MPAJA as the government had been engaged in a forty-one-year war against the communist insurgency. The Communist Party of Malaya did not terminate its armed struggle until 1989. Clearly, the authorities have taken a political decision, having decided it was not possible to satisfy the demands and needs of every ethnic group for historical space and recognition of their communities' past contributions to the country.[6] This is a delicate matter that touches on ethnic sensitivities. On the other hand, the treatment of a Chinese revolt against the Japanese forces in Sabah in October 1943, known as the Double Tenth Uprising, which was supported by other ethnic communities, received a historical understanding that is more accurate and objective. The text reads: "In Sabah, although the population was made of various ethnic communities, they could in a time of emergency unite forces to oppose an enemy which endangered their safety."[7]

THE WAR AS A 'DIVISIVE' ISSUE

It is probable that this change in policy is a reflection that the war still remains a sensitive and psychological issue within Malaysia's multi-ethnic population. In any Malaysian discussion of the war much depends on what one's viewpoint is, who raises it and how the issue is presented. The most contentious issue is really that of collaboration and resistance.

As Willard Elsbree has rightly observed of the war's impact on the peoples of Malaya, "had there been equal proportions of Chinese and Malays in the resistance as well as in collaboration, the bitterness which came in the wake of the occupation would not have had such a pronounced racial tinge."[8] In fact, collaboration affected all communities. However, Malaysian historian Zainal Abidin b. Abdul Wahid has rightly stated that differences in the treatment accorded to the Chinese and the Malays under

Japanese rule, and particularly the use of Malay policemen against the guerrillas in the Chinese-dominated MPAJA, had a negative impact on the development of a united Malayan nationalism and formed the starting point for inter-racial conflicts in the country.[9] American historian Paul H. Kratoska also observes, "In Malaysia, the uneven treatment of the races, the suggestion that the Japanese favoured the Malays, and other aspects of the Occupation are seen as potentially divisive issues."[10]

While most Malaysian Chinese of the older generation would recall unhesitatingly their memories of Chinese suffering, hardship, torture and anti-Japanese resistance during the war, very few would laud the behaviour of Japanese troops or the policies of the wartime Japanese administration towards the Chinese community. Japanese troops are said to have carried out the *sook ching*, the massacre of between 6,000 and 50,000 Chinese in Singapore and in Malaya.[11] Most would find more negative than positive things to say about Japan's wartime role.

The views of Malaysia's Indian, Muslim-Malay, Kadazan, Dayak and other indigenous communities towards the Japanese Occupation, however, would be rather ambivalent. Japanese policies towards indigenous peoples were generally favourable. Initially, Japanese recruitment of Indians for work on the infamous Thai-Burma railway was greatly resented by the Indian community, but later as the Japanese Army recruited Indians to join the Japanese-sponsored Indian National Army [INA] to "liberate" India, many Indians volunteered. As Malaysian Indian scholar P. Ramasamy recalls, "It can be concluded therefore that World War II, and specifically the occupation of Malaya by Japan imposed great hardship and misery on the people.... In the case of the Indian community, while the rank and file was exposed to much hardship and cruelty, their experience with the INA was a very memorable event because it provided a chance of a life-time to settle old scores with their colonial masters."[12] For the Malay community in Kuching (Sarawak), the war, according to historian Naimah S. Talib, did not have far-reaching consequences: "They did not prosper under the Japanese nor did they experience extreme deprivation or hardship."[13] It was a similar experience for the other indigenous communities in Sarawak. Unlike them, however, the Chinese community there was pressured into making a contribution of RM2 million as a "tribute of atonement" to Japan.[14]

Some of the worst inter-racial conflicts in Malaya and in Sarawak occurred at the end of the war. In Malaya clashes between Malays and Chinese occurred in the Batu Pahat and other districts of Johor state as well as in the Telok Anson basin in Perak state. In Kuching and Kanowit in Sarawak, when the war ended in September 1945, latent inter-ethnic tensions erupted. Chinese-Iban clashes and Chinese-Malay clashes broke out in several towns over the issue of collaboration. These clashes were quelled only with the arrival of Australian troops.[15]

When British troops returned to Malaya, they found some 4,000 refugees in Batu Pahat town and 10,000 more in Muar town. In this inter-racial contest, Malays were the "real victors". They had successfully resisted and defeated a wartime armed Chinese-dominated communist movement (MPAJA), which had attempted to seize power in many parts of the country when the Japanese Occupation ended. Subsequently, the Malays also defeated the British government's Malayan Union plan — introduced after its troops had reoccupied the country — to offer non-Malays citizenship and equality of status with Malays.[16]

Thus, from the government's point of view, the war represented a "dark blot" in terms of race relations, much of which is hardly discussed in school history textbooks.

THE 'BLACKOUT' SYNDROME

Relatively speaking, wartime Japanese policy was, indeed, generally favourable towards Malays, who were regarded as the indigenous peoples. The Japanese administration employed a larger number of Malays in government service as well as volunteers for police and paramilitary forces, which were used to hunt down the guerrillas in the MPAJA. But there were also many Malays who suffered great economic hardships or who were ill-treated by Japanese forces. Malay resentment against the Japanese regime really began with the dissolution of the pro-Japanese Malay nationalist party, *Kesatuan Melayu Muda* [the Young Malay Union] in 1942 as the Japanese did not want to encourage a premature flare-up of Malay nationalism. Resentment increased further when Japan transferred the four northern Malay states of Kedah, Perlis, Kelantan and Trengganu to Thailand in 1943.

Consequently, older generation Malays display a certain ambivalence in their recollections of the war. Malaysian historian Abu Talib Ahmad in a recent study captures this ambivalence aptly:

> Against the background of deep anti-Japanese feelings between 1945 and 1957 [the year of Malaya's independence], the Malay elite adroitly downplayed their collaboration with Japan. At the same time, many

began to promote the anti-Japanese aspects of their wartime career and to equate defending Malaya under colonial rule with defending the motherland! This delusory exercise only abated by the mid-1980s when the Malay-Muslim elite who had survived the period began to talk about the positive side of Japanese rule and how this had impacted on their personal career advancement.[17]

Abu Talib also detected what he calls the "Biodata Blackout Syndrome" pertaining to the wartime careers of both Malay and non-Malay elite in the *Who's Who in Malaya* directory between 1957 and 1960. Scanning through these directories, he found ".... there was a conscious effort by an overwhelming majority of the Malay-Muslim elite to avoid public association with the wartime period, although a significant majority did collaborate with the Malayan Military Administration [MMA] ... it was also widespread among the non-Malay elite, notably business and society leaders..."[18]

This effort to blank out their acts of collaboration affected both the elite of the Malay left and the Malay right, and included Malaya's first Prime Minister Tunku Abdul Rahman and the socialist Ahmad Boestamam, who both served in the MMA. Non-Malay celebrities who also blanked out their wartime careers with the MMA were journalist J.V. Morais and Malayan Chinese writer Chin Kee Onn. Abu Talib offers the following rationale for their behaviour:

> For an emerging nation like Malaya, an acceptable definition of "heroic" must relate to the actions of citizens who served the national interests directly, and not the interests of some occupying power. Yet until the 1960s, many Malay-Muslim elite still clung to the erroneous perception that the defence of "Old England" and her imperial possession was "heroic and nationalistic" and more acceptable than fighting for Asiatic Japan, the new invader from the East that many viewed as barbarous, although in reality both powers were equally imperialistic.[19]

This judgment takes little account of the fact that until 1957, Britain still ruled Malaya and would still have viewed wartime collaboration in an unfavourable light. Nevertheless, psychologically, Britain's view [read ghost] did influence the mindset of Malaya's elite and compel them to fall in line accordingly. They could not be free from this mindset until after independence. In the case of Malay socialist Mustapha Hussein, the taint of collaboration affected him so terribly that he had a nervous breakdown. As vice-president of the *Kesatuan Melayu Muda* [Young Malay Union], which collaborated with the Japanese administration, he was arrested and detained twice by the British authorities after the war. On his release, he was not reinstated into government service (he was a lecturer at the Serdang Agricultural College before the war). To fend for himself and his family, he worked as a farmer, a fruit seller, a noodles hawker, a printer and an insurance agent. His health gradually recovered and he spent the rest of his life struggling to prove that he was a Malay nationalist and patriot. He sought recognition from the authorities as such. Before he died in 1987, he delivered a talk to university students about his past, in the course of which he broke down repeatedly:

> I cried along with them as memories of my bitter and grueling experiences came flooding back," (he recalls in his posthumous memoirs, published by his daughter). Involved in World War II as Malay Fifth Columnist leader, detained in several (British) Police lock-ups and prisons, taunted and jeered by Malays who saw me hawking food on the roadside, humiliated by people who slammed their doors in my face, asked to leave my rented cubicle in the middle of the night and even labeled as the Malay who "brought" the Japanese into Malaya... I left them with a tremendous sense of mental and emotional fulfillment. I had sown in these educated young souls the urge to struggle for justice.[20]

In writing these memoirs, Mustapha was clearly able to release and assuage the cries of his own tormented soul for justice and recognition.

THE WAR IN POPULAR CULTURE

In present-day Malaysia, however, the war seems to be a recurrent theme in the public imagination judging by the continuous output of memoirs and books on the war and the production and screening of films about the war. The reasons are varied, ranging from nostalgia to revenge, to trauma, to memories of dramatic events such as mass killings, severe food shortages, deeds of sacrifice and heroism, suffering and tragedy, which affected an untold number of lives. Many of these stories were narrated with mixed feelings. Besides the shock and suffering, the war always taught people lessons.

Malaysian publishers have brought out in recent times a large number of books in Chinese, English and Malay about battle campaigns and stories about wartime resistance. Chye Kooi Loong has narrated what he witnessed of the British troops fighting off the Japanese in Kampar (Perak) in his book, *The History of the British Battalion: The Malayan Campaign,*

1941–1942 (1984). A 365-page volume, *As the River Flows* (2003) is a collection of memoirs by fourteen women who served in the MPAJA, while a pictorial book, *From Pacific War to Merdeka* (2005) is about resistance and romance of Malay guerrillas Abdullah C.D. and Rashid Mydin and their wives Suriani Abdullah (formerly Eng Ming Ching) and Salamah Abdullah (formerly Cao Qi Chu) respectively.[21] Malay film producers have also brought out Malay feature films depicting the war — *Lieutenant Adnan* (2000), *Embun* (2002) and *Paloh* (2003) — each winning awards at the Malaysian film festivals for their respective years of screening. *Lieutenant Adnan* glorifies the sacrifice and heroism of Lt. Adnan Saidi of the Malay Regiment, who put up a spirited struggle in the defence of Singapore at Bukit Timah and Pasir Panjang. *Embun* is about *Kempeitai* (Japanese military police) cruelty towards Malays in a village in Penang state, while *Paloh* (2003) is a love story between a Malay policeman and a Chinese girl, who is involved with the MPAJA, and highlights race relations between Malays and Chinese during the war in the state of Johor.

Attesting further to the war as a popular theme in the people's imagination, the Malaysian daily, *The Star*, commemorated the sixtieth anniversary of the war in 2005 by publishing a series of weekly articles, beginning in January. Every Sunday, the paper devoted two pages to its reporters' interviews with residents of the older generation, of all races, on their memories of the war. The articles were eagerly read, and, in fact, boosted the sales of its Sunday edition. The first article began with residents in the frontline state of Kelantan recalling how they experienced the arrival of the Japanese invasion forces in their villages and in the state capital, Kota Bharu. The newspaper's reporters covered all the eleven states of the Malay Peninsula to record people's experiences. On 10 and 17 July the daily published accounts of those in Sarawak and then of Sabah. The series climaxed on 15 August, the date when Japan surrendered after atomic bombs were dropped on its cities of Hiroshima and Nagasaki.

Most of the articles published by *The Star* described the hardships and suffering of the people and the destruction and dislocation, which the war brought to people's lives, and how the experience taught them many lessons. In 1995, to commemorate the fiftieth anniversary of the war, *The Star* had also published a series of four-page articles, which began in mid-July and ended around the date of the anniversary in August. Later in October 1995 it re-started another series of secondary school students' reports of their interviews with old people on their memories of the war.

The Penang Chinese newspaper, *Kwong Wah Jit Poh,* also held a photographic exhibition on the war at its premises. It would appear that for a section of Malaysian society, interest in the war has not abated.

THE CONTINUING CRISIS OVER JAPAN'S PAST

In Malaysia and in Singapore, the war crimes trials of Japanese military personnel, especially General Yamashita in Manila and other commanders in Singapore and Malaya after the war, did go some way to assuage the pain and bitter experiences of the peoples that had suffered during the war. However, so long as Japan's war past continues to affect relations between Japan and its East Asian neighbours, China and South Korea, similar tensions are unlikely to simmer down in Southeast Asia, including in Malaysia. Although Japanese Prime Minister Koizumi tendered Japan's third apology[22] at the Asian-African summit in Bandung in April 2005 to peoples in Asia and Southeast Asia for what Japan's troops did during the war, the crisis has not yet been resolved. It has merely quietened down. Between the months of May and June 2005, letters to the Malaysian press indicate that readers still felt that Japan had not really "atoned" for its past and until this was done, the issue could not be resolved. Two readers made a telling comparison between the way Germany and Japan dealt with their war crimes:

> ... acknowledging your past sins is always the first step towards gaining forgiveness from the victims you have wronged. Hiding your sins by glorifying wartime criminals and blatantly perverting historical facts ultimately sends a message that you are unrepentant and refuse to recognize the evils of your forefathers.... The Germans apologized and they now have a healthy relationship with their European neighbours. The Japanese did not, and they continue to have a rocky relationship with their East Asian neighbours.[23]

Earlier, another reader had written:

> ... to date, the Germans — unlike the Japanese — have paid billions in reparations to their victims.... As one whose parents and relatives endured the hardships during the Japanese occupation here and had their lives totally disrupted and ruined, I nevertheless harbour no hatred for the Japanese, but only feel more could be done by Japan today to redeem and acknowledge their inglorious past. Then perhaps they will have a new history written for them.[24]

CONCLUSION

While the Malaysian government is anxious to exorcise the ghosts of the World War II, the issue of Japan's past keeps recurring within the public sphere. Until this issue is finally resolved, it is unlikely that it will be forgotten. The issue of Japan's past has been psychologically divisive within Malaysian society, especially among the older generation of Malaysians. Many had been forced to indulge in selective forgetting and remembering of the wartime period. Until the 1980s, many did not dare to come clean with their own wartime past. Right after the war, Malaysian history books had been inclined to play up the victorious Western Allied Powers against Japan, as well as the local anti-Japanese resistance forces like the MPAJA as "heroes", but now there is a trend to look at the war differently, if not to rewrite its history to suit political or national agendas. Textbook accounts about the war remain controversial, as their versions inevitably do not agree with the perceptions of all ethnic groups. Despite the changing government view on the war, however, popular culture still views the war as a "dark blot" in the nation's history. It looks like exorcising the ghosts of the World War II will take a long time.

NOTES

1. Abu Talib Ahmad, *The Malay Muslims, Islam and the Rising Sun: 1941–1945*, MBRAS Monograph no. 34 (Kuala Lumpur, 2003), p. 149.
2. See *The Star* report, "Forget the Past, PM tells Muruyama", 28 August 1994.
3. See *Utusan Malaysia* report, "Kedatangan Jepun Pemangkin Kesedaran Politik" [Japan's Advance was a Catalyst of Political Consciousness], 26 October 1995.
4. *The Star*, 26 May 2005, p. 4.
5. See Sabihah Osman, Muzzaffar Tate and Ishak Ibrahim, *Sejarah Tingkatan Tiga* [History for Form Three] (Kuala Lumpur: Dewan Bahasa dan Pustaka, 1990), pp. 1–20.
6. This issue of history textbooks as a controversial topic is discussed in further detail in Cheah Boon Kheng, "Ethnicity, Politics, and History Textbook Controversies in Malaysia", in *The American Asian Review* XXI, no. 4 (Winter 2003): 229–52.
7. Ibid., pp. 13–14.
8. W.H. Elsbree, *Japan's Role in Southeast Asian National Movements, 1900–1945* (Cambridge, Mass: 1953), p. 149.
9. Zainal Abidin bin Abd. Wahid, "The Japanese Occupation and Nationalisms", in *Glimpses of Malaysian History*, edited by Zainal Abidin bin Abd. Wahid (Kuala Lumpur: Dewan Bahasa dan Pustaka, 1970), pp. 93–98.

10. Paul H. Kratoska, *The Japanese Occupation of Malaya* (London: Hurst and Co., 1998), p. 359.

11. Mamoru Shinozaki, a Japanese official in wartime Singapore, said the Kempeitai (military police) reported 6,000 Chinese killed in "Operation Clean-up" or *sook ching*, while General Kawaguchi placed the death toll in Singapore between 2,000 and 10,000. A Singapore Chinese source, Dr Chen Su Lan, has estimated the number of deaths at between 50,000 and 60,000. See M. Shinozaki, *Syonan — My Story* (Singapore: Asia Pacific Press, 1975), pp. 20–21; Ian Ward, *The Killer They Called a God* (Singapore: Media Masters, 1992), pp. 85, 305–11, and Chen Su Lan, *Remember Pompong and Oxley Rise* (Singapore: Chen Su Lan Trust, 1969), pp. 185–87.

12. See P. Ramasamy, "Indian War Memory in Malaysia", in *War and Memory in Malaysia and Singapore*, edited by P. Lim Pui Huen and Diana Wong (Singapore: Institute of Southeast Asian Studies, 2000), p. 104.

13. Naimah S. Talib, "Memory and its Historical Context: The Japanese Occupation and its Impact on a Kuching Malay Community", in *War and Memory in Malaysia and Singapore* (Singapore: Institute of Southeast Asian Studies, 2000), p. 135.

14. Ooi Keat Gin, "The Japanese Occupation and the Peoples of Sarawak", in *Southeast Asian Minorities in the Wartime Japanese Empire* (London: Routledge Curzon, 2002), p. 142.

15. See Ooi, "The Japanese Occupation and the Peoples of Sarawak", ibid., pp. 144–45.

16. The contest is examined in greater detail in Cheah Boon Kheng, *Red Star Over Malaya: Resistance and Social Conflict during and after the Japanese Occupation, 1941–1946* (Singapore: Singapore University Press, 1987).

17. Abu Talib Ahmad, *The Malay Muslims, Islam and the Rising Sun: 1941–45*, op. cit., p. 149.

18. Ibid., p. 146.

19. Ibid., p. 141.

20. Mustapha Hussein, *Malay Nationalism before UMNO: The Memoirs of Mustapha Hussain*, translated by Insun Mustapha and edited by K.S. Jomo (Kuala Lumpur: Utusan Melayu Publications, 2005), pp. 401–02.

21. See Khoo, *As the River Flows* (Kuala Lumpur: Gerakbudaya Publishers, 2003), and James Wong Wing On, *From Pacific War to Merdeka* (Kuala Lumpur: Strategic Information Research Development, 2005).

22. The first apology was made by Japanese Prime Minister Morihiro Hosokawa in September 1993, and the second by Prime Minister Muruyama on 15 August 1996. While Japan has every year remembered the atom bombings of Nagasaki and Hiroshima, in which thousands of Japanese people died, the sufferings which Japan had inflicted on others during the war, however, had gone unnoticed until 1996 when the Mayor of Nagasaki chose also to

remember those who had been killed by Japanese troops in the occupied territories during the war.
23. See Raphael Ryan, "No Apology, No Forgiveness", *The Star*, 3 July 2004.
24. See Sylvester Goh, "Japan should Own up to WWII Past", *The Star*, 14 June 2005.

REFERENCES

Abu Talib Ahmad. "The Malay Muslims, Islam and the Rising Sun: 1941–1945". MBRAS Monograph no. 34. Kuala Lumpur, 2003.
Cheah Boon Kheng. "Ethnicity, Politics and History Textbook Controversies in Malaysia". *American Historical Review* XXI, no. 4 (Winter 2003): 229–52.
———. *Red Star Over Malaya: Resistance and Social Conflict during and after the Japanese Occupation, 1941–1946*. Singapore: Singapore University Press, 1987.
Chen Su Lan. *Remember Pompong and Oxley Rise*. Singapore: Chen Su Lan Trust, 1969.
Elsbree, W.H. *Japan's Role in Southeast Asian National Movements, 1900–1945*. Cambridge, Mass: Cambridge University Press, 1953.
Khoo, Agnes. *As the River Flows*. Kuala Lumpur: Gerakbudaya Publishers, 2003.
Kratoska, Paul H. *The Japanese Occupation of Malaya*. London: Hurst and Co., 1998.
Kratoska, P., ed. *Southeast Asian Minorities in the Wartime Japanese Empire*. London: Routledge Curzon, 2002.
Lim, Pui Huen, P. and Diana Wong, eds. *War and Memory in Malaysia and Singapore*. Singapore: Institute of Southeast Asian Studies, 2000.
Mustapha Hussein. *Malay Nationalism before UMNO: The Memoirs of Mustapha Hussein*. Kuala Lumpur: Utusan Melayu Publications, 2005.
Sejarah Tingkatan Tiga [History for Form Three]. Kuala Lumpur: Dewan Bahasa dan Pustaka, 1990.
Shinozaki, Mamoru. *Syonan — My Story*. Singapore: Asia Pacific Press, 1975.
Ward, Ian. *The Killer They Called a God*. Singapore: Media Masters, 1992.
Wong, Wing On, James. *From Pacific War to Merdeka*. Kuala Lumpur: Strategic Information Research Development, 2005.
Zainal Abidin b. Abd. Wahid, ed. *Glimpses of Malaysian History*. Kuala Lumpur: Dewan Bahasa dan Pustaka, 1970.

Chapter Six

The Legacies of World War II for Myanmar

Robert H. Taylor

For people of my generation, there is much to remember, much we cannot erase from our memory, try as we may. A stray thought and off we go World War II, the Japanese occupation with all its privations and cruelties, when men's minds became callous and conditioned to pain — the suffering of it, the infliction of it — the tragic, irreplaceable losses; the poignant moments, the adventure, the sacrifices, the baptism of fire making us stronger (we hope).[1]

Dr Maung Maung, 1945 graduate of the Japanese military academy at Mingaladon and President of Burma for one month in 1988.

The legacies of the World War II for Myanmar have been hugely significant. Indeed, evidence of the war are still observable as one travels across the country. It is a significant factor in the politics and economy of the country today as well. Until just fifteen years ago, men who had their formative political and military experiences in the midst of the war still dominated the country's government. The lessons they drew from the war continue to shape the views of their heirs, the present military government. The multiple armed nationalist movements, the ethnically designed separatist insurgencies that have dominated Myanmar's politics since independence less than three years after the end of the war, all had their origins in the war years. The rhetoric of day-to-day politics still owes much to the legacy of the war. As Bayly and Harper wrote of the period of Japanese Occupation, "Nationalism was now more than an aspiration. It became a routine which long outlasted the departure of Nippon's armies."[2] Not only did unbridled nationalism overwhelm the institutions of government, but guns came to replace words as an acceptable means of settling major, and sometimes minor, disputes.

Visibly, the war legacy can still today be seen in Yangon and Mandalay as well as other towns and cities in the chassis and grills of the Myanmar-made wooden buses that ply the streets. Based on Canadian and British-built army trucks, these may now have new Japanese engines but often the gear box and power train, repeatedly patched and mended, survive in day-to-day transport. In 2004 in the northern Kachin State near the jade mining town of Phakan, on a narrow, winding dirt road, I came across a giant six-wheel drive ex-U.S. Army tow-truck still in service pulling ten-wheel Nissans and Hinos up the bank of a river that had to be forded when the bridge was closed. Japanese war reparations are also to be seen on a daily basis in the country in the form of Hino buses and trucks and Mazda "jeeps" and tiny pickup truck taxis (*lei-bein*) that were assembled in Myanmar during the days of socialist autarky in the 1970s and 1980s. Then, they were almost the only "new" vehicles on the roads.

More significantly, many of the political views and attitudes of the governors of Myanmar from the end of the war to the 1990s were shaped by their wartime experiences. As Dr Maung Maung explained in the quotation that opened this chapter, attitudes formed during the war lasted long after it was over. Maung Maung was the last president of Myanmar under the military-socialist regime that General Ne Win created following the 1962 coup, which seized power from Prime Minister U Nu. The president was a graduate of the Japanese military academy at Mingaladon, then on the outskirts of Yangon.[3] He was only one of the many men that served in General Ne Win's governments and political party after 1962, and who had been trained by the Japanese. Certain lessons were drawn from those experiences, none perhaps more telling for the Ne Win years and its legacy than the fundamental lack of trust that exists in contemporary Myanmar perceptions of politics, foreign and domestic.

The Japanese invaded Myanmar in early 1942 via Tanintharyi in the far south of the country with the fledging officer corps of the Burma

Independence Army, the BIA, led by General Aung San. The BIA then
composed of a total of thirty young nationalists from the two factions of
the Do Bama Asiayon (We Burmans) or Thakin (Master) movements
trained on Hainan Island by the Japanese. Told that the Japanese were
coming as liberators to grant Myanmar independence from British colonial
rule, the BIA officers and their growing army of young men were soon
disillusioned by their treatment. Ne Win himself explains one of the key
lessons they learned from their Japanese mentors:

> "We learned our lesson," General Ne Win (as Thakin Shu Maung
> became) would often say in later years, "for the Japanese recruited from
> both our factions, knowing full well the two were far from friendly. So
> long as we were useful, they were willing to use us. Self-interest was all
> that mattered. That remains true today."[4]

POLITICAL DYNAMICS AFTER THE WAR

Lest we believe the view that "self-interest is all that matters" was unique
to the military amongst the major political actors of post-colonial Myanmar,
a brief and separate examination of the continuities in Myanmar's domestic
and foreign politics from the government of U Nu (who had served as
foreign minister and information minister during the Japanese Occupation)
through to the present day will emphasize that this is a widely-shared
attitude. Today, the perception strongly held by the State Peace and
Development Council (SPDC) government is that all of its political
opponents, foreign and domestic, are set upon subverting the country's
independence and breaking its territorial coherence. This perception has
its origins in the lessons of the war. On the other hand, the SPDC's ethnic
minority and Bamar (Burman) political opponents share deeply an absence
of faith that an agreement entered into to the SPDC will be honoured. In
Myanmar, this point has stymied political transition to a new constitutional
order since 1990, if not since 1988.

The development of these attitudes came through the understanding
of the meaning of the war years and their immediate aftermath in the
final struggle for independence and the post-colonial civil war it
engendered. When one hypothesizes about what modern Myanmar would
be like today had the war never reached its borders, one could probably
see a very different country emerging. The war, however, unleashed
domestic political forces that had previously been bottled up or channelled
into political and administrative routines. The war rapidly accelerated

Myanmar's history, leap-frogging a political generation and placing in power in the years of 1942–43 men in their late twenties and early thirties. These men would have had to wait another decade or two for high office had the constitutional evolution begun prior to the war not been terminated by the Japanese in 1942.[5]

A peaceful and equitable political solution to the three greatest issues that effected majority opinion in the country — South Asian labour immigration, land reform and agricultural credit, and the replacement of Indian and British civil servants by trained Burmese — were all in train through legislative and executive action under U Saw's parliamentary government in 1941.[6] Each of these issues was finally to be resolved during and after the war in a manner that left no one better off and most people in greater misery. Thousands of South Asians fled from Myanmar as the Japanese invaded and the British order collapsed.[7] Landowners were little compensated when land reform was introduced after independence and Burmese cultivators became the tenants of the state rather than of foreign landlords. An inadequate state-managed system of agricultural credit was developed as well as a large "private" but extortionate parallel credit market appeared to replace that created by Chettiar money-lenders. And Burmese were thrust into the top posts of the administration with little training or experience as the British and Indian civil servants fled in 1942, most never to return. The one issue that had not yet commenced political resolution before the war was the relationship between the central government and the ethnic minorities in the north of the country. It could also have been resolved through a process of constitutional evolution had the war not allowed that issue to be turned into a battlefield for ethnic conflict rather than a task for constitutional lawyers and compromising politicians.

ECONOMIC DECLINE

Not only did the war halt what one might have thought of as Myanmar's expected political evolution, but it also knocked off course what one would have expected to have been its further economic development. The manner of both the British and the Japanese exoduses contributed to Myanmar's slow and faltering economic recovery after the war. GDP per capita has probably never returned to pre-war standards. By 1959, for example, prior to the introduction of socialist autarky, GDP per capital was still below 1938 levels. It is doubtful whether that level has been achieved even now.[8] The British programme to deny the country's modern economic resources to the Japanese as they withdrew saw the destruction of the country's oil industry, including the wells at Chauk and Yeinangyaung, as well as the oil refinery at Thanlyn (Syriam).[9] Similarly, the British programme scuppered and sunk the ships of the Irrawaddy Flotilla Company, at the time the world's largest inland water transport fleet. As a result of the wartime destruction, the country being fought over twice in the course of three years, and the ending of Myanmar's trading links with South Asia and Europe, total GDP fell by at least 20 per cent or more.[10]

As the economy suffered overall during the war years, the ability of the government to tax and spend also declined precipitously, and arguably permanently. Myanmar to this day generates probably less than 10 per cent of GDP in tax revenues. The average level of government expenditure in the period 1937–41 was 158 million rupees. Despite the massive inflation of the war years, actual government expenditure in 1943–44 was only 30 million rupees. Calculated in rupees at their 1937–41 value, actual expenditure in 1943–44 was only 5 per cent of the pre-war level. Budget estimates for 1944–45 put government expenditure at 3 per cent of the pre-war level.[11]

The cause of the precipitate decline in state expenditure during the war was the dramatic fall in revenue as the state lost the ability to tax. The Japanese military pre-empted revenues from customs, business income tax, and forests. These sources of revenue had together amounted to 42 per cent of government income under the British. Land tax, which had accounted for 30 per cent of tax revenue before the war and had been a major cause of peasant discontent, became the wartime state's major financial base. But the collapse of the administrative system meant that only 12 per cent of pre-war land taxes were collected. This decline was also partially due to the fact that domestic agriculture collapsed because of lack of export opportunities.[12] The state's ability to tax the peasantry directly through land revenue was never subsequently revived and indirect taxation on exports became the major source of state income after independence.

The decline in government revenues directly from the peasant population was mirrored by the decline in agricultural production during the war. In some commodities, production was not to regain pre-war levels for two decades, by which time surpluses for export had shrunk dramatically as the population grew and export markets were lost.[13] Paddy and rice production demonstrated this most clearly. Whereas paddy production had averaged 7.2978 million tonnes between 1935 and 1939, and rice exports had equalled 3.052 million tonnes during the same period, paddy production during the next five years, 1940–44, which encompassed two years of the war, declined to 4.0208 million tonnes. In 1945–49, including the last year of the war, rice production fell further to 3.3846 million tonnes. Export figures are unavailable for these periods but were doubtless negligible, but when large scale exports resumed in the 1950s, exports peaked in the five years from 1950 to 1954 at a mere 1.672 million tonnes, barely half the pre-war figure.[14]

The disruption of rice production was assisted by an outbreak of epidemic diseases amongst the country's draught cattle, killing from one-third to one-half of the country's stock. The plight of the peasantry was made all the more dire by a severe shortage of cooking oil, much of which had to be imported, along with most of the cloth and clothing sold in the country. As a consequence, inflation of the price of basic commodities drove many families into abject poverty. The economy had only begun to recover after the war when the civil war broke out, once more disrupting internal and external trade. Indeed, as independence and the civil war occurred less than two-and-a-half years after the end of the war in Asia, the British had neither time nor resources to restore either the administrative system or the economic order to their pre-war conditions, as they subsequently did in Malaya and Singapore.

ETHNIC CONFLICT

I have so far mentioned three legacies — curtailing of the British-commenced constitutional experiment, arrival in positions of authority of the young nationalists who were the keenest opponents of the existing order, and the economic and administrative decline of the country in the months following the Japanese invasion. None of these compare in their destructive consequence to the initiation of open conflict between the central government and the country's numerous ethnic minorities. As early as March 1942, armed clashes between Christian and Buddhist Kayin (Karen) and BIA troops in the western delta town of Myaungmya occurred. A BIA attempt to impose their authority on the town and confiscate the weapons Kayin had collected evoked a resistance. Only the intercession of two of the leading Kayin politicians of the old order was able to direct the confrontation away from bloodshed, but only temporarily.

Two months later tensions remained high in and around Myaungmya when the BIA discovered a plan by one of the senior Christian Kayin[15] leaders to mount a three-pronged attack on the city in order to liberate his compatriots from their alleged "oppression". Without waiting to investigate the report, the BIA summarily shot one of the senior Kayin leaders in the town, former Senator San C. Po, and his English wife, and took many other Kayin leaders into custody. The three-pronged attack turned out to be a damp squib but this did not stop the BIA from conducting daily executions of Kayin and burning down the Catholic mission headquarters and killing the inmates of an orphanage.[16]

These tragic events exploded in civil conflict less than four years after the end of the war. They were the result of errors of judgment and assessment of motives made possible by years of growing bitterness between those ethnic minorities perceived to be favoured by the British and the Bamar majority that felt their birthright had been denied to them when King Thibaw was driven into exiled in 1885, resulting in the annexation of all of Myanmar by British India. The perception that the British conducted a policy of "divide and rule", favouring with enhanced political and administrative power and opportunities some communities over others, was one the colonial government could neither refute nor, in effect, deny. Whether "divide and rule" had ever been the intention of British policy, it certainly appeared to be the result.[17]

Following the Myaungmya incident, the Japanese sought and gained support from the Kayin community by posing as their protectors. They sponsored Kayin associations in the Delta and conducted a rough census that showed these were twice as many members of the minority in the country than the last British census had shown. As John Cady, the most thorough historian of the Kayin experience during the war years wrote, "The pro-Japanese *rapprochement* on the part of the Karens tended in many instances to take the place of the prewar British-Karen alliance."[18] Thus the overly exaggerated story that the Kayin were loyal to the British during the war years, as demonstrated by the exploits of Major Seagrim's organization of anti-Japanese Kayin guerrillas along the Thai border,[19] was laid bare by the politics of the delta. To counter the pro-Japanese behaviour of the Kayin communities, both Dr Ba Maw's Japanese-sponsored government and eventually the Anti-Fascist People's Freedom League (AFPFL), organized by the Communist Party of Burma and Aung San's army, attempted to organize Kayin groups to cooperate with the Bamar majority. But given the deep animosities and huge degree of mistrust amongst the Kayin community of the majority group, these groups were of little political significance. They did, however, begin a pattern of relationships between the post-independence governments of

Myanmar and the Kayin leading to the fifty years of civil war and the eventual fracturing of the main insurgent group, the Kayin National Union (KNU) in the 1990s. The fracture occurred when the Democratic Kayin Buddhist Army (DKBA) split and entered into a ceasefire agreement with the SPDC.

The perception of a historical antagonistic relationship between the ethnic minorities of Myanmar, not only in the delta where the majority of Kayin resided, but in the northern and eastern border areas, had been taught in Myanmar's schools and religious institutions during the colonial years. The belief that the British occupation had served to protect the minorities from Bamar predations was then widespread. The depth of this belief, despite the lack of a firm historical foundation for these views, was turned into a basis of armed conflict during and after the war as Chin, Kachin, Shan and Kayin in the so-called frontier areas were encouraged to serve as armed levies, scouts and guides for the British. Armed with weapons that had last been used to suppress the 1931–32 Hsaya San peasant revolt, these groups proved vital in assisting the Indian and British populations that fled the country to India in 1942. Their knowledge of the rugged hills and mountains in the north linking Assam and Manipur with Yunnan Province was subsequently crucial for the Americans and the British as they attempted to re-open communications and supply links between China and India.

As the Japanese were never able to take control of the northern stretches of Myanmar, it became possible for British and American commandos to conduct raids into Japanese controlled territory with the assistance of local populations during 1943 and 1944 prior to the retaking of the country in 1945. With newer, advanced weaponry, and eventually a significant build-up of troops, especially around Myitkyina where Kachin assisted the defence of the American Army Air Force based there, local forces became better armed and equipped to assist the allies. Disarming these groups proved essentially to be impossible after the war and thus when the confused politics of the post-independent period lead to civil war, Kachin, Chin, Kayin, Shan other minority armies were quickly assembled to defend their territories against the central government of U Nu[20] and Chinese Nationalist Troops (KMT) fleeing China after the 1949 communist victory.

KMT troops, which had entered northern Myanmar prior to the Japanese invasion to protect the Burma Road supplying Chungking from the port of Yangon, remained in the country for many months after the war. The knowledge they gained there contributed to the ease by which they returned in large number after 1949 and settled down as opium smugglers and potential enemies of the People's Republic of China. This posed one of independent Myanmar's major domestic and international issues in the midst of the civil war in the early 1950s and contributed significantly to the militarization of politics in the Shan state. The fact that the KMT troops were backed by the government of Taiwan and the United States CIA, in conjunction with the military authorities in Thailand,[21] added to the sense of distrust and insecurity of the government of Myanmar.[22]

Another area of ethnic, or perhaps religious, conflict, persists until today and has its origins in events before the war but became more violent with the collapse of the civil administration. This is northern Rakhine (Arakan) "where there had been fierce clashes even before the war between incoming Bengali Muslims and the local Arakanese Buddhists".[23] With the removal of the British administration in 1942, attacks on Muslims became widespread, but when the British returned in 1944, Muslims followed behind to take their revenge on the Buddhists. At the time of Myanmar's independence in 1948, "the *Mujahids*, bands of Muslim adventurers in the extreme north of Arakan, whose terrorist activities were already beyond government control, activities ostensibly devoted to the creation of a separate Muslim state", were actively resisting the government.[24] Their descendants, the so-called Rohingya, an ethnicity unheard of prior to the late 1950s, are still in armed conflict with both the governments of Bangladesh and Myanmar.[25]

The armed conflict, one of the major legacies of the war, was not limited to clashes between minorities and the central government. Conflict amongst the Bamar majority also occurred, most notably between the communists and the government. Even prior to independence, the minor Red Flag Communist band lead by Thakin Soe had taken up arms against the provisional government of U Nu. Three months after independence, the major communist band under General Aung San's brother-in-law, Thakin Than Tun, went underground[26] against the newly independent state. Just as the majority of Kayin troops joined the Kayin insurgency in 1949, so in 1948 troops of commanders loyal to Than Tun abandoned their posts and joined the erstwhile revolution. The government of Myanmar was left with only the support of the 4th Burma Rifles under General Ne Win and half of the 5th Burma Rifles, little more than 10,000 men. In these chaotic conditions, power fell into the hands of local *Bos*[27] who were eventually recruited by the AFPFL government as parliamentary representatives. Soon they became states within the state. Only during the military caretaker government (1958–60) was their autonomous power undermined.[28]

The power of the *Bo* was the result of the collapse of the civil order during and after the war, also made possible by the ease with which arms became available in the country as the Japanese and British assisted their various sometime allies. The distribution of arms across Myanmar in the final stages of the war was seen at the time as planting the seeds of future conflict. When it became clear that the troops of General Aung San's Myanmar Tatmadaw, called the Burma Defence Army (BDA) by Supreme Allied Commander Lord Louis Mountbatten in agreement with Aung San before the end of the war, were about to turn against their Japanese mentors in March 1945, the previous order that the British were not to distribute arms to the Myanmar forces was countermanded. Many on the British side, from Governor Dorman-Smith down, viewed the planned rising of the BDA with their communist allies in the AFPFL as likely to create great problems for the eventual restoration of order in Myanmar. But Lord Mountbatten considered it to be incidental to the assistance that Aung San's forces could provide the British in militarily ending the war in Southeast Asia. The fact that at least four times more weapons were issued to Kayin levies in the Kayin hills along the Thai border than the 3,000 distributed to the BDA was not, however, lost on the Bamar population.[29]

The legacy of the Bo, many of whom rose to positions of power during the Japanese Occupation, is still present in Myanmar. The following anecdote may point toward a pattern to be found across the country. *Wunna Kyaw Htin*[30] U San Myaing was a man who began to build his fortune and his power during World War II. A small-town boy from the village of Ongbwinkwin near Kanbauk between Ye and Dawie in central Tanintharyi, U San Myaing sold timber to the Japanese. After the war, he and his six sons continued in the timber business, shipping logs to their mill in Pazundaung in eastern Yangon. San Myaing quickly amassed a small fortune with which he assisted his nephew, U Nu's Deputy Prime Minister U Ba Swe. He also built a large house in Ongbwinkwin, now nothing more than a large brick foundation, but once having a moat by which dignitaries from Yangon, including Home Minister U Kyaw Nyein, could arrive by boat for lavish entertainment.

After the army took power in 1962, U San Myaing's power began to wane, but was not extinguished. Known as the local *Myosa*,[31] San Myaing fell foul of the new authorities when he was accused of using forced labour from local villagers to build a protective wall against salt-water encroachment on his land and he consequently spent some time in prison. His timber business taken from him under the government's economic nationalization programme during his incarceration, San Myaing nonetheless remained a wealthy man, living after his release in relative obscurity in Dawei, but running a bus and truck line which plied between Dawei, Ye and Mawlamyaing to the north. When, in 1969, U Nu, together with wartime head of state Dr Ba Maw's son-in-law Bo Let Ya, raised a quixotic army to invade Myanmar from Thailand and oust Ne Win from power, at least one of U San Myaing's sons joined with Bo Yan Naing, another of the Japanese-trained Thirty Comrades, to cross the border above Ongbwinkwin and take Tanintharyi for U Nu. U San Myaing's son was killed in the subsequent defeat of the invading force. Maintaining his transport business until his death in the early 1990s, U San Myaing's legacy lives on as another of his sons is now a business partner of a former minister and retired general in the current government.[32]

The point of this anecdote, and that of the preceding point made, is that one can trace back almost any political, military or economic circumstance in Myanmar today to the legacy of the war. Given the impact of the war on Myanmar, it is difficult to point to any one major legacy but forced to do so, one would have to argue that most important was the creation of the army. Born as a political movement to regain the country's independence with the assistance of the Japanese,[33] it later came into frequent conflict with its mentor. This was because the fledging army, immediately after it entered the country, assumed administrative powers in the regions it reached. Distrusting the motives of the "fascist" Japanese from the start, and sympathetic to the arguments of their Myanmar communist allies who were fellow students with the army leadership before the war, the army turned against the Japanese even before their 27 March 1945 march out of Yangon to attack the Japanese in collaboration with the British. But not trusting the British any more than they had trusted the Japanese, and uncertain of the attitudes of the thousands of armed members of the ethnic minorities toward them, it was an army that felt beleaguered from the start. Their strong nationalist sense, combined with their single-minded courage to take on all enemies, despite the odds, contributed to the story that the army tells its new recruits and the entire country at every opportunity. The date 27 March, now Army Day,[34] is perceived as the symbolic beginning of modern Myanmar when the army seized its destiny to forge an independent state despite the odds and despite the enemies which surrounded it. The Myanmar national story has become conflated with the story of its army.

NOTES

1. Maung Maung, *The 1988 Uprising in Burma* (New Haven, Conn.: Yale University, Southeast Asia Studies Monograph, no. 49, 1999), p. 136.
2. Christopher Bayly and Tim Harper, *The Forgotten Armies: The Fall of British Asia 1941–1945* (London: Allan Lane, 2004), p. 314.
3. In *The Forgotten Armies*, Bayly and Harper have confused Dr Maung Maung, former soldier, judge and president, with Tharrawaddy Maung Maung, a pre-war politician, p. 404 and fn. 24, p. 509.
4. Maung Maung, *The 1988 Uprising*, pp. 98–99.
5. For details of the constitutional evolution of British Burma between the first and second world wars, see Robert H. Taylor, "The Relationship Between Burmese Social Classes and British-Indian Policy on the Behaviour of the Burmese Political Elite, 1937–1942", unpublished Ph.D. dissertation, Cornell University, 1974.
6. See Robert H. Taylor, "Politics in Late Colonial Burma: The Case of U Saw", *Modern Asian Studies* 10, no. 2 (April 1976): 161–94.
7. The population of Yangon, nearly half of whom were Indians, fell from half a million to 150,000 between the first Japanese bombing in late December 1941 and the end of February 1942. Dorothy Hess Guyot, "The Political Impact of the Japanese Occupation of Burma", unpublished Ph.D. dissertation, Yale University, 1966, pp. 94–96. Though some Indians came into Myanmar between the end of the war and the imposition of immigration controls in 1947, the South Asian population of the country fell from over one million in 1931 to about 700,000 in 1947–48. R.J. Kozicki, "India and Burma, 1937–1957: A Study in International Relations" (unpublished Ph.D. dissertation, University of Pennsylvania, 1959), p. 225. After independence, South Asians leaving Myanmar annually exceeded those entering the country until the early 1960s when, following Ne Win's sweeping nationalization of almost all businesses, most South Asians who could do so left the country permanently. Robert H. Taylor, *The State in Burma* (London: Hurst, and Honolulu: University of Hawaii Press, 1987), p. 272.
8. Real per capita GDP in constant 1970–71 prices in 1938 stood at Kt. 395.3 but fell 45 per cent because of war time destruction to Kt. 218.1 in 1947/48. Despite economic growth in the 1950s, this figure had still reached only Kt. 335.4 in 1961–62. David I. Steinberg, *Burma's Road Toward Development: Growth and Ideology Under Military Rule* (Boulder, Colorado: Westview Press, 1981), Table 5.1, p. 78. Per capita consumption also declined in 1947–48 to 94 per cent of its 1938–39 standard and fell to 72 per cent of the pre-war level in 1953–54. By 1960–61 per capita consumption had risen to 94

per cent of the pre-war level. Frank N. Trager, *Burma: From Kingdom to Independence* (New York: Praeger, 1966), Table 3, p. 160.

9. Whereas Myanmar produced on average 272 million gallons of petrol in the years 1937/38 to 1941/42, it was only able to produce an average of 17 million gallons in the years 1947–48 to 1951/51. Production during the latter period was disturbed, of course, by the civil war, which in itself was partially a legacy of the war years. Teruko Saito and Lee Kin Kiong, *Statistics on the Burmese Economy: The 19th and 20th Centuries* (Singapore: Institute of Southeast Asian Studies, 1999), Table V-2 (ii) Production of Minerals (1897/98-1993, five years averages), p. 150. Though limited production was resumed by the Japanese during the war, no figures are available but it fell far short of requirements.

10. Mya Maung, "Socialism and Economic Development in Burma", *Asian Survey* IV, no. 12 (December 1964): 1199.

11. Guyot, "Political Impact of the Japanese Occupation", Table 8, p. 208.

12. Ibid., pp. 209–10.

13. A contributing factor to Myanmar's loss of foreign markets was the wartime disruption to spare parts and new milling machinery. Countries such as Thailand which did not face the disruption of the war were able to move into Myanmar's markets after the war.

14. Saito and Lee, *Statistics on the Burmese Economy*, Table II–8, p. 83.

15. Bayly and Harper repeat the often stated, but erroneous, perception that the majority of lowland Kayin were Christians. *Forgotten Armies*, p. 75.

16. John F. Cady, *A History of Modern Burma* (Ithaca: Cornell University Press, 1958), pp. 443–44.

17. For a summary of British policies toward Myanmar, see Robert H. Taylor, "Pathways to the Present", in *Myanmar: Beyond Politics to Societal Imperatives*, edited by Kyaw Yin Hlaing, Robert H. Taylor and Tin Maung Maung Than (Singapore: Institute of Southeast Asian Studies, 2005), pp. 4–16. For a discussion of ethnicity and conflict in colonial Burma, see Martin Smith, *Burma: Insurgency and the Politics of Ethnicity* (London: Zed, 2nd ed., 1999), pp. 40–100.

18. Cady, *History of Modern Burma*, p. 450.

19. See Ian Morrison, *Grandfather Longlegs: The Life and Gallant Death of Major H.P. Seagrim* (London: Faber, 1947).

20. For the story of one of these groups, see Ian Fellowes-Gordon, *The Battle for Naw Seng's Kingdom: General Stillwell's North Burma Campaign and its Aftermath* (London: Leo Cooper, 1971).

21. Thailand had been granted control of the eastern Shan states during the war by the Japanese.

22. See Robert H. Taylor, *Foreign and Domestic Consequences of the KMT Intervention in Burma* (Ithaca, NY: Cornell University Southeast Asia Program

Data Paper no. 93, 1973 and Alfred W. McCoy, *The Politics of Heroin in Southeast Asia* (London: Harper and Row, 1972).

23. Bayly and Harper, *Forgotten Armies*, p. 383.

24. Hugh Tinker, *The Union of Burma: A Study of the First Years of Independence* (London: Oxford University Press, 4th ed., 1967), p. 34.

25. Reuters despatch from Cox's Bazaar, "Bangladeshi Troops Raid Myanmar Rebel Camps", 24 July 2006.

26. Thus contributing a slang legacy for "to go to the jungle" [*tow-ko ko thwa me*], or to go underground, came also to mean to go to the toilet.

27. Bo was previously a generic term for any officer, powerful person, or Caucasian male. It came to mean local bosses or strong men who had amassed a force around themselves with which to protect their town from communists, ethnic insurgents or bandits.

28. See Taylor, *State in Burma*, pp. 267–68. For details, see Mary Callahan, *Making Enemies: War and State Building in Burma* (Ithaca, NY: Cornell University Press, 2003).

29. Bayly and Harper, *Forgotten Armies*, p. 432.

30. An honorary title granted for service to the state.

31. Myosa, literally meaning "eater of the town", was the term used for the officials of the Myanmar kings who held apanage rights under their authority.

32. Based on interviews in Ongbwinkwin and vicinity in February and March 2002.

33. See Dorothy H. Guyot, "The Burma Independence Army: A Political Movement in Military Garb", in *Southeast Asia in World War II: Four Essays*, edited by Josef Silverstein (New Haven: Yale University Southeast Asia Program, 1966).

34. Previously Resistance Day.

Chapter Seven

World War II: Transient and Enduring Legacies for the Philippines

Reynaldo C. Ileto

INTRODUCTION: TWO PASTS IN THE PRESENT

The question of wartime legacies is particularly relevant to the Philippines because a key protagonist of the war in the Pacific was the United States, and the Philippines was its sole colony. Because of this forty-year colonial relationship, coupled with the experience of fighting shoulder-to-shoulder with Americans against the Japanese enemy, it seems a foregone conclusion that the Filipinos would continue to be fixated with the United States ever since. In contrast to the subjects of Britain, France and Holland, who managed to shrug off any special relationship with the former mother country, the Philippines is seen to be very much tied, still, to Mother America. World War II, if anything, would have cemented this relationship.

This image is partly true. As America's colony, the Philippines was inevitably a focal point of World War II in the Asia-Pacific. General Douglas MacArthur had been Field Marshall of the Philippine armed forces at the outbreak of the war. With the surrender of the Filipino-American forces to the Japanese in the Bataan Peninsula, MacArthur left in humiliation, vowing to return. For him, to retake or "redeem" the islands was almost a messianic endeavour. Remembering this promise, a great number of Filipinos, unlike their neighbours in Southeast Asia, continued to thumb their noses at the Japanese administration. Of all the Southeast Asian countries, the Philippines consequently suffered the most in terms of the destruction of life and property and the dislocation of millions of its inhabitants.

A brief rundown is in order for those unfamiliar with what the Philippines experienced in World War II.[1] Political events certainly moved swiftly through the war years: the Japanese takeover, the dogged "last stand" of the defenders at Bataan and Corregidor, the establishment of a new colonial order with its own language, Nihongo, and its own visions of Asian co-prosperity. Then in October 1943 came the granting of independence, three years in advance of the American timetable, a move designed to win the Filipinos over to Japan and jointly defend the country against the imminent return of the United States. But the populace was largely unmoved by this, and guerrilla resistance persisted. Barely a year later came the bombings and massacres that preceded the landing and the liberation by MacArthur's forces in 1944.

Manila was almost totally flattened by the war's end. Tales of torture and killing perpetrated by the Japanese Army and secret police became part of family lore in my father's generation. The Japanese Occupation seemed to be truly a "dark age", in contrast to the so-called golden age of American rule or "peacetime" as the pre-war years were often termed. Soon after liberation came independence from the United States in July 1946, only to be followed by a communist-led insurgency that at one point threatened Manila itself. The whole experience was traumatic for many individuals and families.

Without doubt World War II left many legacies for the Philippines in the decades to come. But I would like to move beyond the commonsense view that the deepest legacy was some kind of permanent bond between the Philippines and the United States. Associated with this is another pervasive view: that the Philippines after independence in 1946 did not see itself as belonging to Asia, and that this view persists even in this age of ASEAN (Association of Southeast Asian Nations). I argue that these are but partial truths, and that the war left a legacy, as well, of nationalist assertion against the United States, and a decisive turn towards fraternity and even identification with Asian states and peoples. The question is, which among these seemingly contradictory wartime legacies is transient, and which one is enduring?

In order to illustrate this, I would like to present two different narrative constructions of Philippine history, two pasts that haunt the present. At odds with each other, these two narratives co-exist uncomfortably within the body politic. The dominant narrative is usually possessed and reproduced by the state and becomes the template through which ongoing events are interpreted by its citizens. The subsidiary narrative survives in the margins — in civil society groups, patriotic religious sects and alternative texts, some hidden, some proscribed. It is relatively powerless in "normal" times but it can surface with a vengeance during times of crisis.

The dominant narrative is that the country was progressing fine towards independence under U.S. tutelage, attaining Commonwealth status by 1935, until the Japanese disrupted the process with their invasion in December 1941. The Filipino-American forces resist them with determination, to no avail. In this view, Japan during the war years is a totally foreign body on Filipino-American soil, the epitome of all things evil. Resistance to it is natural, even divinely inspired. MacArthur's "I shall return" manifesto has apocalyptic overtones that captured the imagination of this predominantly Christian nation. Independence in 1943 is a complete sham leading to a Japanese-sponsored government under puppet president Jose Laurel. It is the guerrilla movement, particularly the units under the command of the USAFFE (United States Armed Forces in the Far East) that keeps the fires of freedom burning until the god-like MacArthur returns.

Finally, the liberated, though wrecked, country elects its leaders and is granted real independence by the United States on 4 July 1946. Special economic and military privileges ensure that the United States would remain in various forms after the formal transfer of sovereignty. In this narrative, one deep-seated legacy of the war is a strong Filipino-American alliance, a special relationship, forged in the battlefield against Japan and further cemented during the Cold War. During the latter, the Philippines is dubbed a daughter republic of the United States and the showcase of democracy in the Far East.

BUSH'S 2003 SPEECH: A JOINT FILIPINO-AMERICAN STRUGGLE

The power of this dominant narrative of the Philippines' wartime past was recently harnessed by no less than U.S. President George W. Bush himself in his speech to Philippine Congress in 2003. "America", he declared, is proud of its part in the great story of the Filipino people. Together our soldiers liberated the Philippines from colonial rule. Together we rescued the islands from invasion and occupation. The names of Bataan, Corregidor, Leyte, Luzon evoke the memories of shared struggle and shared loss and shared victory. (*Applause*)[2]

Furthermore, Bush posits the 1945 liberation of the Philippines and the granting of independence in 1946 as *the* events that parallel or inspire the events of 2003. This is evident if we simply change the "Iraq" in the following quote to "Philippines" and "[Saddam's] cruelest regime" to "Japanese regime": "Since the liberation of Iraq, we ended one of the cruelest regimes in our time… And we're helping to build a free Iraq." He then goes on to posit Iraq as the future beacon of democracy in the Middle East, as the Philippines once was in the Far East:

But democracy has its skeptics. Some say the culture of the Middle East will not sustain the institutions of democracy. The same doubts were expressed about the culture of Asia. These doubts were proven wrong nearly six decades ago, when the Republic of the Philippines became the first democratic nation in Asia. (*Applause*) Since then, liberty has reached nearly every shore of the Western Pacific.

The furious applause by Filipino lawmakers after nearly every point Bush made in his speech testifies to the enduring legacy of the World War II images of a joint Filipino-American struggle against tyranny, the liberation of the country from such, and the installation of an independent, democratic government with U.S. help.

Bush continued to draw parallels between Iraq and the dominant Filipino narrative, this time in reference to the Cold War that immediately followed upon World War II. He called on Filipinos to participate in waging a new joint struggle against what he termed the "new totalitarian threat" against "civilization". He urged his Filipino audience to take sides in the war on terror, just as during the Cold War we had to take sides: "You are either with us or against us," he warned.

Why was the notion of a joint Filipino-American struggle against Japanese tyranny so potent even in 2003, some fifty-nine years after the event, to the extent that Bush could piggyback on it in mobilizing allies for his new war on terror? Well, in the first place, a few veterans of that war were and are still alive, serving to physically connect the present with that past. President Bush in fact made reference to this dwindling group: "Veterans of those battles are here today. I salute your courage and your service," he said.

Secondly, to permanently enshrine the memories of this generation of veterans a large number of monuments, shrines, historical markers and the like were erected in the years that followed. The memorializing of the war against Japan and the various ways this was pressed into the service of politics and policies during the past sixty years could well be the topic of a massive monograph. Here are a few examples.

Soon after liberation, the island of Corregidor was consecrated as the rock on which Filipino-American forces made their last stand; it came to symbolize the rock-stable permanence of the Filipino-American alliance. A memorial was built at Leyte to commemorate the landing of MacArthur's forces, perpetuating the memory of the redemption of the country by the United States from its dark age under the Japanese. And at Capas, Tarlac, one finds a memorial to commemorate the "Death March", the disastrous evacuation by foot of more than 100,000 Filipino and American soldiers from the battlefields of Bataan to the prison camp at Capas, Tarlac. Thousands perished along the way; thus the term "death march".

The dark age of Japanese rule is a well-known event to all Filipino students through their school textbooks. While the veterans of this event were alive, individual life stories were also handed down by parents to their children. Practically every family had a story or two to tell. My aunt's husband, a reserve officer pressed into the guerrilla movement, was captured and executed by the Kempetai after a family visit. Two of my wife's uncles were similarly executed in, of all places, Tanauan, Batangas, the hometown of wartime president Laurel. Private memories of atrocities, deprivation, and suffering by my parents' generation were transmitted to my generation (I was born in 1946). Implicit in their accounts was the other side of this enumeration of Japanese wrongdoing: the saga of liberation and the granting of independence by the "good" Americans. The Filipinos thus incurred a huge debt of gratitude to America, which in turn sought to guide its former wards through the period of reconstruction and development. Thus the notion of a continuing, special relationship was born.

This account of the war was readily promoted and sustained at the national level not just because a whole generation of Filipinos could remember it, but also because most presidents, up to Fidel Ramos in the 1990s, could identify themselves in some way or other with the narrative of resistance, suffering, liberation, and guided independence. The first president of the post-war Republic, Manuel Roxas, had stayed behind and seemingly collaborated with the Japanese by holding public office in the

1943 republic. He was, however, later exonerated by MacArthur, who said Roxas had been ordered by him to work for the Japanese in order to gather information for U.S. intelligence.

Second president, Elpidio Quirino (1947–51), witnessed the tragic slaying of his wife and children by Japanese snipers while they were fleeing their neighbourhood as the Americans approached Manila. Presidents Ramon Magsaysay (1952–55) and Ferdinand Marcos (1966–86), throughout their political careers, fully exploited their credentials as commanders of USAFFE guerilla units. Marcos even went to the extent of faking some, if not most, of his war exploits and decorations. What this shows is how valuable it was for garnering the popular vote to be associated with the epic resistance movement against the Japanese.

But all narratives have their undersides, the untold events that have to be suppressed in order for the dominant story to hold sway. Before President Bush gave his speech, a number of lawmakers walked out in protest. And outside the heavily-guarded hall of Congress, protesters were demanding that the U.S. withdraw its troops from Iraq, Afghanistan, and the Philippines. One group, named Bayan, also called for "a public apology and reparation for war crimes committed by U.S. forces during the Philippine-American War". Is it possible that an earlier war, called the Philippine-American war, might have its own legacies? If so, how do they relate to, and become intertwined with, the legacies of World War II?

THE 'UNFINISHED REVOLUTION' OF 1942–45?

It is apparent, from reading the newspapers, that Philippine politics is ridden with crisis. Today we find President Gloria Arroyo struggling to stay in office as she is bombarded with calls to resign in the light of allegations of vote rigging in the last elections. Not just the opposition politicians but also the church, the military, the left, the students, the unions and so forth are mobilizing against her. Talk of "people power" is again rife. But the United States, recently joining the fray, has said no-no to another people power upheaval to replace Arroyo, now a firm ally in the global war on terror.

For was it not just over four years ago that a people power movement brought down President Estrada before the impeachment proceeding against him had run its course? I remember then-Vice President Gloria Arroyo being sworn into office at a mass rally at EDSA. In her inaugural speech she vowed to continue what she called "the unfinished revolution". A few weeks later, Manila was again plunged into turmoil by another people power demonstration on the part of Estrada's followers. Was it not Estrada who, in 1998, pictured himself as the leader of a new "revolt of the masses" — in reference the country's long history of popular revolts, the mother of all upheavals being the 1896 revolution against Spain?

Wind the clock back to 1986 and we have the original EDSA or people power movement that forced President Marcos to flee to Hawaii and installed as president, Corazon Aquino, widow of assassinated opposition leader Benigno Aquino. Barely a year after Aquino's victory, the politicized military would mount one coup attempt after another also in the name of people power and the unfinished revolution. Are the Filipinos simply a people that cannot get their act together, or, as a commentator has put it, a nation needing a regular "people power" fix in order to keep its political system alive?

Much of today's political commentary on the Philippines is devoid of a deep historical perspective. The past, going back to the conquest and religious conversion by Spain in the sixteenth century, continues to haunt the present. We need not go that far back, however, to recognize the past in the present. The turmoil of post-war politics, it is argued here, is in many ways a legacy of World War II. To recognize this we need to glance at some features of what is earlier termed the subsidiary narratives of Philippine history.

In a talk he gave in March 1967, the late Filipino writer and historian Nick Joaquin concluded, "In a sense, when we speak of the 'Unfinished Revolution', we are not referring to 1896–98 but to 1942–45."[3] Joaquin was alluding to the Japanese Occupation and in particular to the political leadership of Jose Laurel, president of the 1943 republic. Now the term "Unfinished Revolution" conventionally refers to the revolution against Spain in the late 1800s that was interrupted when the United States took over from Spain to "tutor" the Philippines in democracy. When the United States granted independence to its colony in 1946, this was considered to be the completion of the revolutionary/tutelage process — this is certainly how President Bush viewed it in his 2003 speech. But every problem the country has faced since then has led to a resurrection of the "Unfinished Revolution" theme. President Macapagal labelled his leadership as the "Unfinished Revolution". His daughter, Gloria, began her stint as president by alluding to this theme. Always, their historical referent has been the revolution of 1896–98. That is why the elder Macapagal took great pride in having moved Independence Day from 4 July (in reference to 1946) to 12 June, in reference to 1898.

Nick Joaquin was one of the first public intellectuals to take the bold step of asserting that, far from being entirely the dark age pictured in the dominant, official narrative, World War II in the Philippines saw the birth of something positive, even a new revolution. He made this statement upon seeing around him the stirrings of a people power movement that departed from the "joint Filipino-American struggle against tyranny" theme produced by the conventional history. He had witnessed a massive demonstration in front of the U.S. Embassy the previous year, swiftly followed by the mobilization of students for more rallies, the founding of a new Communist Party, and the appearance of a myriad of organizations inspired not just by the Philippines' own historic revolution, but also by the Vietnamese resistance, the Chinese people's revolution, and liberation theology from Latin America.

In 1967, Joaquin could already glimpse the stirrings of an increasingly politicized youth that would lead to the explosion, of early 1970, called the "First Quarter Storm". It was arguably the first modern people power movement in the Philippines, to which President Marcos would respond by declaring martial law in 1972. The assertive nationalism that characterized this groundswell was critical of the special relationship between the Philippines and the United States as a source of the nation's problems. This, to Joaquin, amounted to a resurgence of the unfinished revolution of 1942–45. In other words, the origins of the late 1960s upheaval could be found in World War II.

If this reading of World War II legacies by Nick Joaquin appears startling, if not profane, it is because the dominant Philippine narrative has largely kept from view a previous war in 1899–1902 that cannot be disentangled from the war in 1942–45. We all know that Commonwealth President Manuel Quezon was the single most important Filipino leader during the American colonial period. He was the politician designated and promoted by the Americans to mediate their tutelage, and this relationship is often summed up in his being a *compadre*, or baptismal co-parent, of Douglas MacArthur. But we often forget that the reason Quezon could rise to the occasion and capture the people's imagination was because he was a veteran of the Filipino-American war — a lieutenant colonel in Aguinaldo's republican army. Like Marcos who made political capital out of his heroic exploits in the war against Japan, Quezon did likewise, but in a war just forty years earlier against the United States.

A TALE OF TWO WARS: AGAINST JAPAN AND AMERICA

One dimension that is clearly lacking in the dominant narrative of Philippine history — and that enables the myth of a Philippines eternally fixated to the United States — is the impact of Japan on the pre-war Philippines. To illustrate this, let me continue with Quezon's story. One of Quezon's most serious political rivals was also a veteran of the Filipino-American war, General Artemio Ricarte. When the war ended in 1902, Ricarte refused to take the oath of allegiance to the United States and was imprisoned. But he managed to escape, first to Hong Kong, where he allied himself with Sun Yat-sen's movement, and then to Yokohama. From these locations elsewhere in Asia, Ricarte gave inspiration to Filipino anti-colonialists ranging from party politicians to various secret societies and peasant movements, which awaited his return from Japan to liberate the country from the Americans.[4]

World War II becomes rather more complicated for the Philippines if we factor in not just the earlier war with the United States but also the many decades of dealings with Japan by Filipino nationalists — a narrative that is, of course, still largely suppressed in the wake of Japan's defeat. The U.S. victory over the Filipino nationalists in 1902 was followed by Japan's momentous victory over Russia in 1905. These two events together signal the beginning of American-Japanese rivalry for dominance in the Asia-Pacific. They also signal the beginning of American-Japanese rivalry for the attention of Filipino nationalists. For the rise of Japan as an Asian power did not escape the notice even of the new generation of Filipinos learning English in the American schools. Japan was an alternative destination for higher education. The *bushido* tradition fascinated Filipino nationalists seeking alternative models for nation-building in the 1930s.

The fact that General Ricarte was based in Yokohama heightened among Filipino nationalists the consciousness of Japan as an alternative model of development. Even Quezon, up to the very end, remained in touch with this fellow veteran of the war against the United States. On the eve of the Pacific War, Quezon secretly journeyed to Yokohama to visit Ricarte. Upon his return he pleaded with American officials to permit neutrality as the only recourse of the Philippines faced with a Japanese invasion. The United States would have nothing of this, and Quezon found it fruitless to pursue the argument.

When the Japanese came to occupy the Philippines in 1942, bringing with them Ricarte, it should not come as a surprise that there were quite a few Filipinos who welcomed them as liberators. Understandably, there has not been enough research on this phenomenon. What is well known is that the majority of Filipinos in 1940 regarded the Japanese as invaders and, as I mentioned earlier, fought bravely side-by-side with the Americans to defend the country.

So, returning to Joaquin's thesis of the unfinished revolution of 1942–45, how could such a thing happen in a situation of hostility to the Japanese occupiers? The key is to pursue the logic of the alternative or subsidiary historical narrative that connects the war against Japan with the earlier war against the United States. The Japanese military administration realized that one reason behind Filipino hostility was simply that, as a result of decades of colonial education, the younger Filipinos had forgotten the Filipino-American war. Thus the Japanese cultural corps encouraged an excavation of memories of the revolution and the resistance to U.S. occupation. Veterans and descendants of these events were encouraged to speak freely about the past and to play leading roles in organizations supportive of the Japanese administration.

The recovery of suppressed memory was initiated by no other than the venerable Ricarte himself. Upon his return from Yokohama in 1942, his first speech to his countrymen began with (to paraphrase): I am your brother Ricarte, who fought in the war against the United States forty years ago, a war that led to the deaths of tens of thousands of our people, and the burnings of houses, the arrest, confinement and torture of many, many others by the Americans.... Have the youth today forgotten this war?[5]

If we examine the backgrounds and ideas of some of the leading "collaborators" of the Japanese, we find connections with the forgotten war against United States.[6] President Jose Laurel came from the province of Batangas, a region devastated by U.S. armed operations in 1902. His father had been confined in an American concentration camp and died shortly after his release. A cousin was killed in an encounter with American troops.

Claro Recto, Laurel's secretary of the interior, remembered his mother crying while being interrogated by American officers who were hunting down his uncle, a guerrilla leader in Tayabas Province. Veteran General Emilio Aguinaldo was still around, and he was not playing "pretend" when he graced the independence ceremony in October 1943 and hailed the republic as a fulfilment of the dreams of 1898.

For these leaders of the wartime republic, there was no particular love for their Japanese sponsors, but there was not much nostalgia for U.S. rule either. They remembered the war with Spain, the war with the

United States, and the war with Japan as variations on the same theme: resistance to foreign domination. Their aim was to ensure the survival of the Filipino nation which had become sandwiched in a conflict between imperial powers.

The final six months of the war with Japan were very similar to the final six months of the war with the United States forty years earlier. Homes and buildings were razed, civilians suspected of aiding the guerrillas were tortured and executed; disaster accompanied the path of the contending armies. Personal experiences of the final months of the war were for the most part sad and tragic. This was the ideal environment for the promotion, by post-war presidents Sergio Osmeña (Commonwealth era), Roxas and Quirino, of the official narrative of World War II as a time when Filipino and American soldiers fought and suffered side-by-side to defend the Philippines. Osmeña spoke of Douglas MacArthur's return as a repetition of his father Arthur's arrival in 1898 to free the Philippines from Spain. What was the "Death March", said Quirino, if not the common *pasyon* or Christ-like suffering and death, of Filipinos and Americans, and what was Capas, Tarlac, if not their "Calvary"?

The official interpretation of history propagated in public speeches, radio broadcasts, and the school system, encouraged the public to remember the American colonial period as a golden age when peace and prosperity reigned. This age of bliss was shattered when the Japanese came and plunged the country into a Dark Age, which was only lifted when the liberator MacArthur returned. It was not difficult to establish this official rendering of World War II history because it touched a chord with the countless private memories of death and destruction suffered at the hands of the Japanese Army.

In this official post-war construction of the past, again the Filipino-American war was separated out and turned into a non-event, or at least relegated to the fringes of memory and politics. But it was no longer possible to repress this event, especially since its remembering had been encouraged during the Japanese Occupation. A new generation of nationalist intellectuals had been nurtured during this wartime period — they included writers such as Teodoro Agoncillo, Jose Lansang, Leon Maria Guerrero, Renato Constantino, Nick Joaquin, and many others. For them, both the war against the United States and the war against Japan were to be remembered equally. The Huk army thought the same way. A powerful counter-narrative was thus born.

WAR, REVOLUTION, PEOPLE POWER:
WHAT'S GOING ON HERE?

Within confines, this chapter can only briefly outline some of the trajectories that led from the Philippines' World War II experience to the political crises of recent times. It will focus on the wartime legacies of three phenomena: unfinished revolution, the turning towards Asia, and the political role of the Catholic Church.

One could easily be seduced into accepting the official view that the revolution of 1896 had finally been completed with the attainment of independence from the United States in 1946. But the communist-led Huk rebels, betrayed by the U.S. liberators in the new context of the Cold War, would have nothing to do with this nonsense; their supremo Luis Taruc called it fake independence.[7] The formidable Huk army, originally forged to fight the Japanese occupiers, has undergone a number of mutations since then. In its present form, the New People's Army, it is the only communist armed force outside of Vietnam that is of any consequence in Southeast Asia. What keeps it going ideologically is the notion of the "unfinished revolution".

Wartime president Laurel and his foreign secretary, Recto, were largely responsible for bringing the "unfinished revolution" theme into the politics of the 1950s and, eventually, into the higher education system. The problem as they saw it, even as they languished for a brief period in prison as wartime "collaborators", was that the United States was not about to grant full or real independence as promised. Indeed there were so many strings attached — military, economic, political — to the granting of independence so that in the final reckoning the republic of 1946 turned out to be not much different from the republic of 1943. But at least in 1943 there was available to Laurel and Recto a cultural space for retrieving memories of the Filipino-American war and promoting a form of nationalism that was geared towards local cultures and the wider Asian environment.

Laurel and Recto, as senators in the 1950s, were fond of using history as a weapon in their speeches and debates. Together with the writers mentioned earlier who were all nurtured during the Japanese Occupation, they undertook a massive literary and political campaign to wean public consciousness away from a fixation with America. Alternative history books appeared that would become must-readings for the youth. Laurel even founded the Lyceum, a school (later, university) to promote a pro-Filipino rather than a neo-colonial understanding of the past. From the Lyceum, as well as from Laurel's alma mater, the University of the Philippines, would emerge a new generation of leaders who would leave their mark in the 1970s in the First Quarter Storm, the Moro National Liberation Front, the new Communist Party, and, not to forget, Marcos's New Society movement. Each of these movements, studied closely, can be shown to have their roots in the momentous events of World War II and its immediate aftermath.

Many of the youthful leaders produced in the 1960s and 1970s are the veteran leaders of today — some are in the insurgencies, some in NGOs and civil society movements; some are in the Catholic Church, the military, and even in the halls of Congress. In many, often divergent, ways the question of the unfinished revolution and the role of "the people" continues to be addressed by them. I have been asked why, in Philippine politics, there is so much talk of war, revolution, and people power. We can find the answer by examining the ways these catchwords have actually taken root in Philippine realities, and how interpretations and re-enactments of the great moments of the past have become a way of making politics meaningful to the Filipino public, although palpably strange if not ludicrous when viewed from the outside. How many of us actually bother to listen carefully to the language, the historical allusions, the sentiments, the discursive turns that underlie or shape the debates that are happening this very moment in the Philippines? If we look carefully, we would recognize in all this chatter the various conflicting strands of the past reasserting themselves.

'ASIA FOR THE ASIANS'

World War II has its legacies in foreign relations, as well. One effect of the special relationship between the United States and the Philippines was the pro-American stance showed by Philippine political leaders during the first decade or so after the war. Early attempts to unite the decolonizing nations of Asia and form a neutralist bloc during the Cold War were met with suspicion by the Philippine government. At the Bandung conference in 1955, Foreign Secretary Carlos Romulo, who had proudly stepped ashore at Leyte alongside the liberator MacArthur, was practically given the cold shoulder as a virtual American lackey. The dominant narrative of modern Philippine history is reflected here, as it was in the school textbooks of that period (late 1940s and the 1950s), where the Philippines is pictured unabashedly as the light of freedom in Asia, a bridge between East and

West, America's outpost of democracy, and so forth. This is evidence of the dominant narrative at work.

But as I have been arguing all along, there is always the subsidiary narrative waiting to be resurrected. It definitely surfaced on 5 February 1954, when Undersecretary of Foreign Affairs Leon Maria Guerrero, in a speech titled "Asia for the Asians", called for a fundamental reorientation of Philippine foreign policy toward Asia.[8] This implied a loosening somewhat of the special ties with the United States and making an effort to empathize with the spirit of the forthcoming Bandung conference. A dedicated student of Rizal's[9] life and works, Guerrero was definitely inspired by Rizal's ideas about forming a Malayan confederation. His slogan "Asia for the Asians" was, however, associated by his critics not so much with Rizal's Asian visions, as with the Japanese wartime slogan of "Asian co-prosperity". Guerrero's early career as a diplomat in the 1943 republic was dug up, and he was accused of resurrecting a slogan of the "Dark Age of Japanese Occupation".

Here we find the conflicting legacies of World War II with respect to foreign policy. Wartime President Laurel and Foreign Minister Recto (Guerrero's superior) had taken seriously the call by Japan for Asia to break free from Western colonial shackles. Unless we simply declare that all their messages and letters to fellow Asian leaders were meaningless rhetoric, what these documents reveal is a genuine discovery of common experience and common cause with fellow colonized Asians. What Recto and Laurel also expressed quite boldly to their Japanese patrons was that Japan should not take the road of the Western colonialists, although Japan did, anyway. The fact that Japan itself took the colonialist road does not, however, negate the wartime legacy of Filipino recognition of common cause with other Asian nationalists, an attitude that U.S. colonial education had certainly not promoted.

This "other legacy" of World War II remained in the sidelines during the late 1940s and early 1950s but surfaced with a bang in Guerrero's 1954 speech. President Magsaysay, after consultation with his American advisers, came down hard on Guerrero for preaching neutralism and, ultimately, support for Asian communist states. Some even called Guerrero's views "un-Filipino". In 1948 a Congressional Committee on Un-Filipino Activities had been formed, not just to combat Communism but any other deviation from the official rendering of World War II memories. Recto and Laurel were, of course, solidly behind their longtime friend and associate Guerrero on this issue. And Vice-President Garcia also gave it much needed support from the top. But Congressman Diosdado Macapagal, father of the current president, was among those who slammed it in Congress.

The heated debates that Guerrero's slogan "Asia for the Asians" sparked in Congress and in the media served to ultimately and irreversibly re-orient the nation's foreign policy toward the region in which it was located. President Garcia would take up Guerrero's initiatives in the latter part of the decade. When Macapagal was elected president in the early 1960s, he would change his stance dramatically, flirting with Sukarno's vision of a united Maphilindo and proclaiming the Malayan roots of Filipino civilization and the need to belong to Asia rather than to the United States. From there the line moves straight towards enthusiastic participation in ASEAN on the part of the government, and a love affair with Mao's China on the part of the left — either way, the idea of "Asia for the Asians" was increasingly embraced by Filipinos. We can regard the 1954 controversy over Guerrero's speech, therefore, as a significant milestone in the re-orientation of Philippine foreign relations towards Asia — yet another legacy of the wartime experience under Japan.

Now to our third and final example of a wartime legacy: turmoil within the Catholic Church. "Asia for the Asians" can be said to have taken a religious turn in the post-war period with the campaign for the Filipinization of the religious orders instigated in mid-1957 by rebel priests Fr Ambrosio Manaligod of the Society of the Divine Word (SVD) and the Jesuit Hilario Lim. This clerical revolt drew inspiration from the nineteenth century Filipinization movement led by Fr Jose Burgos that culminated in the 1872 executions of three priests by the Spanish authorities.[10]

The 1957 call for Filipinization was in fact a repeat of what happened during World War II. In 1943 Auxiliary Bishop of Manila Cesar Maria Guerrero (Leon's brother) mounted a coup within the church to take control of the Manila archdiocese from the pro-U.S. Archbishop O'Doherty. Among the staunch Filipino defenders of the *status quo* was O'Doherty's assistant Father Rufino Santos, who was imprisoned by the Japanese for his recalcitrance. Later, Santos would figure in politics as the fierce opponent of any form of clerical radicalism.

The 1957 campaign brought the 1943 issues back on the agenda, becoming national in scope when the rebel priests brought their cause to the attention of the Legislature. Senator Roseller Lim (Father Lim's cousin) sponsored the so-called Filipinization Bill. In the heated debates that ensued, delicate issues were raised including the U.S. colonial regime's collusion with the church hierarchy in ecclesiastical and educational matters, the double standards of the church when it came to leadership by locals, the Catholic interpretation of Philippine history, and so forth. As a conservative cardinal in the 1960s, Rufino Santos would in effect pursue his unfinished business of 1943 by resisting attempts to Filipinize the church or to address questions of U.S. clerical interference.

By the 1970s, a new generation of priests and nuns imbued with liberation theology and building upon the tradition of Fathers Manaligod (1957), Guerrero (1943), and Burgos (1872) before them, would emerge. Some would go to the extent of joining the communists in the hills; most, however would quietly work to defend and mobilize their parishioners against an increasingly rapacious and repressive political leadership under Marcos. From their efforts would emerge the first expression of "People Power" in 1984–86, with the blessing of a new cardinal, Jaime Sin.

The Japanese religious policy of Filipinizing the Catholic Church, a policy wholeheartedly embraced by Bishop Guerrero who undoubtedly had his own agenda, reconnected the church to the burning issues of 1872. This "kick start" in religious policy in 1943 arguably paved the way for the increasing politicization of the church in the succeeding decades.

CONCLUDING REFLECTIONS

To what extent is the image of Filipinos and Americans fighting side-by-side against the Japanese still an effective rallying point for war mobilization, as President Bush attempted in his 2003 speech? Few of the veterans of this war remain alive. None are in any position of power today. And as accounts of the earlier war against the United States continue to enter into our history books, how much longer can World War II hold its status as the darkest age against which every other epoch since should be judged?

It makes sense in the present unipolar world order to read the events of World War II as marking a new and decisive stage in American expansion as defeated Japan became incorporated into the U.S. defence and economic sphere. Forty-three years earlier, in 1902, it was the U.S. Army's triumph over another Asian army — composed of Filipinos — that brought the Philippines into the American sphere and initiated the rivalry with Japan that culminated in America's second war in Asia. Instead of the history of the Japanese Occupation serving to "fixate" Filipinos towards America and establishing the Japanese as the archetypal enemy, would it not be possible to treat as one event the defeats of the Filipino and the Japanese armies by the U.S. Army in 1902 and 1945, respectively?

With the Cold War coming into full swing by the late 1940s, Japan became a valuable ally rather than the defeated enemy of the United States and the Philippines. By the 1990s the increased frequency of travel by Filipinos to Japan for work, education, and marriage had diminished whatever remained of the negative, wartime images of the Japanese enemy. Contrary to commonsense belief brought about by parties eager to extract the most out of wartime reparations and other benefits, Filipinos who had not directly experienced the enemy's brutality were quite willing to "forget" the traumas of the war. In this respect they have been no different from other Asian peoples who had experience Japanese conquest.

During the 1995 commemorations of the victory over Japan, Japanese veterans and dignitaries were invited to grace the occasion in the Philippine events. At that time I was teaching at James Cook University in Townsville, Australia, an important R&R destination during World War II. As to be expected, a massive parade was held in the streets of Townsville to mark the event. But, in contrast to what happened at similar celebrations in the Philippines and elsewhere in Southeast Asia, not only were Japanese people not invited to the Townsville event, but also those who tried to view the parade (such as our students at JCU) were harassed and one or two even physically abused. Here one could see the legacy of World War II in expressions of racial hatred even as late as 1995, whereas such sentiments had long disappeared from the Philippines despite its having borne the full brunt of the Japanese Army's advance into Southeast Asia.

The most enduring legacy of the war, in my view, is that it created the conditions for the possibility of an overhaul in historical consciousness that would eventually undermine the all-to-familiar but transient legacies. The still-current perception of a special relationship between the Philippines and the United States may yet be relegated to a transient legacy of the war. To understand this rather subtle process, we need to reflect more on what Nick Joaquin meant in 1967 about the so-called "unfinished revolution" of 1942–45. We also need to link, as this chapter has tried to do, World War II, or the war against Japan, to the war against the United States some forty years earlier. Together they form a twentieth century legacy of wars that has shaped the Philippine polity into the complex and multi-dimensional phenomenon that it is today, if we dare look beneath the surface.

NOTES

1. For a classic, scholarly account of the war years from an American perspective, see Theodore Friend, *Between Two Empires: The Ordeal of the Philippines, 1929–1946* (New Haven: Yale, 1965). Its Filipino counterpart is Teodoro Agoncillo, *The Fateful Years: Japan's Adventure in the Philippines, 1941–45.* 2 vols. (Quezon City: R.P. Garcia, 1965). A recent collection of essays that incorporates Japanese perspectives is Setsuho Ikehata and Ricardo Trota Jose, eds., *The Philippines under Japan: Occupation Policy and Reaction* (Quezon City: Ateneo de Manila, 1999).

2. The text of the Bush speech is available at <usinfo.state.gov/usinfo/Archive/2003/Oct/18-623282.html>. For a comprehensive analysis of the speech, see Reynaldo Ileto, "Philippine Wars and the Politics of Memory", *Positions: East Asia Cultures Critique* 13, no. 1 (2005): 215–35.

3. Nick Joaquin (Quijano de Manila), "The Law and the Prophet: A Look into the Current Status of the Image of Jose P. Laurel" (1967), reprinted in *The Laurel Legacy*, Memorial Series vol. 2 (Manila: Lyceum, 1986).

4. For details, see Reynaldo Ileto, *Filipinos and their Revolution: Event, Discourse, and Historiography* (Quezon City: Ateneo de Manila, 1998), chapter 6.

5. Artemio Ricarte, *Sa Mga Kabataang Filipino* [To the Filipino Youth], Manila, 1942. Copy in the Garcia collection, Sophia University.

6. For an initial exploration of the parallels between the Filipino-American war and the Filipino-Japanese war, see Reynaldo Ileto, "Colonial Wars in Southern Luzon: Remembering and Forgetting", *Hitotsubashi Journal of Social Studies* 33, no. 1 (2001): 103–18.

7. Luis Taruc, *Born of the People* (New York: International, 1953), p. 208.

8. See Jose Abueva, *Ramon Magsaysay: A Political Biography* (Manila: Solidaridad, 1971), pp. 393–95.

9. Jose Rizal (1861–96) was a Spanish-educated Filipino intellectual who led the campaign for liberal reform in the colony in the 1880s. His two novels critical of Spanish colonialism inspired the budding nationalist movement but led to the author's execution in December 1896, four months after the outbreak of armed rebellion against Spain.

10. See Mario Bolasco, *Points of Departure; Essays on Christianity, Power and Social Change* (Manila: Anvil, 1984), pp. 61–80.

Chapter Eight
Singapore's Missing War

Asad-ul Iqbal Latif

Walter Benjamin's angel of history is turned towards the past out of sympathy for time's victims, but the storm of progress drives him into the future. This image embodies the place of war in the life of a people. So it is with World War II and Singapore.

The main line of descent from then to now lies in the realm of defence. Total Defence Day falls on 15 February, marking the anniversary of the catastrophe in 1942 when Singapore faced a rout that was military, civil, economic, social and psychological: the five aspects of Total Defence. The date 15 February is a metaphorical re-enactment of the truth that a colony remains dispensable even in the mightiest of empires, that what is tactical for the imperial metropole is strategic for the colonized periphery. London lived, but Singapore fell. The motif of betrayal in turn structures a message both simple and powerful: the message being that those who do not take personal responsibility for their common security will soon have nothing left to secure. In making this point, Total Defence Day underscores the particular meaning of World War II for Singapore. It was a classic imperialist war, a gang-fight over turf between an empire that was relatively liberal and comfortable, but over-confident and overstretched; and a

revisionist empire whose outriders bicycled down Malaya in the eager faith
that their emperor was divine. But for the people of Singapore, caught
between two imperia neither of which they were responsible for, their war
began when the fighting stopped with the British surrender of 15 February
1942. For the next three-and-a-half years, the people of this island witnessed
something that they had never known: the capricious sadism of a military
dictatorship. The experience of being a part of Japan's Greater East Asia
Co-Prosperity Sphere was so brutal that it shed almost divine light on the
free-market policies of life and death that Britain had brought to Singapore.
Unlike Britain's laissez-faire imperialism of success and failure, this new
imperialism announced an era of blood and tears. Snatches of that history
can be glimpsed at the War Memorial Park in Beach Road today. Children
who have encountered the war under the censorious eyes of teachers in
school are caught off guard when they stand among war survivors and war
veterans weeping for family, friends and comrades lost in the marchpast of
time. It is a truly moving sight that underscores the legacy of World War
II as the second of three founding events of modern Singapore, the first
being Raffles' arrival in 1819 and the third being independence in 1965.

However, beyond its iconic use as a security motif, World War II is not
a key feature of Singapore's political outlook. Political parties do not
invoke it to influence outcomes in the electoral arena, and political factions
do not form around its legacy. Social groups do not coalesce around their
experience of the war, and it does not figure in negotiations between civil
society and the state. Teachers' unions do not try to score points over how
the war is taught or is not taught in school, and students and intellectuals
do not use the war memories of past generations to make a point against
the government of the day. Given their small numbers, war veterans are
not a demographic constituency, unlike the French veterans who came to
form a prominent political constituency in Gaullist France. The war is
certainly not a key factor in Singapore's foreign policy; even in relations
with Japan, it is but an ambivalent factor. As Diana Wong writes,

> Hardly any traces of the Japanese Occupation can be detected in postwar
> Malayan public memory or, until very recently, in that of the city-state
> island of Singapore. The war has not been memorialized; indeed, it
> would seem that its memory has been directly silenced.[1]

If history is the present's relationship to the past, and if politics
emerges from that encounter, it is tempting to say that World War II has
gone missing in action. It is not an ancestral, inherited and contingent

experience against which the present can be collectively understood, evaluated and judged, a benchmark against which political choices are offered or can be made in the present. This paper seeks to examine why World War II has gone missing in action from the politics of contemporary Singapore — and where it has gone. There are at least four reasons for the absence.

The first has to do with Raffles' arrival being a founding event. This notion is based on an historical reality, of course, and it is one whose general acceptance among Singaporeans is advanced by the bloodless onset of a colonial rule that had its modernizing and reformist aspects. However, that rule was colonial. This being the case, the politics of memory is marked by a perhaps unavoidable contradiction. Singaporeans by and large treat the fall of Singapore in 1942 as perfidious because it revealed Britain's inability to defend its colony, not because the British had colonized Singapore in the first place. Likewise, most Singaporeans cannot welcome the Japanese arrival as heralding the liberation of Singapore because to do so would be to cast Singapore's progress under the British as having been unnatural, undeserved and wrong. Also, of course, such an approach to history would legitimize, even if indirectly, the reign of terror that the Japanese unleashed here. Given that the Japanese "liberation" meant Singapore changing masters but not its destiny, it is difficult to see how a sovereign Singapore state could ratify or even rationalize the Japanese interregnum as a political step forward for this island. Such views of the colonial past may well be patrician because they celebrate Singapore's role in the British empire without paying sufficient attention to how the subaltern withered under the Benthamite gaze of imperial dreamers and schemers motivated by a utilitarian and racist conception of human nature. However, the violent nature of the Japanese Occupation makes it impossible for any serious Singapore politician to declare that uninvited break in colonial history as being propitious. If it were, what form should its political equivalent in today's Singapore take?

The second reason why the war does not feature in contemporary Singapore politics has to do with what happened here during that war. True, 15 February 1942 revealed the limitations of a plural society in which race broadly determined economic function, and it inaugurated an era in which the inhabitants of a plural society were forced to take a stake in one another's fates as they fashioned daily strategies of survival if not resistance to Japanese rule. With that acknowledgement of a collective destiny, provisional though it was, the inhabitants of Singapore took the first unsuspected steps towards eventual nationhood. It is in that context that the formation of Force 136 and the heroic deaths of Lim Bo Seng and Lieutenant Adnan Saidi are commemorated today. However, the war also exacerbated racial divisions latent in a colonial society. As scholars have observed, had there been equal proportions of Chinese and Malays in the anti-Japanese resistance as well as in collaboration, the Japanese Occupation would not have created the racial bitterness that it did in the peninsula of Malaya. In the event, though, what occurred was the racial score-settling that marked the end of the war. It is not a salutary memory.

The third reason for the war's at-best indeterminate political legacy has to do with external influences on what might be called the pre-nationalist phase of Singapore. True, the war created a tentative sense of belonging to Singapore among disparate Chinese, Malays, Indians and Eurasians. But it also witnessed ethnic groups in Singapore and Malaya respond to the diasporic nationalisms of the Kuomintang (KMT) and the Chinese Communist Party (CCP), the Indian Independence League, and the Kesatuan Melayu Muda. The experience of the war years does not contribute, therefore, to the creation of a viable multi-racial identity for independent Singapore. If anything, that identity would require the state to play down the ethnic nationalisms of that centrifugal era. This, it has done. So well has the state blunted the ethnic edges of history that public memories of the pro-Japanese Indian National Army can co-exist with Chinese memories of the KMT and the CCP without Indian and Chinese Singaporeans questioning their forefathers' national affiliations or each other's loyalty to Singapore today. The imagined communities called nations are defined not only by what they choose to remember but by what they choose to forget. A degree of forgetfulness helps to give nations like Singapore a fresh start in a history whose outcomes they did not control.

The fourth reason for the war's absence from Singapore politics is what occurred after the British reconquest of Singapore in 1945. Britain's war with Japan ended, but another war began between the forces of the *status quo ante* and those who had had enough of eternal empires. Buoyed by the success of the nationalist upsurge in India, China and Indonesia, these forces took on the returning imperialists, through either the parliamentary route or the jungle trails to independence. The eventual victory of the parliamentarians in Singapore and Malaya determined the legacy of World War II by excising the contrarian aspects of its aftermath from the popular imagination. The defeat of the communists led to the defeat of their version of the war, the history behind the war, and the history created by the war.

Collectively, these factors have excluded the legacy of World War II from any tangible role in the contemporary politics of Singapore. This absence is clear in its foreign policy.

WAR AND PEACE AMONG STATES

In May 2005, Singapore publicly backed Japan's bid for a permanent seat on the United Nations Security Council. This support came against the backdrop of a particularly nasty row between China and Japan over the publication of the latest revisionist Japanese textbook to gloss over imperial Tokyo's wartime atrocities in Asia. Asked about the permanent Security Council seat, Prime Minister Lee Hsien Loong told visiting Japanese journalists that Japan was "a natural candidate". He cited Japan's international contributions and its ability to contribute to peace, stability and prosperity in the world. But he added that it was regrettable that Tokyo had yet to come to terms with its wartime past. Japanese Prime Minister Junichiro Koizumi's visit to the Yasukuni war shrine that honours war criminals among the war dead was something for the Japanese leader to decide on, he felt. But for countries that had experienced Japanese Occupation, "it raises many unhappy memories" because "it's not just paying respect to war dead, but also it's a shrine which has war criminals". A visit to the shrine, Mr Lee said, was interpreted by many people, including many in Singapore, as being a gesture of not entirely accepting that Japan did wrong during the war. Therefore, he added, when the Yasukuni visits took place, temperatures rose in the region, especially in China and Korea. This was regrettable, Mr Lee declared, because countries should be looking ahead instead of being tied up with the past. But then, he went on, unless the past was acknowledged, it was difficult to move ahead, the way the Germans had done. Germany had come to terms with its war history, repudiated Nazism, and made it a crime even to deny that the Holocaust had occurred. Also, every German child was taught about what had taken place and why it must never recur. "This has not yet happened in Asia and the textbook problem is also to be seen in that context," he said. Nevertheless, Mr Lee saw Japan as continuing to play an active role in the development of the region, particularly Southeast Asia.[2]

These remarks sum up the state of play in Singapore's relations with its erstwhile invader. The key elements are these. Japan's inability to make a clean break with its past compares unfavourably with Germany's example. Instead, Japanese ambiguity is a factor that impedes Asia's unification along European lines. And why not, for imagine what Europe would have looked like today had Germany prevaricated about its wartime past instead of owning up to it unequivocally. Thus, revisionist textbooks and intransigent war shrine visits in Japan are examples of an historical amnesia that does the future no good. Although not as vocal as the citizens of other Asian countries that suffered under the Japanese, Singaporeans have not forgotten the occupation. However, Singapore does not want the past to hold the future hostage. It certainly does not wish to manipulate the past to secure diplomatic or political gains in its relationship with Japan. There is no place here for any kind of officially sponsored protests against Tokyo, or even for spontaneous demonstrations that threaten to get out of hand. All said and done, Japan remains a key player in the peace, prosperity and stability of Asia — a view that reflects the balance-of-power principles and economic pragmatism on which Singapore's foreign policy is founded.[3]

Culture is another important factor in Singapore's rapprochement with Japan. Japan's ability to rise from its ashes — as Singapore did — underlines an ironic similarity between the two former adversaries. Minister Mentor Lee Kuan Yew expresses this strand of Singapore thinking in his two books of memoirs. In the first book, he recalls the horrors of the Japanese Occupation in almost existentialist terms, declaring those years as being the most important in his life because they gave him a first-hand insight into human and social motivations and impulses. Given Japanese depredations, he has no qualms about saying that the atomic bombing of Hiroshima and Nagasaki was necessary. Without it, hundreds of thousands of civilians in Malaya and Singapore, and millions in Japan itself, would have perished.[4] In the second volume of his memoirs, Mr Lee repeats his horror of what the Japanese did here, but he adds that over time he came to respect and admire their solidarity, discipline, intelligence, industriousness and their willingness to make sacrifices for their nation — qualities that make them a formidable and productive force. Given the poverty of their resources, the Japanese will continue to make that extra effort to achieve the unachievable, he declares, noting pointedly their desire for perfection in a range of activities from flower arrangement to sword-making and war. Mr Lee believes that the Japanese will fight as ferociously as they did from 1941 to 1945 if they feel threatened or if they are cut off from critical resources or shut out of their export markets. However, he does not think that Japan can repeat what it did between 1931 and 1945 because China now has the nuclear bomb. Within this larger geo-political picture, Mr Lee draws on almost four decades of interaction with Japanese leaders to place Singapore in an historical perspective that harks back to World War II. Speaking of the rise of China, he recalls most Japanese leaders believing that, in a crunch, ASEAN countries would support Japan. But they were unsure of how Singapore would react.

> They accepted that despite being ethnic Chinese my views and policies towards China were those of a Singaporean whose interests were in Southeast Asia, and that I would not necessarily support China in any conflict. However, they were uncertain how Singapore's majority Chinese population and its future leaders would react under Chinese pressure. I do not think that I succeeded in dispelling their doubts.[5]

It is fair to say that two subsequent leaders of Singapore — Mr Goh Chok Tong and Mr Lee Hsien Loong — have done nothing to detract from Mr Lee Kuan Yew's refusal to take an ethnic-Chinese-based view of relations with Japan. They have adopted a Singapore approach, thereby distancing an island-state from the legacy of a war in which transnational ties of kinship proved to be one source of mass deaths. Instead, and in spite of the economic difficulties that have mired Japan since the late 1980s, there exists in the Singapore elite an admiration for the stoic resilience of a people who move on, no matter what the odds are. Post-war Singapore has something in common with post-war Japan: Both have lived ably to tell the tale. Both have become successful nation-states in a post-colonial world.

THE WAR AND PEACE OF PEOPLES

But there are stories and stories. Wars not only create winners and losers but entire sociological generations on each side. Rapprochement between elites is not replicated automatically among sociological survivors.

Among those survivors are the Eurasians and the Chinese in Singapore. While almost everyone felt the effects of the economic dislocation caused by the Japanese Occupation, these communities were singled out for physical attention by invaders ruling by what can only be called the lawlessness of the law. The Eurasians were a target on account of their putative ethnic affiliation with the British and other Europeans. The Chinese were persecuted because they were Chinese. This historical injustice haunts Chinese Singaporean memories of the war to this day. Today's Chinese readily acknowledge that the Chinese in Singapore and Malaya showed their support for their brethren in China, invaded by the Japanese, by raising money for the China Relief Fund from 1937. Since the Chinese had played the ethnic card, Japan's subsequent treatment of them might make crude sense as the next episode of a racial vendetta. But it does not make sense, enough sense for anyone to rationalize the treatment of the Chinese in 1942. This is because the Japanese did not distinguish between a Chinese patriot and others. As Professor Wang Gungwu observes, a Chinese could have been born in China; he could have arrived in Singapore or Malaya a few years earlier, bearing the raw wounds of the Japanese intrusion; or he could have been local-born, a Chinese who was third-, fourth-, or fifth-generation removed from China. It did not matter. It did not matter even if a Chinese spoke Malay and identified with Malaya: then, he became suspect as a pro-British Chinese hostile to the Japanese empire.[6] When the Japanese arrived, they simply brought the China war here, and the Chinese became natural victims. One depository of memories of victimization is the book, *The Price of Peace: True Accounts of the Japanese Occupation*, a compelling account of what it meant to be Chinese in a genocidal anti-Chinese era. Produced by the Singapore Chinese Chamber of Commerce and Industry, it was first published in Chinese in September 1995 and issued in English in 1997.[7] The book reaches out to non-Chinese Singaporeans, asking them to understand what it meant to be brutalized for no other reason than being born into a race at the wrong time. Such books, which emerge from the subterranean layers of Chinese memory, have the power of archaeological excavations. They force Singaporeans to face the raw reminders of the past, unprotected by the necessarily cautious discourse of the state.

Another source of divergence between the official and folk versions of history is what the war led to. Professor Cheah Boon Kheng speaks of the Japanese Occupation as having had a three-fold effect on Chinese political consciousness in Malaya. It led to Chinese nationalism, communism, and Malayan loyalty.[8] Each of these consequences was to visit the political history of independent Malaysia and Singapore. Nationalist historiography celebrates loyalty to Malaya, or Singapore. However, as the historians Christopher Bayly and Tim Harper remark in *Forgotten Armies: The Fall of British Asia 1941–1945*, a "new phase of the great Asian war" began with Japan's surrender.[9] That phase had many aspects. One is clear in a photograph taken in Singapore at the start of the British recessional. On 1 December 1945, the Malayan People's Anti-Japanese Army (MPAJA) was disbanded, and the British held a ceremony to thank its partisans for their contribution to the war effort. The Malayan Emergency broke out in 1948.

In his memoirs, *My Side of History*,[10] published in Singapore, Chin Peng, the former secretary-general of the Malayan Communist Party (MCP) clearly regards the party as having continued against the British the anti-colonial war that began with the MPAJA taking on the Japanese. In the event, the constitutionalists in Malaysia and Singapore won the post-colonial peace, but Chin Peng is adamant that the MCP played a decisive role in the anti-colonial war. The war in the jungles gave the British a good reason to transfer power while they still had power left to transfer — and thus to deal with the non-communists. To Chin Peng, the MCP's peace treaty with Malaysia in 1989 was precisely that: a treaty signed in peace. It did not detract at all from the MCP's war against the British, whose writ had replaced the laws of the Japanese who had displaced them.

CONCLUSION

World War II has gone missing in action, taking with it some of history's stinging agency, its instinctive urgency. Instead, Singapore's history seems to be dispersed among the many histories that have impinged on this island-state.

When Singapore became Syonan, the year 1942 jumped to 2602 to reflect Nippon's calendar, and the clocks obligingly moved their hands one-and-a-half hours forward to keep pace with Japanese time. As it turned out, Singapore's Japanese future was reversed in three-and-a-half years, and it was restored temporarily to a renewed cycle of imperial British history. The fall of Singapore is a watermark in the tidal fortunes of an island that flourished or survived or scraped through a succession of epochs and eras, from Srivijaya and Majapahit, to the Ming dynasty voyages to Africa, and to the British creation of a trading system of power around the Atlantic and Pacific basins that produced Raffles. Emboldened by an alternative vision of Asian prosperity, the Japanese invaded Singapore, but they failed to destroy its place as an island-state sustained by older maritime cycles of time.

While these facts are true, they add up to a view of Singapore as a port of call on others' voyages through time. That view explains perhaps why World War II does not have the resonance here that national moments have elsewhere. These are moments when all time stops to watch what is happening in some corner, courtyard or corridor of the nation. Jallianwala Bagh is a national moment in the sense that, though it took place in 1919, it is still "taking place" in the lives of Indians who, whether they are princes or paupers, extend to Dyer's victims the companionship of Indian time, the comradeship of Indian history. Over in China, popular memory has incorporated Hong Kong's handover to the mainland into the historical footprint of the Opium War to the mid-twentieth century, a time span within which Republican China emerged, the May Fourth Movement broke out, and the Long March commenced. Even the defeated cling to their national moments. Thus, Colonel Masanobu Tsuji, who helped to plan Japan's Malaya campaign, concedes that Tokyo was defeated in the war, but he declares defiantly that India, Pakistan, Ceylon, Burma, the Dutch East Indies, and the Philippine Islands gained independence. "The reduction of Singapore was indeed the hinge of fate for the peoples of Asia," he proclaims.[11] That a soldier should write with such conviction after losing a war says something about history as a definitive, inescapable and inexhaustible experience.

As for Singapore, notwithstanding World War II having gone missing in action, private and public memories of that catastrophe came together in 1965 when the calligrapher, poet and educator Pan Shou penned his lines for the civilian victims of the Japanese Occupation. He wrote:

> The people of Singapore are always with the peoples of the world, including the people of Japan, who are peace loving and who oppose aggression, imperialism and colonialism. May the souls of the civilian victims of the Japanese Occupation rest in eternal peace and accept this epitaph dedicated to them by the people of Singapore.[12]

The Japanese Occupation was one of the many wars that marked the course of World War II. But it was that particular war on the innocents which, today, stands as the benchmark by which Singapore must judge its living past. If handled sensitively, coming to terms with the agony of the times should strengthen Singapore's political fabric by reminding Singaporeans that the blood of unknown martyrs seeped into the soil of a colony without even knowing that it was watering the saplings of a nation. In return, all that the martyrs of the occupation ask for is the right to remembrance and respect in a national lineage so much of which is about other nations, their global reach, the life spans of their imperial dreams, and the death spasms of their colonial follies. Mocking the impertinent power of imperialism for having arrogated to itself the privileges of immortality, the dead martyrs seek the companionship of Singapore time and await the comradeship of Singapore history.

Meanwhile, Walter Benjamin's angel of history keeps its restless watch.

NOTES

1. "Memory Suppression and Memory Production: The Japanese Occupation of Singapore", in *Perilous Memories: The Asia-Pacific War(s)*, edited by T. Fujitani, Geoffrey M. White and Lisa Yoneyama (Durham: Duke University Press, 2001), p. 222. One reason for the silencing, Wong observes, is that Singapore's "unremitting narrative of survival" has been "anchored in the present" (Ibid., p. 230). But she adds that, after about three decades of independence, Singapore's existence as a "city-, island-, nation-state" no longer appeared an anomaly, and an earlier sense of fragility gave way to the "conviction of success" (Ibid., p. 234). The year 1992, the fiftieth anniversary of the onset of the occupation, appeared to mark the "reinsertion of history into Singapore's public culture" (Ibid., p. 230).
2. "Singapore Backs Japan's Bid for UN Council Seat", Sue-Ann Chia and Kwan Weng Kin in Tokyo, *Straits Times*, Singapore, 19 May 2005.
3. For an analysis of Singapore's diplomatic relations with Japan, see Michael Leifer, *Singapore's Foreign Policy: Coping with Vulnerability* (London: Routledge, 2000), pp. 124–27. For an analysis of economic and political factors in Singapore's foreign policy choices, see Linda Y.C. Lim, "The Foreign Policy of Singapore", in *The Political Economy of Foreign Policy in Southeast Asia*, edited by David Wurfel and Bruce Burton (Hampshire and London: Macmillan, 1990), pp. 124–45.
4. *The Singapore Story: Memoirs of Lee Kuan Yew* (Singapore: Times Editions, 1998), pp. 59–60.
5. *From Third World to First: The Singapore Story, 1965–2000, Memoirs of Lee Kuan Yew* (Singapore: Times Media Private Limited, 2000), p. 576.
6. "Memories of War: World War II in Asia", in *War and Memory in Malaysia and Singapore*, edited by P. Lim Pui Huen and Diana Wong (Singapore: Institute of Southeast Asian Studies, 2000), p. 17. This volume consists of papers presented at a workshop organized by ISEAS to commemorate the fiftieth anniversary of the war, and two additional papers.
7. Compiled and edited by Foong Choon Hon, translated by Clara Show (Singapore: Asiapac, 1997).
8. Cheah Boon Kheng, "Memory as History and Moral Judgement: Oral and Written Accounts of the Japanese Occupation of Malaya", in *War and Memory in Malaysia and Singapore*, op. cit., p. 28.

9. Christopher Bayly and Tim Harper, *Forgotten Armies: The Fall of British Asia, 1941–1945* (London: Allen Lane, 2004), p. 462.

10. Chin Peng, *My Side of History, as told to Ian Ward and Norma Miraflor* (Singapore: Media Masters, 2003).

11. Masanobu Tsuji, *Singapore 1941–1942*, translated by Margaret E. Lake, edited by H.V. Howe and introduced by H. Gordan Bennett (Singapore, Oxford and New York: Oxford University Press, 1988), p. 281.

12. Tan Beng Luan and Irene Quah, *The Japanese Occupation 1942–1945: A Pictorial Record of Singapore During the War* (Singapore: Times Editions, 1996), p. 186.

Chapter Nine

World War II and Thailand after Sixty Years: Legacies and Latent Side Effects

Thitinan Pongsudhirak

INTRODUCTION[1]

Unlike its neighbours in Southeast Asia, Thailand emerged from the ravages of World War II relatively unscathed. Although the government of then-Prime Minister P. Phibunsongkram (henceforth Phibun) officially sided with Japan and exploited irredentist claims of territories in Malaya, Laos and Cambodia from Great Britain and France, Thailand was forced to pay only minimal war indemnities. Owing to an influential anti-Japanese Seri Thai [Free Thai] underground movement, led by Pridi Bhanomyong, Thai leaders at war's end were able to secure American support in the face of British reparatory, punitive demands for Thailand's wartime efforts against the Allies. Spectacularly victorious after the war, the United States government persuaded its British counterpart to soften its stand on Thailand. The leaders of Seri Thai were also able to negotiate the release of financial assets in Japan and the United Kingdom for domestic economic recovery and revitalization. Notwithstanding the relatively favourable post-war settlement, the domestic political scene in the wake of the war was tumultuous, fragmented and fractious.

Following the downfall of Phibun's wartime government in July 1944, a series of shortlived and unstable democratic governments spearheaded by Pridi and his associates came to power over the next three years. During this period, the civilian leadership under Pridi drawn from political parties with socialist and leftist leanings as well as from the Seri Thai movement held sway, as the military and conservative élite under Phibun were in retreat. However, the threat of communist expansionism associated with Pridi's socialist ideas and crucial domestic developments, including the Supreme Court's exoneration of Phibun and his associates on war crimes charges in April 1946, the mysterious death of the young King Anand two months later for which Pridi was held accountable by the public, and Pridi's genuine support for anti-colonial nationalist movements in Southeast Asia, undermined the former Seri Thai leader's political legitimacy.

Soon thereafter, the brief post-war interval of parliamentary democracy came to an end. The military seized power in the November 1947 *coup d'état*, with Phibun at the helm of the Coup Group. A civilian was installed as the caretaker prime minister for five months. By April 1948, Phibun, whose previous government had allied with Japan during the war, was back in power. His political resurgence marked the onset of Thailand's longest period of military-authoritarian rule. After Phibun's reign ended in 1957, his erstwhile allies in the military, Sarit Thanarat, Thanom Kittikachorn and Praphat Charusathien, extended military-authoritarian governments until the early 1970s. Not until the late 1980s did participatory democratic government reappear, and it was halted briefly by yet another *putsch* and a military-installed government during 1991–92. The political reform movement since the overthrow of military rule in May 1992, however, has ushered in the reform-driven constitution of 1997 and robust democratic rule that lasted until another *putsch* in September 2006.

Against this brief historical backdrop, it is instructive to delineate several latent ramifications from Thailand's experience during WWII. In retrospect, Thailand's post-war outcome appears serendipitous. Forced to choose sides, one group of the ruling elite joined Japan, whereas the opposing group took up with the Allied powers. Thailand was destined to land on the winning side however the war turned out. Yet this *ex post* view is oversimplified. In fact, Thailand prior to the outbreak of war underwent trials and tribulations in search for the optimal strategic response to weather the oncoming clash between the Axis and Allied camps. This chapter draws attention to several foreign policy and domestic political trends that can be traced back to what happened in Thailand during

WWII. In particular, it focuses on Thailand's "non-neutrality" imperatives, clientelistic alliances under exigent circumstances, military-authoritarianism and the accompanying economic development, foreign policy opportunism under certain conditions, and the role of the monarchy.

NON-NEUTRALITY IMPERATIVES

Following the bitter memory of losing territories in Indochina to France in 1893, the consensus among the Thai foreign policy elite was to avoid entanglements with the great powers. The confrontation with France yielded the chief lesson that Thailand cannot rely on a single world power to come to its aid in times of need, as Great Britain had failed to assist Thailand in thwarting French imperialist demands. Britain itself also gained territories in northern Malaya from Thailand in a treaty settlement in 1909. Overtures for intervention from Germany and Russia came to naught. Neutrality among, or "equi-distance" from, the great powers thus became the new *modus operandi* among Thai foreign policy-makers.[2] This was the mindset of Thai leaders as they faced the onset of World War II.

Although the Phibun regime in the late 1930s harboured fascist characteristics, it did not intend to side with Japan from the outset. Indeed, Thailand earnestly sought to maintain the policy of neutrality. Faced with the inexorable march of war, Phibun tried in vain to ascertain Japanese intentions towards Thailand and to gain reassurances from Britain and the United States of military and financial aid in the event Bangkok's neutrality is challenged by a Japanese invasion. In the end, Thailand was mistrusted by both sides. Britain and the United States saw Bangkok as Japan's closet ally given Phibun's fascist preferences and Thailand's own irredentist grievances and border demarcation issues with France, whereas Tokyo doubted the Phibun government's intentions in view of the pro-Western elements in cabinet. When Japan issued its ultimatum to Thailand on 8 December 1941, fighting broke out for three days after Japan launched a multi-pronged attack. Phibun had issued a standing order to military officers to stand their ground in the event of a Japanese attack. However, it became clear that the Japanese onslaught would overrun Thailand in a matter of days.

To avoid an outright invasion and occupation, Phibun had initially opted for the granting of passage rights to Japan. When Japan's occupational intentions were manifested, the prime minister was compelled on 11 December to sign a military cooperation agreement. In return, Thai sovereignty and independence were preserved, Thailand was not considered an occupied nation, and the Thai army did not have to be disarmed.

As the pro-Western faction in government quickly organized the Seri Thai movement, the perils of neutrality became clear. With the imperatives of World War II, Thai neutrality became untenable, and the country ultimately had to choose sides. This is the lesson that was reinforced by Thailand's previous confrontations with the European powers in the 1890s and early 1900s. When push came to shove, Thailand was on its own. Unless it went to one side or the other, it was bound to end up absolutely worst off. Playing on both sides — Japan and the Allies — by Phibun and Pridi's Seri Thai underground movement was merely coincidental.

STRATEGIC CLIENTELISM

When Phibun re-entered top office in April 1948, he had apparently learned his lesson. In view of the post-war liberation movements and communist expansionism in China, Indochina and other parts of the developing world, the fast-emerging environment of the Cold War gave Phibun a second chance. This time, he shunned neutrality and enthusiastically hopped on the anti-communist bandwagon under the stewardship of the United States and the so-called "Free World". Phibun's decision to become an American client was unsurprising. In his first term, he had already exhibited anti-Chinese prejudices. Standing up to communist China thus came naturally to him. Moreover, Phibun's power base in the military also advocated a closer alliance with the United States for the benefit of growing American economic and military aid, some of which ended up in the private pockets of military officers. Intimate ties to the United States further bolstered the military's institutional power in domestic politics. Thus from the onset of the Cold War through to the communist victory in China and the Korean and the Indochina wars, Thailand unambiguously picked the anti-communist camp and gradually became America's client state on mainland Southeast Asia.

During the Korean War, for example, Thailand sent troops to fight alongside the American-led UN forces. In 1954, Thailand joined the Manila Pact along with Australia, New Zealand, Britain, France, the United States, Pakistan, and the Philippines in the formation of the Southeast Asia Treaty Organization (SEATO). In 1962, the Thai foreign minister and his American counterpart issued a joint communiqué to reaffirm their united, anti-communist stand. Thailand supported anti-communist struggles in Laos, Cambodia, and South Vietnam, and despatched a division of troops to fight against the Viet Cong on the side of the Americans during the Vietnam War. For the United States, Thailand became the last "domino" on mainland Southeast Asia in desperate need of substantial economic and military support.[3] Following the communist victory in South Vietnam and America's withdrawal from mainland Southeast Asia in the mid-1970s, Thai policy became adrift and superficially returned to an "equidistance" position. Yet the alliance with the United States endured, given the increased amounts of military and economic aid pouring into Thailand in the late 1970s.[4] With the end of the Cold War and the democratic transition in the late 1980s, and with the re-emergence of China, the imperative of choosing sides became less apparent. Thai foreign policy in the 1990s thus became more fluid and less clear-cut.

Picking sides became imperative again with the 11 September 2001 terrorist attacks on the World Trade Centre and the Pentagon in the United States. President George W. Bush made it clear to the world community that "you are either with us or against us". Overlooked by many, Prime Minister Thaksin Shinawatra's first impulse was to declare Thailand's "strict neutrality" in the face of America's imminent invasion of Afghanistan after 9/11. When Thailand's foreign and security policy planners reminded Thaksin of the longstanding treaty alliance between Thailand and the United States, the prime minister back-pedalled. Thailand ultimately honoured its treaty obligations with the United States and took part in the UN-led, post-war reconstruction effort in Afghanistan. Eighteen months later, the commencement of hostilities in Iraq posed a similar challenge to Thaksin and Thailand's foreign policy and security establishment. With the U.S. administration and the UN Security Council at odds over the disarmament of the Iraqi regime, the formulation of Thailand's position naturally became a conundrum. Thaksin made clear from the opening day of the war in Iraq that Thailand remained committed to the UN framework. But he also took the concurrent measure of expelling eleven Iraqis who were deemed a liability to Thailand's security interests, and Thailand sent troops to join the American-led forces in Iraq. The Thai position thus became two-sided, standing by the UN and sticking to the United States.

But this balancing act changed by June 2003 when Thaksin visited President Bush at the White House. A deal was struck. With President Bush's blessing, Thailand soon became a major non-Nato ally (MNNA). Bangkok signed on to the Container Security Initiative (CSI), and trade ties under the limited Thai-U.S. Trade and Investment Framework Agreement were broadened. In addition, a full-fledged bilateral free trade agreement between the two countries was to be negotiated at Thaksin's request. Two months later, Thai authorities arrested Riduan Isamuddin, better known as Hambali who was the operations chief of Jamaah Islamiyah, and handed him to the United States. The Hambali arrest marked a turning point in Thailand's post-9/11 position. It was no longer a bystander in tacit support of the United States but became an overt American ally in the war on terror. When push came to shove, even the nationalist Thaksin had to take sides.[5]

MILITARY-AUTHORITARIANISM AND ECONOMIC DEVELOPMENT[6]

Perhaps the most profound side effect of World War II was the entrenchment of military-authoritarian rule. As Phibun regained the premiership in April 1948, he had to contend with factional rivalries between General Sarit Thanarat and Police General Phao Sriyanond. Sarit's power base was in the army, whereas Phao's was in the police force. Their legendary conflict in domestic politics and clashing vested interests in the fast-growing economy preoccupied Phibun throughout his tenure, culminating with the September 1957 *putsch* by Sarit on the pretext of a fraudulent general election held earlier in the year. Sarit and his chief allies in the army, General Thanom Kittikachorn and General Praphat Charusathien, thus took charge of government. During the twenty-five years that the Phibun-Sarit-Thanom military-authoritarian governments were in operation, the Thai political economy underwent tremendous changes, underpinned by strong and steady economic growth rate of more than seven per cent per annum.

Without the necessary expertise to engineer economic growth and manage the macroeconomy, the military dictators relied on a small coterie of technocrats, most of whom were educated abroad with specialized expertise mainly in economics. The military and the technocracy soon developed an "implicit bargain" whereby the military provided the necessary policy-making autonomy and political insulation to the technocrats in exchange for technocratic expertise. The military needed a growing economy for political legitimacy and for sources of rent, whereas the technocrats needed the military's permission and authorization to put their expertise in motion. During the Sarit period in the early 1960s, the institutional management of the macroeconomy was reformed and became outward-oriented along neo-liberal lines. A clutch of macro-policy agencies became the guardians and drivers of the macroeconomy, featuring the National Economic Development Board, the Bureau of the Budget, the Ministry of Finance, and the Bank of Thailand. A symbiotic relationship between the military and the technocracy was thereby established.

Following the political upheavals of October 1973 and October 1976, this military-technocracy arrangement was gradually eroded by the rising tide of democratization. By 1988, the election of the Chatichai Choonhavan government essentially sidelined and politicized the technocracy, eventually leading to the policy mismanagement that helped pave the way for the 1997 economic crisis. Accordingly, the present Thai political economy has its origins under military-authoritarian rule, which was the outgrowth of wartime and post-war conditions. The correlation between the authority of the military and that of the technocracy is unmistakable. The more entrenched the military, the more autonomous and effective the technocracy. Unsurprisingly, as democratization made greater headway over the past two decades, the technocrats' days were numbered. They are hardly visible under current political economy conditions in Thailand.

FOREIGN POLICY OPPORTUNISM

As previously mentioned, foreign policy opportunism is not alien to Thai policy-making circles. The Thai participation in World War II alongside Japan was premised partly on the reclamation of territories in the Shan state of Burma, northern Malaya, and several provinces in both Laos and Cambodia that had been ceded to colonial France and Britain. Although these territories were promptly returned to Britain and France as part of Thailand's post-war settlement, they represented Thai leaders' willingness to take advantage of opportunities. Since World War II, territorial issues have receded in importance, but the subliminal notion of reclaiming lands that once belonged to the Siamese empire may not have been abandoned altogether.

In the late 1980s under the government of Prime Minister Chatichai Choonhavan, Thai foreign policy shifted from a firm alliance with the United States to friendliness towards China and Indochina.[7] Advised by a small group of academic experts in international affairs, Chatichai sought to turn Indochina from "battlefields into marketplaces" just as the curtain of the Cold War was drawing to a close. A "baht zone" policy was promoted in dealing with Indochina. Egged on by General Chavalit Yongchaiyuth, the then army chief and future prime minister during 1996–97, the Chatichai government harboured the idea of Thai preponderance on mainland Southeast Asia, harking back to the "Golden Land" or "Suvarnabhumi" concept of past Siamese empires. However, this grandiose scheme was shortlived as Chatichai was toppled in a *coup d'état* in February 1991.

More recently, former Prime Minister Thaksin Shinawatra's implementation of the Ayeyawady-Chao Phraya-Mekong Economic Cooperation Strategy (ACMECS) also testifies to the notion of a pan-Thai domination of mainland Southeast Asia. ACMECS was spawned when Thaksin met with his counterparts from Myanmar, Laos and Cambodia in April 2003 (Vietnam joined the scheme in May 2004). That initial discussion led to a leaders' meeting in Myanmar in November 2003. Significantly, ACMECS sprung up at a time when Thaksin was being seen in some quarters as a potential regional leader in view of Malaysian Prime Minister Mahathir Mohamad's retirement.[8] The advent of ACMECS is reminiscent of the Chatichai period and of Phibun's attempt to restore the old parts of the Siamese empire.

As an economic development plan for mainland Southeast Asia, ACMECS called for Thailand to provide financial assistance to reduce the development disparity between itself and Myanmar, Laos and Cambodia. A Thai fund of THB10 billion was pledged to this end, combining soft loans with twelve-year repayment periods at three per cent interest with outright aid transfers. At the same time, Thaksin declared Thailand to be an aid donor and no longer an aid recipient. This was a stunning departure from Thailand's past status as an aid recipient. It also marked the first time Thailand became a financial donor of a considerable sum. The THB10 billion package did come with strings attached. The credit line for development projects in the three recipient countries was required to be denominated in Thai baht, and procurement contracts were required to be sourced with Thai firms. Using the Thai baht in this fashion also recalled Chatichai's attempt to create a "baht zone"[9] on mainland Southeast Asia. In some ways, Thaksin's ACMECS can be seen as irredentism by economic and developmental means.

THE MONARCHY

The institution of the monarchy was nowhere to be seen during World War II. Following the 1932 overthrow of absolute monarchy by the "People's Party", led by a foreign-educated bureaucratic elite comprising military and civilian wings, respectively headed by Phibun and Pridi, constitutional rule was introduced. As the monarchy was in eclipse while the newly empowered military and civilian leaders increasingly widened their power bases, King Prachadipok (Rama VII) decided to abdicate in March 1935 and went into exile in Britain, where he passed away in the midst of World War II.[10] The governing People's Party chose Prince

Ananda Mahidol, then a schoolboy studying in Switzerland, as the new monarch. King Anand's post-war return to Thailand lasted merely six months by which time he was found dead under a cloud of controversy and mystery. His younger teenage brother became King Bhumibol Adulyadej (Rama IX), the present monarch.[11] From the time of King Prachadipok's abdication to King Anand's death and King Bhumibol's ascension to the throne, the institution, role and prestige of the monarchy were at its nadir. Its future in the aftermath of the war was most uncertain.

In fact, King Bhumibol faced daunting challenges from the outset. Although the 1949 constitution empowered him to appoint the senate, Phibun stripped away this authority just as King Bhumibol was returning to Bangkok from abroad in late 1951 to assume his royal duties. Citing the communist menace and widespread corruption, Prime Minister Phibun abruptly replaced the 1949 constitution with its precursor from 1932. This change of charter enabled the government to do away with the bicameral legislature and re-introduced a single, appointed National Assembly. Thus the new monarch's power was clipped even before he began to exercise it. During the early 1950s, the Thai monarchy was rudderless without a clear sense of direction.

The September 1957 coup and the rise to power of Field Marshal Sarit Thanarat, however, provided the monarchy with a new lifeline.[12] He organized an incumbency[13] coup in October 1958, abolishing constitutional rule and governing through decrees issued by the Revolutionary Council. As prime minister during 1958–63, Sarit reconstituted the monarchy by reordering the Thai social hierarchy. Instead of channelling citizen loyalty to the concept of the state and the constitution, Sarit redirected the focus to the institution of the monarchy, restoring the king to the apex of the moral, social, and political order. The close association with the monarchy lent political legitimacy to Sarit and the military government. A new symbiotic relationship was thereby established, allowing the monarchy to be reconstructed and flourished to this day. The genesis of the current monarch's immense authority, prestige and popularity thus goes back to the periods during, prior to, and in the aftermath of World War II.

CONCLUSION

This chapter has tried to discern the broad contours of Thailand's contemporary foreign policy and domestic politics that are traceable to World War II. It has argued that Thai leaders emerged from the war with a fervent bias against the policy of neutrality. With this lesson in mind, Thai leaders from 1948 to the mid-1970s did not hesitate to side staunchly with America's anti-communist crusade, serving as an outpost on mainland Southeast Asia. The origins of Thailand's longest period of military-authoritarian rule during 1957–73 are located in the domestic politics of wartime and the immediate post-war periods when the civilian leadership was unable to hold on to power. In turn, the military-authoritarian rule ushered in vibrant and sustained economic development, steered by autonomous technocrats with specialized expertise. As with the irredentism witnessed during World War II, foreign policy opportunism is discernible in the modern period in the late 1980s under Chatichai, and more recently under Thaksin in their attempts to make Thailand a preponderant power on mainland Southeast Asia through economic ways and means. Finally, the chapter has noted the absence of the monarchy during World War II, and pointed out that its resurgence has derived from the efforts of a military strongman who rose to prominence during the tumultuous post-war aftermath.

NOTES

1. This section draws on Songsri Foran, *Thai-British-American Relations During World War II and the Immediate Post-war Period* (Bangkok: Thai Khadi Research Institute, Thammasat University, 1981); Wyatt, David K., *Thailand: A Short History* (New Haven, CT: Yale University Press, 1984); Kobkua Suwannathat-Pian, *Thailand's Durable Premier: Phibun through Three Decades, 1932–1957* (Kuala Lumpur: Oxford University Press, 1995); Niksch, Larry Allen, "United States Foreign Policy in Thailand's World War II Peace Settlements With Great Britain and France", Ph.D. dissertation, Georgetown University, 1976; Direk Yayanama, *Siam and World War II*, trans. by Jane Godfrey Keyes (Bangkok: Social Science Association of Thailand Press, 1978); Thawi Bunyaket, "Additional Facts on Incidents in Thailand During World War II", in *Thai Politics: Extracts and Documents 1932–1957*, edited by Thak Chaloemtiarana (Bangkok: The Social Science Association of Thailand, 1978), pp. 324–48.
2. See Kobkua Suwannathat-Pian, *Thailand's Durable Premier: Phibun through Three Decades, 1932–1957*, chapter 5; Benjamin Batson, "Siam and Japan: The Perils of Independence", in *Southeast Asia Under the Japanese Occupation*, edited by Alfred W. McCoy (New Haven, CT: Yale University Southeast Asian Studies, 1980).
3. On American economic and military assistance to Thailand, see Muscat, Robert J., *Thailand and the United States: Development, Security, and Foreign Aid* (New York, NY: Columbia University Press, 1990).

Thitinan Pongsudhirak

4. See Suchit Bunbongkarn and Sukhumbhand Paribatra, "Thai Politics and Foreign Policy in the 1980's. Plus Ca Change, Plus Ca la Mîme Chose?", in *ASEAN in Regional and Global Context*, edited by Karl D. Jackson, Sukhumbhand Paribatra, and Soedjati Djiwandono (Berkeley: Institute of East Asian Studies, University of California, 1986).

5. Paul Chambers, "U.S.-Thai Relations after 9/11: A New Era in Cooperation?", *Contemporary Southeast Asia*, December 2004.

6. This section draws on Sathien Chantimatorn, *Chatchai Chunhawan: taharn nak prachatipatai* [Chatichai Choonhavan: A "Democratic" Soldier] (Bangkok: Plan Publishing, 1989); Thitinan Pongsudhirak, *Crisis From Within: The Politics of Macroeconomic Management in Thailand, 1947–97*, Ph.D. thesis, London School of Economics, 2001; Muscat, Robert J., *The Fifth Tiger: A Study of Thai Development Policy* (Armonk, NY: M.E. Sharpe, 1994); Ammar Siamwalla, "Can A Developing Democracy Manage Its Macroeconomy? The Case of Thailand", paper presented at the East Asian Crisis Workshop, Institute of Development Studies, Brighton, 13–14 July 1998; Christensen, Scott, David Dollar, Ammar Siamwalla, and Pakorn Vichyanond, *The Lessons of East Asia: Thailand — The Institutional and Political Underpinnings of Growth* (Washington, D.C.: World Bank, 1993); Thak Chaloemtiarana, *Thailand: The Politics of Despotic Paternalism* (Bangkok: Social Science Association of Thailand, Thai Khadi Institute, Thammasat University, 1979).

7. Sukhumbhand Paribatra, *Beyond Cambodia: Some Thoughts on Southeast Asia in the 1990s* (Bangkok: Institute of Security and International Studies, Chulalongkorn University, 1989).

8. See "Thaksin Asserts Regional Ambitions", *Bangkok Post*, 16 July 2003.

9. See "Regional role possible for baht", *The Nation*, 26 January 2004.

10. For the replacement of absolute monarchy by constitutional rule, see Batson, Benjamin, *The End of the Absolute Monarchy in Siam* (Singapore: Oxford University Press, Ithaca, NY: Cornell University, 1977).

11. See Kershaw, Roger, *Monarchy in South-East Asia* (London: Routledge, 2001).

12. For more details on Sarit's role in the reconstitution of the monarchy, see also Thak Chaloemtiarana, *Thailand: The Politics of Despotic Paternalism* (Bangkok: Social Science Association of Thailand, Thai Khadi Institute, Thammasat University, 1979); Hewison, Kevin, "The Monarchy and Democratisation", in *Political Change in Thailand: Democracy and Participation*, edited by Kevin Kewison (London: Routledge, 1997).

13. The incumbency coup was against Prime Minister Gen. Thanom Kittikachorn, who was put in office as caretaker until Sarit could return from medical recuperation abroad to take over the premiership himself.

Part Three

Northeast Asia and India

Chapter Ten

Remembering World War II: Legacies of the War Fought in China

Huang Jianli

INTRODUCTION

The war fought in China against Japan during World War II has never been forgotten by the Chinese people. Voluminous writings, memorial shrines, museum exhibitions and annual commemorations on the war are the staple diet in this nation of historically-conscious people. However, memories of the Sino-Japanese War had for a substantive period of time faded in the international arena outside of China because of a number of closely related events. There was the founding of the Communist People's Republic of China (PRC) in 1949, the descend of the bamboo curtain after the outbreak of the Korean War in 1950, as well as the reversing of American occupation policy in Japan soon after. The hegemonic rhetoric of the Cold War and the corresponding self-isolation of a Chinese Communist regime had resulted in an essentially Anglo-Saxon remembrance of World War II, with the Sino-Japanese War relegated to the fringe of mainstream commemorative events around the world. This relegation lessened only after China's re-entry into the international community in 1972 and even more so after the opening and reform of the Chinese economy from 1978.

Consequently, one significant fragment of neglect at the international level is that not many people are sufficiently conscious that World War II has a fractured timeline, and China was actually the earliest of all nations to be caught up in a full-scale war, beginning with the outbreak of fighting in 1937 near the Marco Polo Bridge located just outside of the city of Beijing. China was alone in its war with Japan for nearly two full years before the German invasion of Poland had the unintended effect of meshing the Sino-Japanese War together with the outbreak of fighting in continental Europe, making this a much more global war than the Euro-centric World War I of 1914–18. The ending of a sense of desperate isolation among the lonely Chinese defenders and the expanding scale of the global war became even more visible with the Japanese bombing of Pearl Harbor in December 1941 and the reluctant entry of the United States into war. From then on, the three discrete entities of the Sino-Japanese War, the World War II and the Pacific War metaphorically fused into one. This chapter refers to the war fought in China in the loose sense of covering the theatre in China in the period from 1937 to 1945.

The year 2005 marked the sixtieth anniversary of the end of all fighting and provided the *raison d'etre* and occasion to reflect on World War II's transient and enduring legacies. There was a transformation of the socio-economic structure of China during the war which led to the emergence of an interventionist state, a shift in balance of power which left an imprint on current cross-Straits relations, a metamorphosis of Chinese diasporic relations, a resultant pattern of cycles in Sino-American relations and, last but not least, a legacy of turbulence in Sino-Japanese relations up to the present day.

SOCIO-ECONOMIC TRANSFORMATION AND THE INTERVENTIONIST STATE

China today is undergoing a historic change from a socialist command economy to one that is much closer to the Western model of a capitalist, free market. The jury is still out on whether this current exercise will be a successful one.[1] This subject is attracting international attention for various reasons, the most important being whether the Chinese case would be a model for an economics-first approach in the reform of any communist country. All eyes are currently on China to see if it can pull off the first ideological reversal on the practical level in human history, moving from Marxism-Leninisism-Maoism to modern-day capitalism, without toppling the party-state machinery. More noteworthy is an erroneous view that the origins of a planned, centrally-controlled Chinese economy is to be traced solely to the ascent to power by the Chinese Communist Party (CCP) in 1949 and its emulation of the Soviet developmental model during the 1950s. In reality, the post-1949 socio-economic structure had an earlier beginning during World War II.

The wartime years should indeed be considered exceptionally important for dating the origins of Chinese state dominance in economic activities and welfare provision.[2] It was only during the war that the ruling party Kuomintang (KMT) came under extreme pressure but also acquired sufficient national clout to nationalize key sectors of the economy and to mobilize major resources for fending off the invaders. It was not an easy task. The war was the first full-scale, countrywide modern war, with China losing almost the entire eastern coastal region and key centres of industry, modernity and knowledge production. The major cities of Beijing, Shanghai, Tianjin, Nanjing and Guangzhou fell to Japanese forces in quick succession. At least sixty million people were displaced, arguably the largest ever migratory exodus in human history in terms of number, spatial distance and time. The sheer size of such dislocation imposed unprecedented demands on the state to cater to the basic welfare of these people. Moreover, the loss of the relatively more urbanized and industrialized regions in the early stages of the war had created the necessity for the hinterland agrarian sector to shoulder the fiscal responsibility and for a rapid jump-start of a new industrial base. This was attempted partly by using whatever factory machineries that had survived the relocation inland through congested waterways and difficult terrains.

Therefore, prompted by the need to mobilize scarce resources for wartime production and to fight raging hyperinflation (sparked partially by an imbalance in the demand and supply of goods and services),[3] the KMT regime evoked state control over a wide range of economic activities. Through its powerful wartime National Resources Commission and other governmental agencies, it greatly expanded direct state participation in the economy, especially within the sectors of manufacturing and mining. By 1943, nearly 70 per cent of the 3,700 factories in the rear area were state-owned. As a proportion of total Chinese factory production, state ownership had risen from a mere 10 per cent in 1935 to as high as about 50 per cent in the rear area by 1944. Of these, petrol, electrical copper, tungsten and pure tin were fully state produced, while steel and textile production became dominated by the state. Such a lion's share of production within the national economy by the state was unprecedented and represented a structural change for the Chinese economy. This structure laid a strong foundation and became the model for planned economies on both sides of the Taiwan Straits after 1949. In a similar vein, various welfare measures implemented by the KMT for its state factory workers, in addition to wartime relief packages for civil servants, soldiers and educators, were also forerunners of the latter-day Communist China "*danwei*" (work place units) system and the Taiwanese semi-state welfare system.[4]

The interventionist state, however, has been at best a transient legacy because both the PRC and Taiwan have been moving away since the 1980s and 1990s from such state-interventionist practices. While recognizing that the state's role cannot be eliminated, both have been restructuring their socio-economic foundations to one which is much more responsive to free market dynamics.

SHIFT IN BALANCE OF POWER AND IMPACT ON CROSS-STRAITS RELATIONS

Before the outbreak of war in China during 1937, the KMT held the upper hand in the balance of power in China, with the CCP as the much weaker underdog. The rise of the KMT could be traced to its rejuvenation by the mass-based, anti-imperialistic nationalism culminating in the May Fourth Movement, as well as the help rendered by the Soviet Union in its reorganization. Although the party was plagued almost immediately by the problems of residual warlordism and intra-party factionalism after it came to power in 1927, it was able to maintain a semblance of national unification. It slowly extended its power beyond the coastal provinces of Jiangsu and Zhejiang, in particular advancing into Sichuan province in the southwestern corner of China, where its army pursued the Chinese Communists through "anti-bandit" campaigns. Indeed, the Chiang Kai-shek led-KMT government at this stage consciously gave a much higher priority to defeating its internal rivals, both warlords and Chinese Communists, rather than to meeting the challenge posed by the external threat of Japanese incursions. Chiang initially opted to rely on diplomatic channels to resolve conflicts with the Japanese military, especially in seeking the help of the League of Nations. "First to pacify within, then to resist the outside forces" [*Xianannei, hourangwai*] became his operating principle.[5] Public unhappiness with this approach was reflected by the frequent occurrence of student protests and an eventual military rebellion that led to the kidnapping of Chiang during his military inspection of Xian city.[6] His quick release and triumphant return to Nanjing on Christmas day in 1936 indicated the lack of a viable alternative leadership, and this by default reaffirmed the KMT's position in the position of power just before the war started. But beneath the surface, Chiang's release marked his recognition of the simmering public demand for resistance against further Japanese incursions. As a condition for his release, he was nudged towards the forging of an alliance (the second in history) with the Chinese Communists, which became an operational reality when skirmishes at the Marco Polo Bridge on 7 July 1937 escalated into a full-scale war.

The engagement of the KMT regime in battles against Japan and the agreement of a second united front during the war tied the hands of the KMT considerably. This gave its long-time communist rival critical breathing space to revitalize and shift to a relatively strong position with the aim of tipping the balance of power if and when the opportunity to do so emerged, which arrived after Japan had surrendered.[7] Otherwise, the CCP would have remained weak and barely alive. Ever since the breakdown of the first united front (1924–27) and the bloody purges of the communists by the KMT in the latter half of 1927, the CCP had been on the run, first away from urbanized centres such as Shanghai and then from its rural hideout in Jiangxi. The much mythologized Long March was in reality a long retreat away from KMT military attacks and a painful run during which the CCP reportedly lost nearly 90 per cent of its marching participants. By the time the CCP landed up in the poor northwestern rural area of Yanan in Shaanxi Province at the end of 1935, it was a pale shadow of its former self. Its survival was further at stake as the KMT was regrouping its forces and taking aim for a final, decisive strike against Yanan that would annihilate its communist enemy.

The war against Japan and the consequent necessity for a public display of national unity in the face of an external threat provided the CCP with the gift of life. Such an opportunity also gave it eight years of breathing space to rejuvenate itself, through a series of administrative and rural socio-economic reform programmes as well as by conducting credible guerrilla campaigns against Japanese forces which enabled it to lay claim to a nationalist mandate.[8] This potent mixture of nationalism and Communism, as well as the rebuilding of a peasant-based army led by a lean administrative-politico machinery, arguably won for the CCP by 1945 a near-parity of power *vis-à-vis* the KMT. The communists subsequently took advantage of the rapidly declining state of civic and military morale in post-1945 China caused primarily by KMT mismanagement and raging hyperinflation. After the CCP decisively won three large-scale, civil war battles fought in northern China, the fate of the KMT was sealed. The communists emerged victorious and declared the founding of a new republic in October 1949, while the KMT fled into exile on the island of Taiwan.[9] World War II was therefore crucial in shifting the balance of power within China, facilitating the reconsolidation, reform, and ultimately victory of the CCP, and the founding of the PRC. This new political map for China has been an enduring legacy with broad implications even from the vantage point of 2005.

For a long time thereafter, despite the political division across the Straits of Taiwan, the Beijing leadership and the exiled KMT leaders remained jointly committed to the romantic ideal of bringing about eventual political reunification. However, with every passing year of political separation and divergent economic and cultural development paths, a separate sense of belonging emerged on the island of Taiwan. By the late 1980s and early 1990s, Taiwanese indigenous nationalism harbouring the desire for an independent Republic of Taiwan had appeared and matured within mainstream politics. The banner of Taiwanese separatism has been raised and it is a threat to making the post-war political division a permanent reality.[10] The banner has become a major source of tension in East Asia, especially after the independence-inclined Democratic Progressive Party (DPP) under the leadership of Chen Shui-bian managed to dislodge the KMT and captured the presidency in the 2000 and 2004 presidential elections. The dangerous scenario of a Taiwanese declaration of independence, very likely to be followed by instantaneous PRC military retaliation, has somewhat receded after the DPP failed to maintain its winning momentum and was unable to secure an absolute majority in the legislative elections held in late 2004. The "homecoming visits" of the pro-unification as well as *status quo* party leaders from the KMT, the People's First Party and the New Party to China in the first half of 2005 has created a new atmosphere for possible reduction of tension in cross-straits relations.

The war has resulted in another — this time permanent — change in the political map of China. Due to diplomatic negotiations between the KMT and the Soviet Union during the closing months of World War II, Outer Mongolia's declaration of independence in October 1945 was recognized by the KMT.[11] When the KMT regime fled to Taiwan and became an ally of the American camp in the Cold War, however, it attributed its loss of mainland China to a Soviet master conspiracy and revoked its recognition of Outer Mongolia independence, henceforth reclaiming the Outer Mongolia as Republic of China (ROC) territory. Until 1961, the ROC even repeatedly exercised its veto as a permanent member of the United Nations Security Council to deny Mongolia's admission into the United Nations. On the part of the PRC, anxious to seek allies during its early infant years as well as to forge a strategic partnership with the Soviet Union, it upheld the post-war recognition of Mongolian independence. It maintained this stance even after the Sino-Soviet split in the late 1950s.

This divergence in the foreign policies of the PRC and ROC towards Outer Mongolia has come full circle with the rise of Taiwan's independence sentiments. Half a century of Taiwanese claim to sovereignty over both China and Mongolia ended in 2002 when the Democratic Progressive Party-led government, in its eagerness to test the boundaries of independence for Taiwan, detached Mongolia from the jurisdiction of the ROC by amending state statutes and suspending the publication of any official map of China.[12] This was a politically sensitive and controversial move, regarded by anti-independence critics as unconstitutional and a dangerous step towards the eventual disowning of Chinese sovereignty. Another fragmentary legacy of World War II has thus been drawn, in an unexpected manner, into the complicated dynamics of current cross-straits tensions.

METAMORPHOSIS OF CHINESE DIASPORIC RELATIONS

The war also changed the nature of Chinese diasporic relations. Until recent times, the bulk of the Chinese migrants overseas chose to settle in Southeast Asia, notably Singapore and the Malay Peninsula, with only a minority going out of the region. Historically, relations between China and Chinese communities in Southeast Asia shifted from a state of benign neglect to one of close rapport, ever since the late nineteenth century, caused by a rivalry for overseas Chinese loyalty and financial support. It was a hot contest between the Qing dynasty government and two groups of its enemies: the exiled institutional reformists led by Kang Youwei and Liang Qichao, and the roving band of Republican revolutionaries led by Sun Yat-sen.[13] Far from being moderated after the Qing dynasty fell with the October 1911 Revolution and the Chinese Republic founded in January 1912, this "drumbeat of the Motherland" to engage and tie the overseas Chinese communities to China intensified even more from the 1920s to 1940s under the leadership of the KMT.[14] Chinese schools throughout Southeast Asia increasingly used textbooks originating from China, with students taught mainly by teachers trained in China and supervised by school inspectors dispatched by the KMT government. This Sino-centric focus and Chinese nationalist sentiment beyond the shores of China reached a crescendo with the widespread organization of anti-Japanese national salvation movements within and without China to counter the expansion of Japanese imperialist ambitions in the 1930s. When war eventually broke out in 1937, the KMT military effort was in part funded by generous donations raised in various parts of Southeast Asia and was assisted by thousands of overseas Chinese war volunteers who served in various capacities such as soldiers, truck drivers, pilots, mechanics, nurses, welfare workers, and many more.[15]

Following the end of World War II, two major developments brought this China-overseas Chinese relationship to a grinding halt. One such event was the onset of the post-war decolonization process. Many countries in Southeast Asia gained independence from their colonial masters and the overseas Chinese residents were pressured into severing of ancestral or motherland ties and re-orienting their activities and mindset towards their respective newly emerging host nation-states. The other development that added to the forced shift in loyalty was the beginning of the Cold War and the political danger of being associated with the new communist regime in China. In the eyes of Cold War warriors, the PRC was in league with the Moscow-based Communist international movement to manipulate Chinese overseas communities into fifth columns to support jungle insurgencies and urban subversion against the newly independent nation states. At the 1955 Bandung Non-alignment Conference, Chinese Premier Chou Enlai urged Chinese overseas communities to re-orient and adapt to their new residential environment. The call mitigated but did not eliminate the Cold War concerns.

This freezing of close links between China and the Chinese diasporic communities lasted for nearly three decades. The thawing came about only after China rejoined the international community with the Sino-American rapprochement of the early 1970s and even more so after its market reform and opening up to foreign investment in late 1978. The abrupt ending of the Cold War, signalled by the collapse of the Berlin Wall and the Soviet Union during 1989–91, gave further encouragement to the Chinese overseas (especially the ideologically agnostic businessmen) to reconnect with mainland China, now with much less fear of being seen as communist stooges, or of losing their citizenship rights, and in fact with some degree of endorsement from their Southeast Asian governments who had also become keen to tap into the China market. Aware of the usefulness of tapping into this pool of Chinese overseas capital, PRC citizens themselves have been assertive in renewing the attraction of ancestral linkages, mixing it with the promises of a vast Chinese consumer market. There have been numerous recent publications playing up the past linkages between the Chinese overseas and China. One case has revolved around the "Tiger Balm King" named Aw Boon Haw. He was originally tainted as a Japanese collaborator during World War II, partly because of his business connections with the Japanese, and that he had flown to Tokyo to meet with Japanese Prime Minister Tojo Hideki at the height of the war. In the 1980s and early 1990s, lured by lucrative business connections between China and Sally Aw's Hong Kong business empire inherited from her father, Tiger Aw was promptly rehabilitated by mainland China as a true-blue "patriotic overseas Chinese leader".[16]

Beyond business networks and at the popular culture level, there has been the emergence of a "Greater China" with a multi-loci Chinese culture spearheaded by China, Taiwan and Hong Kong, and shared by many other Chinese overseas communities. On the one hand, this educational-entertainment network embedded within the knowledge-based global economy and driven partly by the technological explosion started during World War II, has given the Chinese diaspora an unprecedented platform to engender a sense of togetherness in terms of Chinese identity. On the other hand, the pluralistic nature of information technology and the contradictory localization-globalization tensions of globalized capitalism have also fractured the identity of being Chinese into multiple meanings and uncertain hybridity.[17] Changing residential and migratory population dynamics have also brought forth a process of self-transformation in terms of having more local-born and mixed marriages and less of a numerical migratory weighting on Southeast Asia, especially when many of the new migrants from the re-opening of China have been flocking towards the seemingly more exciting "other worlds" of the United States, Europe and Australia rather than hopping just to another "Asian" country. In sum, the picture on Chinese diasporic relationship is getting much more complicated with every passing year. The vestiges of pre-war, wartime and immediate post-war diasporic influences are receding further into the background.

CYCLES IN SINO-AMERICAN RELATIONS

Over the last sixty years, the relationship between the United States and the CCP/PRC has undergone various cycles of highs and lows that can be related to the effects of World War II and its aftermath. American journalists reporting on China during the 1920s to 1940s played a key role in laying the foundation for post-war Sino-American relations. Edgar Snow had literally carved a journalistic and writing career for himself by succeeding in making pioneering Western contacts with the Chinese Communists and getting to interview Mao Zedong and other key leaders hiding in rural sanctuaries.[18] Other American journalists that later played a similar role in introducing the Chinese Communists to the American audience included Graham Peck, Agnes Smedly, Theodore White and Jack Belden.[19] Their sympathetic airing of the Chinese Communist cause stood in contrast to the negative images revolving around KMT/ROC corruption and demoralization, providing a positive environment for U.S. policy makers of the Roosevelt administration to view the Chinese Communists more as friendly social reformers rather than hardcore puppets of Moscow.[20] Indeed, due to an anxiety to draw in wider Chinese participation so as to build up a capacity to launch a counter-attack on Japan, the United States made official contact, especially through the Dixie Mission, to try to forge some form of cooperation and joint operation with the Chinese Communists during the war.[21] Apart from the military side of the government, the U.S. State Department also had a corps of diplomatic officials who were sympathetic to the CCP, including John K. Fairbank.

Thus when World War II ended and China plunged into four years of civil war between the KMT and CCP, the Americans tried to be even-handed, stepping back from the fray and refusing to commit substantial military and financial assistance to the KMT despite repeated and near-desperate appeals by Chiang Kai-shek.[22] Even as the Chinese Civil War (1945–49) was decided in favour of the CCP in October 1949, there was a chance that the United States would join Great Britain in extending official recognition to the new state of the PRC. However, the abrupt outbreak of the Korean War in June 1950 and the dawning of the Cold War in Asia destroyed such a possibility. Domestically, the witch-hunt of the McCarthy era nearly shut out all sympathetic voices to the PRC from within the U.S. administration for the next two decades.

John K. Fairbank was one of those that left the diplomatic service and returned to academia to work under the cloud of McCarthy witch-hunting.[23]

From within the academic world, he achieved the distinction of contributing significantly to the build-up of a generation of new American scholars with the necessary language facility and a broader understanding of modern China from late Qing dynasty up to the contemporary era. It was partly due to such scholarship, which was engendered for two decades during the 1950s and the 1960s, that when the opportunity came during the early 1970s for President Richard Nixon (1969–74) and his Secretary of State Henry Kissinger to reverse America's China policy and seek a rapprochement with the PRC, Sino-American relations were able to swing upwards quickly and attained normalization of full diplomatic relations in 1979.[24]

The story of Sino-American relations, however, would be incomplete without the mentioning of KMT again and its eventual exile and anchorage on the island of Taiwan. This is because cross-straits relations between China and Taiwan remain a flashpoint in international relations today and a major thorn in Sino-American relations. Although the KMT generally received unfavourable press coverage among the American audience in the late 1930s and 1940s, it was not without its share of American media support. Henry Luce of Time Incorporated was one such firm believer. He subscribed to the view that Chiang Kai-shek was the saviour of the Chinese people and the only one with courage and ability to lead China in the fight against internal and external enemies. Luce thrice featured Chiang on the cover story of *Time* magazine — in 1931, 1933 and 1936. Luce's support for Chiang remained unwavering throughout the whole of World War II.[25] After the war, this foundation of goodwill, laid by Henry Luce and by those that bought into the McCarthyist rhetoric of anti-communism, portrayed Chiang's KMT as a valuable anti-communist ally and built up a powerful American congressional lobby to protect the ROC government in exile on Taiwan.[26]

This lobby group again made an impact at a critical point when the United States normalized its relations with the PRC in January 1979 by persuading the American Congress to pass a Taiwan Relations Act shortly after. It is the passage of this act and the varying interpretations promoted by a diverse range of political groups in the PRC, United States and Taiwan over the past twenty-five years that have planted the dimension of "strategic ambiguity" in Sino-American and cross-straits relations. This is because the United States has not clearly laid out the terms under which it would intervene in the defence of Taiwan should the situation in the straits become militarily confrontational. This allows the United States room for policy manoeuvring. Together with three U.S.-PRC communiqués of

1972, 1978 and 1982, the Taiwan Relations Act underpins the American foreign policy towards Taiwan. The communiqués have been somewhat reinforced by President Bill Clinton's enunciation of the so-called "Three No's" policy during his state visit to China in June–July 1998. These are not supporting "independence for Taiwan, not endorsing two Chinas or one Taiwan-one China" and not believing that "Taiwan should be a member of any organization for which statehood is a requirement", a pledge made in the aftermath of the dangerous missile face-off of 1995–96.[27] The ascendance of the neo-conservatives within the George W. Bush administration initially led to a hardening of the foreign policy line towards China, almost to the point of having a neo-containment colouring. But the EP-3 spy plane incident of April 2001 and the increasingly visible rise of China as a major economic power forced the George W. Bush's administration to continue with a policy of constructive engagement, especially in his second term of office. The relationship between China, America and Taiwan thus obviously hinges on current political and economic strategic interests, but this triangular relationship is not one without its historical baggage from World War II. This is especially so when Japan was a player in the complex relationship and is now also an interested party in the state of U.S.-PRC relations.

TURBULENCE IN SINO-JAPANESE RELATIONS

For the turbulence surrounding Sino-Japanese relations, Taiwan has also featured prominently. The island was ceded to Japan when China was defeated during the First Sino-Japanese War of 1894–95. After being governed as a Japanese colony for fifty years, it was returned to China at the end of World War II. However, half a century of Japanese colonial rule in Taiwan produced one to two generations of local Taiwanese that could not identify themselves with the incoming KMT regime. After a few decades of struggle against authoritarian KMT rule, a Taiwanese independence movement has emerged, which at times solicited support from the Japanese public and government.

On the part of Japan, apprehension about the emergence of China as a major economic and military power in recent years has led it to an alignment with pro-independence factions in Taiwan as a useful means of "balancing and checking" Chinese aspiration. The United States, who have provided a nuclear umbrella to protect Japan and forced it to demilitarize, has also reassessed the role Japan should play in the shifting security dynamics in East Asia.[28] Beginning with international peace-keeping participation, the United States has steadily drawn Japan into committing a higher amount of military spending and into playing a larger international role. In a major review of the U.S.-Japan Security Treaty in 1996 in the aftermath of China's missile test, Japan pledged to provide a greater amount of support for American forces deployed from bases in Japan to meet security contingencies in East Asia. In February 2005, after a meeting of the U.S.-Japan Security Consultative Committee, Washington and Tokyo went one step further to issue a joint statement declaring the Taiwan issue to be within the ambit of their mutual security concerns.[29]

However, the bigger hurdle in smooth Sino-Japanese relations has not been the issue of Taiwan independence, but the fundamental dispute over the issue of responsibility for Japanese atrocities committed in China during World War II. A number of sub-issues are entangled here. First and foremost, the wounds of war have remained painful for many Chinese, with the conflict fought across vast stretches of China. An estimated fifteen to twenty million Chinese in China died as a result of eight years of war.[30] Probably more than sixty million Chinese were forcibly relocated, making it the largest migration in human history. In their eagerness to push hard and fast and to force an early surrender by Chiang Kai-shek, and in their expression of anger against the previous decades of rising anti-Japanese urban public protests, the Japanese armed forces committed mass killings of Chinese in the major cities they seized, especially in the capital city of Nanjing, where the reported scale of massacre has ranged from 150,000 to 300,000.[31] In stark contrast to Germany's public and frequent admissions of guilt over its involvement in World War II and in the Holocaust through commemorative forums, the erection of memorials and the payment of financial compensation, Japan acquired an image of being unrepentant, despite the issuing of occasional apologies and the grant of substantial economic and financial aid to victim countries after World War II.[32] The perception that there has been a lack of sincere repentance is pervasive across a large cross-section of the Chinese public, even though their government officially waived the claim of war reparations as part of the normalization of diplomatic relations in 1972. Furthermore, Deng Xiaoping, in a strategic move to forge a new era of East Asian relations, agreed to put the war firmly in the past and pushed bilateral Sino-Japanese relations forward, culminating in the Sino-Japanese Treaty of Peace and Friendship in 1978. Some Chinese citizens have regarded such goodwill gestures as misplaced and have considered them as mistakes by the PRC government. In April 2005, violent anti-Japanese protests occurred in several Chinese cities due to cumulative public dissatisfaction about ongoing territorial, energy and history textbooks disputes. Recalling deep wounds, a history expert at the Chinese Academy of Social Sciences offered the view that World War II had retarded China's modernization by as long as about fifty years, and direct and indirect economic losses during the war had amounted to as high as US$500 billion. A market research poll of unspecified sample size had then found that the percentage of Chinese that rated Sino-Japanese relations positively had fallen from 57.1 per cent in 1999 to just 15.8 per cent.[33]

This lack of a palatable general resolution to the issue of war responsibility had a spill over effect into many related areas. The Tokyo War Crime Trials (1946–48) were meant to close a chapter of World War II but they quickly became mired in its own controversy of inappropriate credentials, questionable legitimacy and dissenting views. The issue of a 1,235-page dissent judgment report by Justice Radhabinod Pal of India depicting the trials as merely victor's justice has often been seized upon as evidence of unfairness.[34] Official visits to the Yasukuni Shrine, honouring Japan's 2.5 million war dead inclusive of the souls of fourteen of the Class-A war criminals convicted by the Allied tribunal, have become diplomacy flashpoints, especially because Prime Minister Junichiro Koizumi has insisted on going to the shrine every year since taking office in April 2001, despite five ex-prime ministers of Japan counselling against such a move before his 2005 visit.[35] The revision of some Japanese school textbooks, especially in relation to passages depicting Japanese war actions, has stirred up yet another related storm of controversy, beginning from the early 1980s and picking up momentum from 2001. The initial domestic disagreements over textbooks between Japanese left and right wing activists dragged on for many years through laborious Japanese court proceedings and policy changes within the Ministry of Education. Originally an issue of domestic politics, the fight over textbooks has since escalated into an unpleasant international dispute containing cross accusations of avoidance of war responsibility and of interference in Japan's domestic affairs.[36] In May 2005, a last minute cancellation of Chinese Vice-Premier Wu Yi's visit to the office of Prime Minister Koizumi and the categorical denial of China's support for Japan's bid to secure a permanent seat on the United Nations Security Council constituted the latest calibrated Chinese responses to this series of seemingly intractable problems.[37]

Despite the stormy weather, both sides have apparently recognized the need to maintain sufficient diplomatic effort to keep Sino-Japanese relations afloat above troubled waters. This endangered relationship clearly has had something to do with how Japan, the world's second ranking economic power and a close ally of the United States, has struggled for a way to cope with the strategic emergence of China as a new economic superpower possibly by the middle of the twenty-first century. However, the real Gordian knot between the two antagonists continues to be the forgetting and the remembering of the war fought in China in the 1930s and 1940s. In this way, the turbulence in Sino-Japanese relations can possibly be considered as the most enduring legacy of World War II.

EXAMINING LEGACIES: PRESENT AND PAST

The year 2005, being the sixtieth year after World War II, provided the occasion for more than the usual number of commemorative events across the globe. It was also an opportunity for deeper reflections about the transient and enduring legacies of the war. The approach in this chapter has been to emphasize the impact that the war had on contemporary politics and foreign policy of China and other neighbouring states in the Pacific region. In leaning towards a more present-minded line of inquiry, historical details and discourse have been kept to a minimum and the analysis is centred on the contemporary setting.

On the contemporary stage, the present may well have the capacity to develop a life of its own and craft a new future. Nonetheless, in pursuing the angle of legacies, it is also obvious that the present would have much less meaning or significance unless it is contextualized and linked to its past. This is especially the case when there is a need to exercise judgment in deciding on which legacies are to be considered as transient and which are to be regarded as more enduring. It is only through a deliberate detachment from the present immediate happenings, a reflective measurement against the shifting sands of time, and a conscious effort to place things within the context of changes and continuities over the long duration, that the significance of the War fought in China can be better appreciated.

Historical sensitivity to the war fought sixty years ago contributes to a greater understanding of the development of an interventionist state in the Chinese economy even before the communist seizure of power, the contemporary political divide between PRC and Taiwan and their diverging policy towards Mongolia, the waxing and waning of diasporic relations between China and Chinese communities overseas, the cycles in Sino-American relations and the current tension between China and Japan.

NOTES

1. An example of the lack of consensus is the case of the contrasting views postulated in William Overholt, *China: The Next Economic Superpower* (London: Weidenfeld & Nicolson, 1993) and Gordon Chang, *The Coming Collapse of China* (New York: Random House, 2001).

2. This line of argument is laid out in a recent publication by Morris L. Bian, *The Making of the State Enterprise System in Modern China* (Cambridge, Mass.: Harvard University Press, 2005). The first major academic works trying to break through the 1949 barrier were those of Paul Cohen, "The Post-Mao Reforms in Historical Perspective", in *Journal of Asian Studies* 47, no. 3 (August 1988) and "Reflections on a Watershed Date: The 1949 Divide in Chinese History", in *Twentieth Century China: New Approaches: Rewriting Histories*, edited by Jeffrey N. Wasserstrom (London: Routledge, 2003). Currently, there is a research project at the Institute of Modern History at the Academia Sinica, Taiwan, probing into "China and Taiwan in the 1950s", and examining changes and continuities across the 1949 time divide.

3. For details on the devastating hyperinflation, see Chang Kia-ngau, *The Inflationary Spiral: The Experience in China, 1939–1950* (Cambridge, Mass.: Harvard University Press, 1958) and Arthur Young, *China's Wartime Finance and Inflation, 1937–1945* (Cambridge, Mass.: Harvard University Press, 1965).

4. For a useful discussion on "*Danwei* system" in PRC, see Lu Xiaobo and Elizabeth J. Perry, eds., *Danwei: The Changing Chinese Workplace in Historical and Comparative Perspectives* (Armonk, NY: M.E. Sharpe, 1997).

5. Akira Iriye, "Japanese Aggression and China's International Position, 1931–1949", in *The Cambridge History of China*, edited by John K. Fairbank and Albert Feuerwerker, vol. 13 on Republican China, 1912–49, part 2, pp. 492–519 discusses the pre-1937 Sino-Japanese international relations.

6. For student movements and KMT responses, see John Israel, *Student Nationalism in China 1927–1937* (Stanford: Stanford University Press, 1966); Huang Jianli, *The Politics of Depoliticization in Republican China: Guomindang Policy towards Student Political Activism, 1927–1949* (Berne: Peter Lang, 1996). On the Xian incident, see Wu Tien-wei, *The Sian Incident: A Pivotal Point in Modern Chinese History* (Ann Arbor: Center for Chinese Studies, University of Michigan, 1976).

7. On the importance of the united front strategy for the CCP, see Lyman Van Slyke, *Friends and Enemies: The United Front in Chinese Communist History*

(Stanford: Stanford University Press, 1967); Tetsuya Kataoka, *Resistance and Revolution in China: The Communists and the Second United Front* (Berkeley: University of California Press, 1974); Shum Kui-Kwong, *The Chinese Communist Road to Power: Anti-Japanese National United Front, 1935–1945* (London: Oxford University Press, 1988).

8. The issue of whether socio-economic reforms were more important than nationalism in the CCP's successful battle for the hearts and minds has been debated among Chalmer Johnson, *Peasant Nationalism and Communist Power: The Emergence of Revolutionary China, 1937–1945* (Stanford: Stanford University Press, 1962); Mark Selden, *The Yenan Way in Revolutionary China* (Cambridge, Mass.: Harvard University Press, 1971); Chen Yung-fa, *Making Revolution: The Communist Movement in Eastern and Central China, 1937–45* (Berkeley: University of California Press, 1986); Mark Selden, *China in Revolution: The Yenan Way Revisited* (Armonk, NY: M.E. Sharpe, 1995).

9. For a comprehensive English-language account of the civil war, see Suzanne Pepper, *Civil War in China: The Political Struggle, 1945–1949* (Berkeley: University of California Press, 1978); Odd Arne Westad, *The Chinese Civil War, 1946–1950* (Stanford: Stanford University Press, 2003).

10. Tien Hung-mao, *The Great Transition: Political and Social Change in the Republic of China* (Stanford: Stanford University Press, 1989); Denny Roy, *Taiwan: A Political History* (Ithaca: Cornell University Press, 2003). For a study of how Taiwanese independence sentiments affected the commemoration of the war in 1995, see Chang Jui-te, "The Politics of Commemoration: A Comparative Analysis of the Fifteeth Anniversary Commemoration in Mainland China and Taiwan of the Victory in the Anti-Japanese War", in *Scars of War: The Impact of Warfare on Modern China*, edited by Diana Lary and Stephen McKinnon (Vancouver: University of British Columbia Press, 2001).

11. Outer Mongolia had several declarations of independence and the one in October 1945 is what matters most in the context of this discussion. For a brief overall view of Kuomintang-Soviet Union relations during the war, see R.K.I. Quested, *Sino-Russian Relations: A Short History* (Sydney: George Allen & Unwin, 1984), ch. 9 and 10. For a detailed treatment of the immediate post-war period, see Brian Murray, "Stalin, The Cold War, and the Division of China: A Multi-Archival Mystery", Working Paper 12, Cold War International History Project, Woodrow Wilson International Center for Scholars, Washington D.C., June 1995.

12. Lin Fang-yan, "Taiwan, Mongolia Expand Relationship" in *UB Post*, 3 April 2003.

13. Yen Ching Hwang, *The Overseas Chinese and the 1911 Revolution: With Special Reference to Singapore and Malaya* (Kuala Lumpur: Oxford University Press, 1976); Yen Ching Hwang, *Coolies and Mandarin: China's Protection of*

Overseas Chinese during the Late Ch'ing Period, 1851–1911 (Singapore: Singapore University Press, 1985); Zheng Liren, "Overseas Chinese Nationalism in British Malaya, 1894–1941", Ann Arbor, University Microfilms International, 1997; and Huang Jianli, "Writings on Sun Yat-sen, Tongmenghui and the 1911 Revolution: Surveying the Field and Locating Southeast Asia", in *Tongmenghui, Sun Yat-sen and the Chinese in Southeast Asia: A Revisit*, edited by Leo Suryadinata (Singapore: Chinese Heritage Centre, 2006), pp. 61–107.

14. Png Poh Seng, "The Kuomintang in Malaya, 1912–1941", *Journal of Southeast Asian History* 2, no. 1 (March 1961); C.F. Yong and R.B. McKenna, *The Kuomintang Movement in British Malaya, 1912–1949* (Singapore: Singapore University Press, 1990).

15. Pang Wing Seng, "The 'Double-Seventh' Incident, 1937: Singapore Chinese Response to the Outbreak of the Sino-Japanese War", *Journal of Southeast Asian Studies* 4, no. 2 (September 1973); S.M.Y. Leong, "The Malayan Overseas Chinese and the Sino-Japanese War, 1937–1941", *Journal of Southeast Asian Studies* 10, no. 2 (September 1979); Zheng Ruiyan, *Huajiao yu kanri zhanzheng* [Overseas Chinese and Sino-Japanese War] (Chengdu: Sichuan University Press, 1988); Huang Xiaojian, Zhao Hongying and Cong Yuefeng, *Haiwai jiaobao yu kangri zhanzheng* [Chinese Overseas Compatriots and Sino-Japanese War] (Beijing: Beijing Publishing Company, 1995).

16. For further reading on the renewed emphasis on Chinese overseas patriotism and contribution, see the two Chinese-language publications cited in the previous footnote. On Aw's roller-coaster reputation, see Huang Jianli, "Entanglement of Business and Politics in the Chinese Diaspora: Interrogating the Wartime Patriotism of Aw Boon Haw", in *Journal of Chinese Overseas* 2, no. 1 (2006): 79–110.

17. Tu Wei-ming, ed., *The Living Tree: The Changing Meaning of Being Chinese Today* (Stanford: Stanford University Press, 1994); Ien Ang, *On Not Speaking Chinese: Living between Asia and the West* (London: Routledge, 2001); Wang Gungwu, *Don't Leave Home: Migration and the Chinese* (Singapore: Eastern University Press, 2003).

18. Edgar Snow, *Red Star over China* (Middlesex: Penguin Books Ltd, reprint 1972, first in 1937) and *Red China Today: The Other Side of the River* (Middlesex: Penguin Books Ltd., reprint 1970, first in 1962). For an overview of Snow's career, see S. Bernard Thomas, *Season of High Adventure: Edgar Snow in China* (Berkeley: University of California Press, 1996).

19. Graham Peck, *Through China's Wall* (London: Collins, 1941) and *Two Kinds of Time* (Boston: Mifflin Co., 1950); Agnes Smedley, *China Correspondent* (London: Pandora Press, reprint 1970, first in 1943) and *The Great Road: The Life and Times of Chu Teh* (New York: Monthly Review Press, 1956); Theodore H. White and Annalee Jacoby, *Thunder Out of China* (New York: William

Sloane Associates, 1946) and Theodore H. White *The Mountain Road* (London: Cassell, 1958); Jack Belden, *China Shakes the World* (New York: Monthly Review Press, reprint 1970, first in 1949).

20. For insights into the role played by journalistic reporting on Sino-American relations, see T. Christopher Jespersen, *American Images of China, 1931– 1949* (Stanford: Stanford University Press, 1996); Peter Rand, *China Hands: The Adventures and Ordeals of the American Journalists who Joined Forces with the Great Chinese Revolution* (New York: Simon & Schuster, 1995).

21. Carolle J. Carter, *Mission to Yenan: American Liaison with the Chinese Communists, 1944–1947* (Lexington: University Press of Kentucky, 1997).

22. *United States Relations with China: With Special Reference to the Period 1944–1949* (Washington, D.C.: The Department of States Publications, 1949); Shaw Chonghai, *The Role of the United States in Chinese Civil Conflicts, 1944–1949* (Salt Lake City, Utah: Charles Schlacks, Jr Publisher, 1991); Nancy Bernkopf Tucker, *China Confidential: American Diplomats and Sino-American Relations, 1945–1996* (New York: Columbia University Press, 2001).

23. John King Fairbank, *Chinabound: A Fifty Year Memoir* (New York: Harper & Row, 1982), especially part 5 on "The Fallout from World War II" covering "China Policy and Area Study" and "Fighting McCarthyism", pp. 315–51.

24. Nancy Bernkopf Tucker, *China Confidential: American Diplomats and Sino-American Relations, 1945–1996*; John W. Garver, *The Sino-American Alliance: Nationalist China and American Cold War Strategy in Asia* (Armonk, NY: M.E. Sharpe, 1997).

25. Henry Luce's pro-Chiang Kai-shek mentality and his romantic notions of an American century and Americanized China are analysed in T. Christopher Jespersen, *American Images of China, 1931–1949*, prologue, chapters 1, 2 and 5.

26. Ross Y. Koen, *The China Lobby in American Politics* (New York: Macmillan, 1960).

27. Michael Y.M. Kau, "Clinton's 'Three No's' Policy: A Critical Assessment", *The Brown Journal of World Affairs* 6, no. 2 (Summer/Fall 1999): 16–17; "Enough with Strategic Ambiguity" in *The Wall Street Journal*, 3 May 2001.

28. Qingxin Ken Wang, "Taiwan in Japan's Relations with China and the United States after the Cold War", in *Pacific Affairs* (Fall, 2000); Gregory May, "Taiwan's Role in the China-Japan-U.S. Trilateral Relationship", in *Major Power Relations in Northeast Asia: Win-Win or Zero-Sum Game*, edited by David Lampton (Tokyo: Japan Center for International Exchange, 2001); Greg Austin and Stuart Harris, *Japan and Greater China: Political Economy and Military Power in the Asian Century* (London: Hurst & Co., 2001).

29. Frank Ching, "Japan and U.S. up the Ante on Taiwan", in *Japan Times*, 7 March 2005.

30. For a brief discussion on conflicting war casualty data, see Lloyd Eastman, "Nationalist China during the Sino-Japanese War, 1937–1945", in *The Cambridge History of China*, edited by Fairbank and Feuerwerker, Vol. 13, Republican China, 1912–1949, Part 2 (Cambridge: Cambridge University Press, 1986), p. 147.

31. Reflecting the increased tempo of controversy, there has been a flood of recent literature on the Nanjing massacre. For a sampling of views, see Joshua A. Fogel, *The Nanjing Massacre in History and Historiography* (Berkeley: University of California Press, 2000); Iris Chang, *The Rape of Nanking: The Forgotten Holocaust of World War II* (New York: Basic Books, 1997); Honda Katsuichi, *The Nanjing Massacre: A Japanese Journalist Confronts Japan's National Shame* (London: Penguin Books, 1999); Tanaka Masaaki, *What Really Happened in Nanking: The Refutation of a Common Myth* (Tokyo: Sekai Shuppan, Inc., 2000); Gao Xingzu, *Rijun qinhua baoxing: Nanjing datusha* [Japanese War Atrocities: The Nanjing Massacre] (Shanghai: Shanghai renmin chubanshe, 1985); Zhang Kaiyuan, *Nanjing datusha de lishi de jianzheng* [An Eyewitness's Historical Records of the Nanjing Massacre] (Wuhan: Huazhong shifan daxue chubanshe, 1995).

32. "Why Japan Failed Where Germany succeeded", in *Straits Times Interactive*, 10 May 2005.

33. "China Marks Anniversary of Japan's WWII Invasion", in *Straits Times Interactive*, 7 July 2005.

34. Timothy Brook, "The Tokyo Judgement and the Rape of Nanking", in *Journal of Asian Studies* 60, no. 3 (August 2001): 673–700. Brook's concern here is not with discerning which version of events is correct but with demonstrating how those differing accounts fit into various narratives and how Justice Pal had contributed to the framing of international laws. See also Timothy Brook, ed., *Documents on the Rape of Nanking* (Ann Arbor: University of Michigan Press, 1999); Richard H. Minear, *Victor's Justice: The Tokyo War Crimes Trial* (Princeton: Princeton University Press, 1971); B.V.A. Roling, *The Tokyo Trial and Beyond* (Cambridge: Polity Press, 1993).

35. "Ex-Prime Ministers Hit Yasukuni Visits", *Japan Times*, 2 June 2005; "Much More to Yasukuni Shrine than War Criminals" and "Top Leaders Ask Koizumi to Reconsider Yasukuni Visits", *Straits Times Interactive*, 28 May and 2 June 2005. Despite such criticism, Koizumi's 2005 visit to the shrine still finally took place on 17 October.

36. "Japan History Texts Anger E Asia", *BBC News*, 5 April 2005; "Japanese Schoolbooks Anger S. Korea, China: Militaristic Past is Seen as Whitewashed", *Washington Post*, 6 April 2005; "Japan's Textbook Controversy: Read It and Weep", *Straits Times Interactive*, 13 May 2005; T. Fujitani, Geoffrey M. White and Lisa Yoneyama, eds. *Perilous Memories: The Asia-Pacific War(s)* (Durham, North Carolina: Duke University Press, 2001); Y. Nozaki, *War*

Memory, Nationalism and History in Japan: Ienaga Saburo and the History Textbook Controversy, 1945–2005 (London: Routledge, 2006). Although the new textbooks had been approved, only 48 of Japan's 11,035 (0.4 per cent) public and private schools for students aged 13 to 15 had adopted the controversial textbook for the school year starting in April 2005. See "Most Schools Shun Japan's Controversial History Text", *Straits Times Interactive*, 1 September 2005.

37. "Wu Yi the Woman who Stumped Japan", *Asahi Shimbun*, 28 May 2005.

Chapter Eleven

How to Assess World War II in World History: One Japanese Perspective

Takashi Inoguchi

THE SIGNIFICANCE OF WORLD WAR II IN MODERN HISTORY

This chapter assesses the impact of World War II through the following lenses: (1) World War II as a fight between democracy and Fascism; (2) winning World War II meant independence from colonial powers for many countries; and (3) World War II as another fight by democracy against tyranny. The chapter assesses the legacies of World War II especially as they relate to East and Southeast Asia. Lastly, it attempts to make a combined assessment from all these three lenses.

THREE FACES OF WORLD WAR II

Democracy against Fascism

That the United States played a leading role in defeating Fascist allies in World War II is the standard narrative about the significance of World War II (Butow 1954, 1961; Gaddis 1987; Leffler 1992; Ikenberry 2000).

According to this version, World War II was the war of democracy against Fascism embodied by Germany and Japan. All the Allied Powers fought against them, and the Soviet Union ruled by the Communist Party contributed no less immensely to the defeat of Fascism. Hence democracy was taken in a broad sense of the word. In other words, any kind of anti-Fascism was democracy, including anti-Fascism by people's democracy, which was actually totalitarian rule. That was the broad understanding on the basis of which the United States, the Soviet Union, Great Britain, France and China were convened at Yalta in 1945 (Yergin, 1978). They were all also victors in World War II. France and China were not as strong as they wished in fighting this war in the first place. Yet to bring the semblance of unity and solidarity of all Allied Powers to the fore, the United States wanted to include all these five as parties to the Yalta accord. All five became the permanent members of the Security Council of the United Nations, which was founded in 1945. The United Nations Charter requires its members to uphold the spirit of democracy against Fascism. All newly independent countries were naturally mostly welcomed to enter the United Nations, because part of the struggle of democracy against Fascism was the struggle of an emerging Third World to gain independence after World War II.

Yet the competition between the United States and the Soviet Union about who should be credited for defeating Fascism most effectively continued to take place even before the war ended. At Yalta, Franklin D. Roosevelt was able to keep the anti-Fascist coalition united. But beneath the amicable conversation was a discord that led to the Cold War after 1945. Immediately after President Roosevelt's death, President Harry Truman, along with Secretary of State James Burns, was most conscious of this competition (Alperovitch 1995; Torii 2005). Truman's idea was to take dramatic and decisive action *vis-à-vis* Japan before the Soviet armed forces, pulled from the European front and assigned to the Far Eastern front, could defeat Japan. Truman wanted to drop newly developed atomic bombs on Japan before the Soviet Union violated the Non-Aggression Treaty with Japan and occupied Manchuria, Sakhalin, the Kuriles and northern Korea. Truman had barely finished dropping bombs on Hiroshima on 6 August 1945, when two days later Stalin ordered the Soviet Army to occupy the Japanese imperial territories in the Far East. At stake in Truman's mind was hegemonic leadership of the post-World War II world. He thought this leader should not be the Soviet Union, and he was worried; the Soviet Union looked most effective in getting Germany defeated in Europe. Further, at Yalta, Stalin expressed his intention to bring his army from the Western front (because the anti-German war was over in June 1945) to the Far Eastern front to defeat Japan. Truman consequently gave an ambiguous message to Japan as to the terms of surrender so that Japan would procrastinate over the terms of surrender and not surrender too fast. It was strange to discuss the terms of surrender when the Allied Powers led by the United States government issued the message calling for an unconditional surrender. But the Japanese government was in no mood to allow Emperor Hirohito to be executed. The United States government decided therefore to keep Emperor Hirohito alive and to let the Japanese bureaucracy run the country under the auspicies of the Supreme Commander of Allied Powers (Torii 1985–2003; Iokibe 1985). While negotiations on these terms were going on, atomic bombs were dropped on 6 and 9 August. The Soviet Army was not ready to invade the Japanese imperial territory before 8 August. What was critical in getting Japanese leaders to make their surrender decision was not atomic bombs but the Soviet invasion of Manchuria and threat to bring troops into China (Hasegawa 2005). Their calculations went as follows: First, the Soviet Army had devastated the Japanese Guandong army in Manchuria. Second, if the Soviet Union had brought troops further south into China, that would have facilitated the Chinese Communists' accession to power since the Japanese Imperial Army's troops stationed in China had already given a devastating blow to the Chinese Army under Chiang Kai-shek in 1944, after the complete defeat of the Japanese Imperial Navy had become obvious by mid-1944. Japan's aim was to prepare what it envisaged as a decisive war against the United States over the Japanese archipelagoes by recalling the Japanese Army in China without worrying about being driven out by Chinese troops, whether Kuomintang or Communist.

Therefore, pursuing hegemonic ambitions, the United States demonstrated its unprecedented power to the world through its nuclear bombs. This lens of history still wields strong influence today. One possible manifestation of this lens is the United States government rejection of the Group of Four's (Japan, Germany, India and Brazil) push for permanent membership in the United Nations Security Council. Japan and Germany are two countries whose sins have not been fully accommodated by the West (Maier 1988).

Anti-Colonialism against Colonialism

The second significance of World War II is the victory of anti-colonialism. The United States and the Soviet Union had already heralded the era of anti-imperialism in the wake of World War I (Iriye 1968). The spirit was not lost in the wake of World War II. The United States persuaded old European powers to decolonize their imperial territories after the war. Germany and Italy were forced to do so because of their defeat. Great Britain and France did so somewhat begrudgingly. Japan's defeat effectively liberated its colonies. The United States proceeded to decolonize its colonies in the Caribbean and the Pacific. The struggle of anti-colonialism started to produce the massive concrete results of independence after World War II. The architect of the United Nations Headquarters on the Hudson River bank in New York in 1945 thought that the maximum number of members of the United Nations would be fifty. His prediction and thus space design of the headquarters failed utterly. By the end of the 1950s the number of members easily exceeded fifty. By the end of the 1960s it exceeded 100. By 2005 it had become 191. History registers this disappearance of colonialism in the mid-twentieth century like the disappearance of slavery institutions in the mid-nineteenth century.

Without fully reflecting on the disappearance of colonialism and its post-colonial development after World War II, any discussion on the impact of World War II on contemporary society would be amiss. Freedom and equality of peoples, nations and states were achieved, at least in international law and the United Nations Charter. In Asia, for instance, the dream of Rabindranath Tagore, Jose Rizal, Sun Yat-sen and Okakura Tenshin was at long last achieved. The struggle by Mahatma Gandhi, Mao Zedong, Ho Chi Minh, Sukarno, Aung San won its final victory. The United Nations Charter registers the equality of nations in the form of one member, one vote in the General Assembly. Members' efforts at empowering themselves took various forms of getting together and voicing dissents on issues that were unfavourable to the Third World or former colonial countries.

The question yet to be fully answered is: who ignited the dismemberment of colonialism? It is important to recall that while Germany attacked old Europe itself at home, Japan attacked old Europe in its colonies or semi-colonies as well as the United States. Japan attacked Hawaii and Southeast Asia almost simultaneously. Christopher Thorne (1985) attributed the dismemberment of colonialism especially in the Far

East to the Japanese attack of old Europe through its colonies or semi-colonies although Japan did not intend the genuine liberation of the colonies including those of its own.

Democracy against Tyranny

The third way to assess World War II is to frame it in terms of a fight against tyranny. It began with the legacy of the "new diplomacy" of Woodrow Wilson and Vladimir Lenin in the wake of World War I, and the legacy of the Yalta compromise between Franklin Roosevelt and Joseph Stalin. In other words, when Wilson and Lenin were decrying old European power politics, they were hiding their profound differences. In a similar vein, when Roosevelt and Stalin reached the accord at Yalta, they were hiding their fundamental divergences. All four actors did so for the sake of fighting tyranny. Their discord erupted soon after, when Harry Truman became U.S. president. He tried to demonstrate the United State's post-war hegemonic leadership role in the form of dropping atomic bombs in 1945 when the Soviet entry into the anti-Japanese war was imminent. By pre-empting the Soviet Union's likely-to-be-decisive victory against the Japanese Imperial Army in Manchuria and possibly further into China, Truman achieved his dream of giving devastating blows to the Japanese government, which had been procrastinating about when to surrender "unconditionally". The Japanese government negotiated for preservation of the "national polity" and a constitutional monarch.

The legacy of the "new diplomacy" is inherited by ideological reformulations of a new line of thinking about the world in the wake of 9/11. These were attempted in several ways. Simplistic yet powerful is the formulation by George W. Bush in his speech in Riga, Latvia (Bush 2005), commemorating the sixtieth anniversary of the victory of the anti-Nazi war:

> Sixty years ago, on the 7th of May, the world reacted with joy and relief at the defeat of fascism in Europe. The next day, General Dwight D. Eisenhower announced that "history's mightiest machine of conquest has been utterly destroyed." Yet the great democracies soon found that a new mission had come to us — not merely to defeat a single dictator, but to defeat the idea of dictatorship on this continent. Through the decades of that struggle, some endured the rule of tyrants; all lived in the frightening shadow of war. Yet because we lifted our sights and held firm to our principles, freedom prevailed.

Now, ladies and gentlemen, the freedom of Europe, won by courage, must be secured by effort and goodwill. In our time, as well, we must raise our sights. In the distance we can see another great goal — not merely the absence of tyranny on this continent, but the end of tyranny in our world. Once again, we're asked to hold firm to our principles, and to value the liberty of others. And once again, if we do our part, freedom will prevail.

It is a picture of democracy against all sorts of tyranny. Attracted immensely by the simplicity and clarity of the democracy message that strikes a chord with his "fundamentalist" Christian faith, George W. Bush is advancing his strategy of democracy promotion on all fronts: in failed states such as Afghanistan, Iraq, North Korea and Sudan, in former and currently communist states such as Ukraine, Kyrgistan, Georgia, Russia and China, and in resiliently authoritarian states like Myanmar and Iran. The thrust of the Bush speech at Riga was simple and forceful; it addressed what Bush regarded as the key common denominator — tyranny — shared by Osama bin Laden, Saddam Hussain, Kim Jong Il, and the rest. Early in April 2005 Secretary of State Condoleezza Rice delivered a speech in Tokyo, calling for an Asian league of democracies (Rice 2005).

> Because one day, an American President and a Japanese Prime Minister will sit across from democratic allies in Iraq and Afghanistan and Palestine. And they, too, will chart a better future for our children and for the children of the world. They will do so on the basis of democratic values and they will do so because there is no stronger friendship than that that is born of a common commitment to democratic values, to liberty and to freedom.

The Rice speech is consistent with the Bush speech that came after. The immediate post-Cold War euphoria over the end of ideology (Francis Fukuyama 1992) was substantially toned down. Rather, a post-Cold War and post-9/11 ideology has placed the United States at the centre of the world in an intermittent struggle against the deniers of freedom and democracy. This ideology was no doubt influenced by Natan Sharansky, who portrayed the vision of a future always beset with struggles against tyranny, which is bound to triumph unless freedom and democracy intermittently fight their way forward (Natan Sharansky 2004). The events of 9/11 gave George W. Bush a well-defined enemy against which he would direct his nation and all the peoples in the world to fight against. In his first term of 2001–04, he concentrated on the anti-terrorist war. In the second term, he continued his anti-terrorist war, and found himself facing two other fronts as well: (1) the rise of China (Kokubun and Wang 2004; Lardy 2003) and (2) ever-rising anti-Americanism (*The Economist* 2005; Goldsmith, Horiuchi and Inoguchi 2005). These led him all the more to sweeping slogans and messianic messages.

EAST AND SOUTHEAST ASIA SEEN FROM THREE LENSES

We have examined the picture of the legacies and impacts of World War II, as seen from three global angles. This section takes a closer look at East and Southeast Asia through the three lenses or perspectives just sketched above. The question here is: who are our enemies? Who are our friends? The answers differ when the lenses change.

Democracy against Fascism

What is democracy? What is Fascism? In 1945 when the Yalta conference was held, China was governed, albeit tenuously, by Chiang Kai-shek. Through this lens, the U.S. government preferred to work with the Kuomintang over the Communist Party. Chiang Kai-shek represented democracy in their eyes, and Kuomintang China was the beacon of democracy in the East when in American eyes, Japan was clearly Fascist. That was why the United States assisted Chiang despite great difficulties. That was why it dropped the bombs on Hiroshima and Nagasaki before the Soviet Union could march into Manchuria (Hasegawa 2005). An alternative to Kuomintang China was Communist China, an alternative attractive to some but clearly not acceptable to the mainstream in the U.S. government at that time. Yet China under the Kuomintang was arguably a *quasi*-Fascist, quasi-Leninist regime (Eastman 1991). The Communist Party portrayed the Kuomintang regime in a similar fashion.

On the other hand, Japan was clearly Fascist in 1945 in the eyes of the United States. Japan had to be dealt a fatal blow. It had to be literally flattened by incessant bombings on cities and military facilities. It had to transform itself into a Switzerland of the Far East, by which General Douglas MacArthur meant Japan becoming a geographically small, politically quiet and militarily insignificant entity. But Japan transformed itself into a democracy, thanks to the American intervention. Japan has nothing to be ashamed of this, as Lawrence Whitehead tells us that only three countries before it had developed democracy endogenously — Great Britain, Switzerland and Sweden (Whitehead 2002). Japan has registered a record of mature democracy for sixty years, thanks again to the American largesse as well as to the Japanese strategy called the Yoshida Doctrine, which instructed Japan to keep a low profile diplomatically, rely on the United States for security, while working hard to excel economically. The combination of the Peace Constitution (forbidding Japan from using force for the settlement of international disputes) and the Japan-United States Security Treaty (enabling the United States to use facilities and services in Japan almost as freely as it wishes) helped to engender this transformation (Dower 1999; Swenson-Wright 2005).

Anti-Colonialism against Colonialism

Most colonies in East and Southeast Asia, among them Japanese and German ones, had decolonized by the end of the 1950s. The United States played a positive role in persuading or forcing otherwise reluctant European colonial powers to give up their colonies. By 1955 the spirit of anti-colonialism was greatly hailed, as the Afro-Asian conference at Bandung had demonstrated. Sukarno, Jawaharlal Nehru, Zhou Enlai and their contemporaries demonstrated outstandingly that colonialism represented the past whereas anti-colonialism was the future.

Yet as time passed, what came to be called neo-colonialism was on the rise as the United States competed with the Soviet Union, each trying to help their "client" regimes consolidate themselves in East and Southeast Asia as well (Gurtov 1974). South Korea and South Vietnam were cases in point (Cumings 1981 and 1989; Kahin 1986). As a reaction to the Cold War, the Non-Aligned Movement asserted itself *vis-à-vis* the United States and the Soviet Union for many decades. At present, anti-colonialism is not vehemently expressed in East and Southeast Asia. Rather, countries in the region have been riding high on a developmental momentum that caught on to globalization's virtuous cycle. In view, however, of the allegedly neo-colonialist role that the United States played on the Korean Peninsula and in Vietnam, the United States has been accepted only in a lukewarm fashion in the region (Inoguchi, et al. 2006, *The Economist* 2005).

Democracy against Tyranny

The third wave of democratization (Huntington 1993) and the terrorism of 9/11 set the stage for democracy against tyranny in East and Southeast Asia as well. Virtually every country rode on the bandwagon of anti-terrorism in the wake of the 9/11 terrorism. This bandwagoning behaviour is due to the way in which terrorism can be defined to serve the regimes' purposes. Among these bandwagoning countries are authoritarian or authoritarian-leaning regimes, enthusiastic in using anti-terrorism as an excellent cover for suppressing what they defined as terrorist groups. Outwardly, these regimes also wanted to be on friendly terms with the United States in a unipolar world. Shortly after 9/11, however, the course of anti-terrorism started to go hand-in-hand with anti-tyranny ideas, concomitant with the rejection and eradication of weapons of mass destruction. The ideological shift of the U.S. government towards issuing a *quasi*-messianic call for freedom and democracy, backed up with super-high-tech weapons in dealing with rogue states, has added momentum to the promotion of democracy in the Third World.

The question is: in East and Southeast Asia, where is the tyranny? In Tokyo in April 2005, when United States Secretary of State Condoleezza Rice called for a league of democracies in East and Southeast Asia, she had this question in mind. The Human Rights Report by the United States State Department, Human Rights Report by Amnesty International and Freedom House's Freedom in the World Report all point to a similar set of countries that suffer from a shortage of freedom and democracy. Condoleezza Rice's conspicuous absence at the annual Association of South East Nations meeting in mid-2005 demonstrates the clear discomfort the United States feels with the ASEAN policy of allowing what it regards as a tyrannical country to preside the meeting. Subsequently, Myanmar gave up its chairmanship of ASEAN. It is not at all clear whether recent events that took place in Georgia, Ukraine, and Kyrgistan have anything to do with democratic promotion from outside. But those leaders of regimes of a tyrannical bent must be at least mildly apprehensive of the possibility of their regimes being subverted from within with help from afar, in the cause of freedom and democracy.

CONCLUSION

Using the three lenses to look at World War II, its impact on Japanese foreign policy and domestic politics is not difficult to identify. It is not an exaggeration to say that the first lens of democracy fighting against Fascism remoulded Japanese foreign policy and domestic politics since 1945. Japan itself was democratized and disarmed. It has become the longest-standing democracy outside the West, along with India. Japan has not waged any war with any country since 1945. Furthermore, thanks in part to the arrangements of the Peace Constitution and the Japan-United States Security Treaty, Japan has become a very wealthy country.

Yet, while a substantial number of Japanese find it agreeable to view World War II as a struggle by democracy against Fascism, beneath this agreement lurks, no matter how weakly, the view that what World War II boiled down to was a fight among imperialist powers. While one may argue that Japan was one of these powers, ultimately a vanquished Japan disarmed, democratized and became allied with the United States. The Japan-United States Security Treaty has been performing most effectively in East and Southeast Asia its role as the regional linchpin of stability and prosperity (Inoguchi and Bacon 2006).

Through the second lens of anti-colonialism, we have seen decolonization materialize since 1945. Most Japanese agree with the view that World War II effectively prepared the death of colonialism, the freedom of nations and liberation of Asia. Yet a footnote that is usually inserted is Japanese pride in daring to Westernize itself thus avoiding falling prey to Western colonialism and imperialism. A further footnote that is also usually added, says that it was the Japanese who dared to destroy the Achilles heel of Western colonialism and imperialism — their colonies and semi-colonies. The first footnote is probably easy to accept. It is the beautiful story of a non-Western country in East Asia learning ideas, institutions and industrialization from the West and even outperforming the original masters. The second footnote, however, is more troublesome. The reasons are as follows.

First, Japan was itself imperialist and colonialist, causing havoc and calamities in East and Southeast Asia. Second, equating Japan and the Allied Powers is problematic. This equation contradicts the first lens that all the Allied Powers and thus all the United Nations' member countries adhere to till today. Maintaining that Japan was brave and should be lauded is a silly view. Inserting this footnote bespeaks the ambivalence of the Japanese identity. In the minds of the majority of Japanese, their modern history is a success story of Westernization, beginning from the coerced opening of the country by Commodore Perry of the United States Navy in 1853 through to the Meiji Restoration in 1868. Since then, the Japanese worked industriously and ingenuously at the task of civilization and enlightenment to achieve "rich country and strong army" status. Although the digression and derailment from the course took place in the 1930s and 1940s, Japan has gotten back on track, and has succeeded as a nation. In the minds of the Japanese therefore, there is a historical continuity well kept and alive dating from the mid-nineteenth century until the twenty-first century (Inoguchi 2005). Thus, Japanese modern identity is formed through their focused memory of their assiduous Westernization without losing their Japanese-ness. This line of identity construction has historical continuity justifying what Japan had done wrong during the war — that of aggression and seeking its own colonies. It thus cannot sit well with how World War II is interpreted outside Japan.

The third lens seems at a glance to go down well with the Japanese. After all, the democratic and peaceful credentials of Japan abound — no authoritarian rule for six decades since 1945; none killed in war combat since 1945. The Japanese worry is, rather, that the fight against tyranny in the twenty-first century could ignite clashes surrounding Japan, dragging it into these conflicts and posing to it difficult choices in view of its steadfast alliance with the United States. In a permissive environment of unipolarity, the United States' promotion of democracy in China, North Korea and Myanmar has seen it take a vindicationist rather than an exemplarist strategy, following the characterization of Jonathan Monten (2005). This strategy is militarily aggressive; it is also politically inadequately contextualized and therefore imprudently unilateralist. This strategy aimed to alter the politics and economics of many target countries all at once by overwhelming military strikes. More alarming was the fact that since late 2005, U.S.-Japan political and defence cooperation has linked Japan far more tightly to the United States than before. In situations of dilemma, such as military confrontation over the Taiwan Straits or the Korean Peninsula, Japan might well procrastinate. No more wars in Asia must be one of the principles that Japan should strive for. It should not want to further aggravate the relationship with China or North Korea. Yet its alliance with the United States must be kept steadfast. Until it has to choose sides in the future, Japan is pursuing democracy as the way for the future in Asia, under which Asians should live with each other peacefully and prosperously. The Japanese preference for "shared values" rather than "diversity of values" in such places as the Network of East Asian Think Tanks unmistakably points to this goal.

When asked about the impact of the French Revolution, Zhou Enlai answered that it was too early to assess its impact (Schama 1997). This could well be true for the impact of World War II on Japan and East Asia. All in all, the significance of World War II is great and complex to Japan. Its current foreign policy and domestic politics cannot be discussed without even a most cursory reference to World War II. The three lenses that have been influential to varying degrees in time and space often pose difficulties to the Japanese government and people. Life would be much easier for the Japanese if one, or two, or all three lenses fit nicely with their construction of their memory, history and identity. When 15 August approaches every year, emotions and private histories about the wartime period, thoughts about the state and war burst forth among Japanese in newspapers, magazines, televisions and radios, and more recently, on blogs. Within this outpouring, one can see the struggle among the three lenses laid bare in the relentlessly hot mid-summer sunlight, as they did on 15 August 1945. And no less relentlessly does summer stomp in every year.

REFERENCES

Alperovitch, Gar. *The Decision on to Use the Atomic Bombs*. New York: Vintage Books, 1995.

Armstrong, Charles, et al. eds. *Korea at the Center: Dynamics of Regionalism in Northeast Asia*. New York: M.E. Sharpe Inc, 2005.

Bush, George W. "President Discusses Freedom and Democracy in Latvia". A speech made at the Small Guild Hall, Riga, Latvia, 7 May 2005, <http://www.whitehouse.gov/news/releases/2005/05/print/20050507-8.html>.

Butow, Robert. *Japan's Decision to Surrender*. Stanford: Stanford University Press, 1954.

———. *Tojo and the Coming of the War*. Stanford: Stanford University Press, 1961.

Cumings, Bruce. *Origins of the Korean War*, 2 vols. Princeton: Princeton University Press, 1981 and 1989.

Dower, John. *Embracing Defeat: Japan in the Wake of World War II*. New York: W.W. Norton, 1999.

Eastman, Lloyd E., Jerone Ch'en, Suzanne Pepper, and Lyman P. Van Slyke. *The Nationalist Era in China, 1927–1949*. New York: Cambridge University Press, 1991.

The Economist. "Still not Loved. Now not Envied", 25 June 2005.

Fukuyama, Francis. *The End of History and the Last Man*. New York: Free Press, 1992.

Gaddis, John. *The Long Peace*. New York: Oxford University Press, 1987.

Goldsmith, Benjamin, Yusaku Horiuchi and Takashi Inoguchi. "American Foreign Policy and Global Opinion: Who Supported the War in Afghanistan?" *Journal of Conflict Resolution* 49, no. 3 (2005): 408–29.

Gurtov, Melvin. *The United States against the Third World: Antinationalism and Intervention*. New York: Praeger, 1974.

Hasegawa, Tsuyoshi. *Racing the Enemy: Stalin, Truman, and the Surrender of Japan*. Cambridge: Belknap Press, 2005.

Huntington, Samuel. *The Third Wave*. Norman, Oklahoma: University of Oklahoma Press, 1993.

Ikenberry, G. John. *After Victory*. Princeton: Princeton University Press, 2000.

Inoguchi, Takashi. "The Evolving Dynamics of Japan's National Identity". In *Global Governance: Germany and Japan in the International System*, edited by Saori Katada, Hanns Maull, Takashi Inoguchi. London: Ashgate, 2005.

————. *Human Beliefs and Values in Stiriding Asia-East Asia in Focus: Country Profiles, Thematic Analyses and Sourcebook Based on the AsiaBarometer Survey of 2004*. Tokyo: Akashi Shoten, 2006.

Inoguchi, Takashi and Paul Bacon. "Japan's Emerging Role as a 'Global Ordinary Power' ". *International Relations of the Asia-Pacific* 6, no. 1 (2006).

Iokibe, Makoto. *Beikoku no Nihon senryo seisaku* [United States Occupation Policy in Japan]. Tokyo: Chuo koronsha, 1985.

Iriye, Akira. *After Imperialism*. Cambridge, Massachusetts: Harvard University Press, 1968.

Kahin, George. *Interview: How America Became Involved in Vietnam*. NY: Knopf, 1986.

Kokubun, Ryosei and Wang Jisi. *The Rise of China and a Changing East Asian Order*. Tokyo: Japan Center for International Exchange, 2004.

Lardy, Nicholas. "The Economic Rise of China: Threat or Opportunity?" Cleveland: Federal Reserve Bank of Cleveland Research Department, 2003, <www.clevelandfed.org/Research/Com 2003/0801pdf>.

Leffler, Melvin. *A Preponderance of Power: National Security, the Truman Administration, and the Cold War*. Stanford: Stanford University Press, 1992.

Maier, Charles S. *The Unmasterable Past: History, Holocaust, and German National Identity*. Cambridge: Harvard University Press, 1988.

Monten, Jonathan. "The Roots of the Bush Doctrine: Power, Nationalism, and Democracy Promotion in U.S. Strategy". *International Security* 29, no. 4 (Spring 2005): 112–56.

Rice, Condoleezza. Remarks by Secretary of State Condoleeza Rice at Sophia University, 19 March 2005, <http://japan.usembassy.gov/e/p/tp-20050321-04.html>.

Schama, Simon. *Citizens: A Chronicle of the French Revolution*. NY: Vintage Books, 1997.

Sharansky, Natan. *The Case For Democracy: The Power of Freedom to Overcome Tyranny and Terror*. New York: PublicAffairs, 2004.

Swenson-Wright, John. *Unequal Allies? United States Secretary and Alliance Policy toward Japan, 1945–1960*. Stanford: Stanford University Press, 2005.

Thorne, Christopher. *The Issue of War: States, Societies and the Far Eastern Conflict of 1941–1945*. London: Hamish and Hamilton, 1985.

Torii, Tami. *Genbaku o toka surumade Nihon o kofukusaseruna* [Never Let Japan Surrender Until Atomic Bombs Be Dropped]. Tokyo: Soshisha, 2005.

———. *Showa 20 nen* (Year 1945), 11 vols. Tokyo: Soshisha, 1985–2003.
Whitehead, Laurence. *Democratization: Theory and Experience.* Oxford: Oxford University Press, 2002.
Yergin, Daniel. *Shattered Peace: The Origins of the Cold War and the National Security State.* Boston: Houghton Mifflin, 1978.

Chapter Twelve

Obstacles to European Style Historical Reconciliation between Japan and South Korea — A Practitioner's Perspective¹

Andrew Horvat

INTRODUCTION

On 19 November 2006, the Asian Women's Fund (AWF) convened a symposium in Tokyo to mark its own demise. Established in 1995 on the initiative of the Japanese government to compensate women who had been recruited to provide sexual services for Japanese soldiers during World War II, the AWF's mandate ended on 31 March 2007. Dogged by controversy from its inception, the organization was able to provide compensation to 285 former *ianfu* (comfort women) in eleven years. Right wing politicians and critics in Japan, who had long insisted that all comfort women had been "voluntary paid prostitutes", denounced the AWF for attempting to address a non-existent issue.² As for the Asian feminist and nationalist women's organizations who had embraced the *ianfu* as symbols of their various causes, virtually all had pressured the elderly women they supported not to accept funds from the AWF. To the *ianfu* support groups, the AWF was an attempt on the part of Japanese government to avoid taking full legal responsibility for state-sanctioned sexual enslavement of hundreds of thousands of Asian women.

Throughout its short existence, the AWF represented in a microcosm the failure of Northeast Asian nations to forge a shared perception of a negative past in spite of the passage of more than half a century since the end of World War II. Perhaps it was fitting that the farewell symposium should end with a heated exchange between a representative of a Japanese women's NGO and a Korean[3] academic, one of very few to have come to the AWF's aid. Just as the moderator was about to declare the final session of the symposium closed, Nishino Rumiko,[4] representative of the Japanese NGO VAWW-Net (Violence Against Women in War Network) stated: "This summing up session has been carried out without regard for the victims. The victims don't want money. Their sufferings cannot be settled with financial compensation."

Park Yu-ha, professor of Japanese literature at Sejong University in Seoul, author of books and articles advocating reconciliation between Japan and Korea responded: "As I agree with you that it is the victims who are the central characters in this process, perhaps it would be best if we allowed them to speak for themselves." Park's comment referred to the pressure that *ianfu* support groups had put on the former comfort women to refuse money offered by the AWF. In a rare example of transnational cooperation between NGOs, VAWW-Net worked closely with Korean nationalist organizations to oppose the work of the AWF. A Korean *ianfu* support group had publicly denounced seven Korean former *ianfu* for having accepted money from the AWF.[5]

The AWF, its demise, and the heated exchange which punctuated it, are all testimony to the obstacles faced by Japan and Korea while seeking to deal with the legacy of war and colonial subjugation. Although the AWF's farewell symposium was by no means the most dramatic example of Northeast Asians exchanging harsh words over an unresolved past in recent years, the incident is nonetheless significant because it offers an opportunity to assess the role of non-state actors in transnational history-related dialogue. Thanks to pioneering research by political scientist Lily Gardner Feldman, we now know that the day-to-day work of post World War II reconciliation in Europe was accomplished not by such visionary political leaders as Jean Monnet, Robert Schuman, Konrad Adenauer and Willy Brandt, whose names we associate with the process of European integration, but rather by a multitude of organizations and individuals behaving as "transnational non-state actors" (TNAs).[6]

For the most part, the TNAs Gardner Feldman categorizes correspond more or less with present-day definitions of civil society organizations.[7]

Gardner Feldman's conclusions about how TNAs worked with or against their governments in the context of post-war European reconciliation, described below, lead us to ask about the likelihood of a similar process taking place in Northeast Asia. The reason is six decades after the end of World War II, unresolved issues stemming from invasion and colonial rule continue to act as barriers to regional integration and, according to some, contribute to the risk of future conflict.[8] Moreover, if, as Gardner Feldman's research indicates, TNAs do play a key role in post-conflict reconciliation and that civil society organizations do make up a significant portion of a country's TNA resources, then is it fair to conclude that countries with vibrant and active civil societies will stand a better chance of reaching out to their neighbours and engaging in the kind of grass-roots activities that will lead to overcoming a negative past? In other words, does the post World War II European experience offer lessons for Northeast Asia, specifically for Japan and Korea, the two countries in the region which can be described as having active civil society sectors? Or are there other factors such as the geopolitics of the Cold War, legal and financial constraints on the growth of NGOs, or the particular historical and social conditions of each country, which mitigate against a European-style solution to the region's history problem?

CIVIL SOCIETY IN KOREA AND JAPAN

On the positive side, we can see that in both countries, the civil society sector has flourished since the early 1990s albeit for different domestic reasons. In Korea, thanks to the transition from a succession of authoritarian military-backed regimes to popularly elected ones, NGOs have come to play active roles not only in domestic politics but also in foreign relations including the implementation of policies aimed at the reunification of the peninsula. In the case of Japan, the devastating Kobe earthquake of 1995 and the long period of economic stagnation triggered by the bursting of the stock and real estate bubble in the early 1990s showed that a highly centralized bureaucratic state (though well suited for promoting economic development and expansion) is ill equipped to respond quickly to the needs of citizens after a natural disaster or to take care of the weakest members of society during an economic crisis. The above trends necessitated a reappraisal of government–civil society relations in Japan, which culminated in the introduction in 1998 of a new law permitting relatively easy incorporation of non-profit organizations.

Nevertheless, questions remain whether the new Japanese NPO law marks a genuine departure from strict oversight of civil society by the state enshrined in the 1898 Civil Code. Moreover, in spite of the rapid growth of CSOs in both Korea and Japan, the 1990s also saw the rise of nationalism in both countries and with it, the widening of the gap in approaches to a shared, difficult past. This gap was showing signs of deepening not only between Japanese and Koreans but also domestically within the two societies. For example, under President Roh Moo Hyun, a law was enacted to punish Koreans who had collaborated with the peninsula's Japanese colonial administrators, even though any traitors who might be found alive would be 90 or more years old.

In Japan as well, while millions of viewers have been glued to TV sets watching Korean soap operas since their introduction in 2003, just two years earlier rightwing political activists succeeded in gaining official approval for a history textbook to be used in Japanese junior high schools. The textbook, asserting a national narrative aimed at countering what its authors saw as a far too apologetic attitude toward the teaching of the past, so offended Koreans that the Korean organizers of the Japan-ROK project to jointly host the 2002 FIFA World Cup soccer matches threatened to pull out of the games less than a year before they were scheduled to take place. Only the rejection of the textbook by more than 99 per cent of Japan's local educational committees reassured the Koreans of the Japanese public's good intentions and permitted resumption of preparations for the games.

The success of the World Cup games in which Japanese fans, once their own national team had been eliminated, rooted for the Korean team, offers an alternative vision to the failure of the AWF to address the *ianfu* issue. State actors do have a track record of promoting reconciliation in Northeast Asia. One example is that between Japan and the United States after World War II.[9] Although more modest than the post-war European movement for historical rapprochement, Northeast Asia has seen its share of state-inspired international exchanges in such fields as sports, popular culture and education. But while one cannot underestimate the superior resources available to the state in convening symposiums, supporting academic exchange, and funding major sports and cultural events, at least in the European case, non-state actors have demonstrated an ability to act more effectively than state organizations.[10]

TRANSNATIONAL NON-STATE ACTORS —
THE EUROPEAN EXPERIENCE

In her analysis of the German government's attempts to improve relations with France, Poland, Israel and the Czech Republic after World War II, Gardner Feldman creates four categories of TNA-state relations: TNAs can act as catalysts, complements, conduits or competitors. Gardner Feldman writes:

> As catalyst or competitor, it is the TNA that dictates the terms of reference, with the German government performing in a more reactive mode. When TNAs are complements the government sets the overall tone. The role of catalyst or competitor involves relations of tension with the government, whereas activity as complement or conduit by TNAs suggests harmonious relations.[11]

There are also TNAs that are religious bodies, academic organizations, labour unions, chambers of commerce, international friendship groups, student unions, political foundations, as well as prominent individuals — journalists or retired political leaders — who act in the public sphere to promote reconciliation. Gardner Feldman offers many examples of faith-based catalytic activities such as the outreach by the French Protestant church to German POWs in the immediate post World War II period, the missives of the German Evangelical church to Poland in the 1960s, the exchange of letters between German and Polish Catholic bishops, similar attempts between German and Czech Catholic leaders, and the formation of the Societies of Christian-Jewish Cooperation promoting ties between Germany and Israel. Although strictly speaking not a religious group, Moral Rearmament played a crucial role in bringing together German politicians and French leaders (including members of the Resistance) for reconciliation meetings at MRA headquarters in Caux, Switzerland, in the late 1940s. One prominent German to participate in the meetings was Konrad Adenauer.

With regard to TNAs as complements, Gardner Feldman focuses on the various schoolbook commissions whose aim was to "decontaminate"[12] school history textbooks by removing from them one-sided nationalistic versions of the past. Also in the complement category are TNAs, mostly NGOs, engaged in the promotion of exchanges including "youth associations, sports clubs, language centers, training centers, trade unions, schools, universities and town twinning organizations".[13]

As for TNAs in the role of conduits, an example is provided by the activities of the German political foundations, of which the three most prominent are: the Friedrich Ebert Stiftung (Social Democratic Party), the Konrad Adenauer Stiftung (Christian Democratic Party) and the Friedrich Neumann Stiftung (Free Democratic Party). While all of these foundations are supported from the public purse, they function independently of the state. All three have offices outside Germany and engage actively with the public and opinion leaders of former enemy countries, holding symposiums, administering scholarships and generally promoting activities stressing shared values of democracy, free markets and human rights.

With regard to competition, Gardner Feldman makes reference to the clandestine activities of former Nazi scientists who tried to help Egypt in the 1950s to develop nuclear weapons for use against Israel, and the recent public questioning of Germany's Middle East policies by a younger generation of Germans sympathetic to the Palestinian cause. In the case of Poland and the Czech Republic, German governments have faced internal opposition to rapprochement from large groups of expellees, ethnic Germans forced to flee from Silesia, an area with a formerly mixed German-Polish ethnic population which became virtually entirely Polish after 1945, and the Sudetenland from which ethnic Germans were driven out after World War II by the Czechoslovak government.

ARE THERE NORTHEAST ASIAN TNAs?

Although the above "patterns of reconciliation" reflect a European reality, they provide a grid against which it is possible to compare progress (or lack of it) in Northeast Asia's history debates. First of all, it is possible to see that religious organizations play a much smaller part in transnational activity in Northeast Asia in general, and on historical issues in particular. Unlike in Europe where Catholic and Protestant believers can easily find co-religionists in neighbouring countries, there are no large transnational religious organizations to speak of in Northeast Asia. Granted, the Japanese and Korean *ianfu* support groups do have connections with the Christian churches of their respective countries, but their relationship is highly asymmetrical: some forty per cent of the Korean population describe themselves as Christians while less than one per cent of Japanese claim affiliation with any Christian denomination.[14]

When it comes to Buddhism, the relationship between Koreans and Japanese is even more tenuous. Although Buddhism was transmitted to

Japan from China *via* Korea in the seventh century, the last time Koreans and Japanese shared that faith was in the fourteenth century. Buddhism was suppressed by the Choson dynasty (1392–1910) which used Confucianism to bolster its legitimacy. The legacy of seven centuries of a shared belief in Buddhism between Japanese and Koreans consists today of about one hundred Koryo Period (935–1392) Buddhist paintings now in the possession of a number of Japanese temples.[15]

We can also eliminate from Gardner Feldman's patterns the conduit roles played by Germany's three largest political foundations.[16] No such organizations exist in Japan, Korea or the PRC. In the case of Japan, most transnational activity in international relations is either in the hands of government supported organizations or else a handful of large foundations which, according to law, must report to "competent governmental agencies".[17] The AWF is typical of a government-initiated foundation with close relations to its "competent agency", the Ministry of Foreign Affairs. As explained below, the overwhelming strength of the state in comparison to civil society has inhibited the development of large, independent Japanese NGOs and therefore has made it extremely difficult for all but a handful of civil society organizations to function as TNAs.

One of very few Japanese NGOs that can be described as having a significant track record as an active TNA in historical issues is Peaceboat, which organizes cruises to various parts of the world holding on-board seminars aimed at achieving better understanding of the viewpoints of Japan's neighbours. Peaceboat supports its activities through fees it collects from cruise participants.[18] Founded in 1982 when attempts to remove from Japanese history textbooks references to aggression on the Asian mainland triggered anti-Japanese demonstrations in Seoul and an official protest from Beijing, Peaceboat has grown into a mainstream, national organization with broad-based support throughout the country. Posters advertising its cruises to such trouble-spots as North Korea, the Middle East, and Cuba can be seen on the walls of restaurants, coffee shops, language schools and colleges even in remote communities. The fact that individual Japanese spend as much as $10,000 each to take part in the cruises indicates a willingness to invest both time and money in getting to know the often negative views of one's neighbours.[19] In taking on the task of holding shipboard conferences in ports of both Koreas, Taiwan, the PRC and Russia — countries with which Japan has historical and territorial disputes — Peaceboat has the potential of acting as a catalyst for future government action. One of its former leaders has recently been re-elected to the Japanese parliament. Its ship-board lecturers represent a broad cross-section of Japanese society, from leading public intellectuals to television cooking instructors.

VAWW (Violence Against Women in War Network Japan), the feminist NGO mentioned above, is a typical small-scale Japanese NGO, unusual only in that it is one of very few to function successfully as a TNA. Organizer of a mock trial in December 2000 which found the late Emperor Hirohito guilty of war crimes, VAWW acts as a competitor to the Japanese government. Nicola Piper states, "VAWW-NET Japan is one of the few Japanese groups active on behalf of gendered violence generally, and the 'comfort women' issue in particular, which has strong transnational links. The original, and possibly still the main impetus for concrete lobbying at the international level, however, seems to come from Korean groups." Although a comprehensive comparison of the Japanese and Korean civil society sectors is beyond the scope of this chapter, Piper is correct in highlighting the far greater level of activity on the part of Korean NGOs, especially on the issue of the former comfort women.[20]

Structural Constraints on Advocacy NGOs in Japan

Peaceboat and VAWW present unique examples of independent transnational NGO activity in Japan in the field of political advocacy. Strictly speaking, Peaceboat is not totally a non-profit organization; rather it acts as an ingeniously conceived corporation whose business model (travel agency and cruise line) allows it to be a self-supporting enterprise totally independent of the state and free from reliance on charitable donations. VAWW, on the other hand, consists of a highly committed small group of volunteers who belong to the minority of Japanese citizens capable of functioning across boundaries of language and culture.[21]

Peaceboat and VAWW are to a certain extent the exceptions that prove a rule. When comparing the role of European *versus* Northeast Asian NGOs in addressing problems of history, the most important difference is the legal and financial constraints that have been imposed on civil society activity of any kind in Northeast Asia. Until very recently, in all three countries in the region, Japan, Korea and the PRC, the coming together of ordinary citizens for the kinds of activities that might benefit historical reconciliation with neighbouring countries has been strictly controlled by the state. For this reason, TNA activity in any of the four categories cited by Gardner Feldman can be expected to take place on a far smaller scale between Japan and Korea, than for example between Germany and France, even though in the former case the two neighbours have a combined population well in excess of the latter two.[22] In Japan, until the coming into effect of a new Non-Profit Organization Law in 1998, advocacy groups, environmental organizations, in fact all but large-scale corporate foundations had virtually no hope of obtaining legal status. Without legal status NGOs could not rent offices, lease telephone lines, open bank accounts (needed to receive donations) or hire employees.

Although Article 34 of the Japanese Civil Code — the law defining the activities of NGOs and NPOs — has been in force virtually unchanged between 1898 and the present day, the definition of permitted activities for private non-profit groups was actually narrowed in the 1970s and would not be broadened for almost thirty years — not until the passage in 1998 of a new NPO law. Until that time, Article 34 limited non-state or non-profit activity to so-called *kôeki hôjin,* literally "public benefit juridical persons" commonly translated as "public benefit corporations", or "foundations". An international survey of the non-profit sectors of some forty countries described the challenges facing Japanese wishing to take part in civil society activities in the latter part of the twentieth century in the following words:

> In order to establish a *kôeki hôjin,* approval by the "competent governmental agency" is required. ...[I]t is a very difficult and time-consuming process, except when the government itself takes the lead in establishing a *kôeki hôjin.* Moreover, approval is also subject to the discretion of the officer in charge of the application case, and no clearly stated and standardized criteria for incorporation exist. One of the major obstacles to creating a *kôeki hôjin* is the substantial amount of financial assets required by the public authorities prior to the actual establishment of the organization. The actual amount may vary from case to case, but it is very difficult for groups of citizens to accumulate assets of 300 million yen (US$2.3 million) or more, as required by the Ministry of Foreign Affairs.[23]

An example of the negative impact that an overwhelmingly state-centred political system can have on transnational civil society activity in reconciliation is the refusal in 1997 by the Japanese committee of UNESCO to accept an invitation from its Korean counterpart to initiate a dialogue on the teaching of history in high schools. In proposing the textbook talks, Korea was following the precedent of UNESCO mediation between West Germany and Poland on history issues that had begun in 1972 and concluded successfully four years later. According to a Japanese news report, in turning down the Korean request to enter into talks, the Ministry of Education's school textbooks department and the Japan UNESCO committee stated, "This sort of research should be delegated to private historians. It is not the role of governments." The Japanese UNESCO Committee, however, is part of the Ministry of Education and is staffed by the ministry's own bureaucrats. As this example shows, in a state-centred society, there is little room for non-state actors.[24] The West German-Polish negotiations also prove that what non-state actors, working in harmony with the state, can achieve in the historical field breakthroughs which for structural reason, may elude representatives of the state.

Although the new NPO Law permits NGOs to obtain legal status through a much simplified reporting procedure, it still takes as long as three months to obtain approval. Moreover, tax exempt status has to be applied for separately; it is granted only rarely and often after long months of negotiations with officials. Since tax exempt status is reviewed once every two years, the lengthy procedure has to be repeated regularly. No wonder the majority of Japanese NGOs have opted not to obtain legal status even under the new much more liberal NPO Law.

Korean NGOs — Nationalism *versus* Human Rights

Given that Korea's modern legal system owes its origins to the period of Japanese colonial rule, the Korean non-profit sector bears some remarkable similarities — at least in form — to that of Japan. Names of the various types of non-profit organizations (including that term itself) are derived from the same Chinese character compounds that were absorbed into the Korean vocabulary during the thirty-five years when Japanese administrators ruled the peninsula. The structure and agenda of Japanese and Korean civil society began to diverge in the 1980s. Civil society advocacy groups came to be formed in the latter stages of authoritarian military-backed rule when rapid growth triggered "discrepancies in almost every aspect of society: between city and country, between classes, between regions, and between sexes".[25] But economic expansion under Korea's state-guided economy also spawned the growth of a middle class, whose members were now keen to address social ills.

In contrast to Japan, civil society in Korea exercises strong influence on government. President Roh Moo Hyun owes his election — and his return to office after his impeachement — to the support of Korea's powerful civil society sector. As Kim Inchoon and Hwang Chansoon state:

> Civil society organizations are new actors in Korean society especially after the economic crisis of 1997. Sometimes they influence the behaviour of the state and business. The reason the role of civil society organizations is highlighted in the reform process is that political parties cannot serve as a leading force of reform.... . Cases in which civil society organizations express their views on pending policy issues became more frequent and their influence on the policy-making process more powerful. Furthermore, the pressure they exert on the government and parties to adapt their policy alternatives [has] intensified. Major civil society organizations have equipped themselves with research institutes and policy commissions to strengthen their policy-presenting capacity.[26]

Korean civil society has also undergone rapid expansion and a broadening of its agenda with the sudden shift in the late 1980s from military-backed regimes to elected governments. But, the flowering of advocacy activism in Korea would amplify differences between Japanese and Korean NGOs, not only in their relations with the state but also in political orientation. Perhaps no statistical comparison between Japanese and Korean advocacy groups is more relevant for the purposes of this discussion than the one released in 2006 by the Johns Hopkins Comparative Nonprofit Sector Project. By the early part of this decade, the proportion of civil society workforce engaged in advocacy in Korea had risen to 9.9 per cent, compared with 0.5 per cent for Japan. Even accounting for the much larger size of Japanese civil society, nearly 2.9 million "full time equivalent" (FTE) employees, there were an estimated 53,000 Korean FTEs active in highly political Korean NGOs, compared with an estimated 14,000 similar workers in Japan. As a ratio of the total population of the two countries, the figures are even more meaningful: In the case of Korea, there is one civil society advocacy activist per 885 members of the population whereas in Japan there is one for every 9,285 citizens.[27]

The asymmetry between Japanese and Korean advocacy NGOs is further compounded by divergent agendas. Commenting, for example, on the willingness of Korean NGOs to continue to work in North Korea long after European and North American counterpart organizations had given up, Chung Oknim stated: "For Korean NGOs, nationalism, unification, and reconciliation [with North Korea] are the main motivations for relief activities that extend beyond simple humanitarianism."[28] It was this same tendency to place a higher priority on nationalism than on human rights which would bring about a split between Japanese and Korean NGOs working on behalf of the comfort women. The main reason for the rift, according to Chung Jin-sung, was the decision by the Korean Council for Women Drafted for Military Sexual Slavery by Japan, a coalition of Korean women's organization to prefer to form alliances with so-called "anti-feminist [Korean] nationalist organizations" even at the risk of alienating the Japanese feminist groups with whom the council originally joined forces in the early 1990s.[29]

Chung quotes an unidentified Japanese woman activist commenting at a joint Japan-Korea meeting of *ianfu* support groups as saying, "If Korea strongly raises nationalistic issues it will be difficult to form alliance [sic]."[30] When the Korean Council shifted priorities in the early 1990s away from demanding compensation for the aging *ianfu* to campaigning for the punishment of officials who had been responsible for the coercive recruitment of the women and their maltreatment at "comfort stations", the schism between the Japanese and Korean NGOs widened, causing several of the former to side with the AWF which stressed compensation for the aging comfort women while they were still alive over pursuing the legal responsibility of the state. The Japanese women justified their compromise with the AWF on pragmatic grounds and argued that the goal of obtaining a full legal apology from the state is so time-consuming that given the advanced age of the *ianfu*, pressuring them to demand an apology and to refuse compensation actually violated their human rights. As of time of writing, there seems little hope for reconciliation between the Japanese and Korean women's NGOs on the comfort women issue. On the contrary, the demand for a full legal apology from Japan has become so firmly embedded in Korea's domestic politics of grievance, one suspects that even if the Korean NGOs wanted to compromise, they would find it difficult to do so as long as feelings of nationalism remain at present high levels in Korea.

It would be a mistake, however, to suggest that Korean NGOs are more responsible for the heightened sense of nationalism in Korean society today than other groups. History talks between Japan and Korea came to an impasse in June 2005 when Korean scholars, appointed by the government, insisted that the Japanese members of the committee agree that the Treaty of Annexation concluded between Korea and Imperial Japan in 1910 had been illegal and therefore the entire thirty-five-year period of Japanese colonial rule that followed was contrary to international law. One could argue that the fact that the Japan-Korea history talks had been set up by the governments of the two countries and all the delegates were officially appointed, did not give much of an opportunity for participants from either country to work out compromises which might be embarrassing to the governments that appointed them. But since non-governmental talks between Japanese and Korean historians have also broken down in the past for similar reasons, Korea's domestic politics of grievance has to be seen as a factor greatly limiting the potential of civil society TNAs for work toward Japan-Korea reconciliation.[31]

What's in a Name?

As the name of the Korean Council indicates, the dominant Korean vision of the *ianfu* is: a) that they were victims of colonial exploitation; b) that all were coerced into providing sexual services; and c) that the vast majority were Korean. Although this view of the *ianfu* is widely held among Koreans, not all of these points are accepted by all scholars who have studied Japan's wartime military "comfort stations".[32] The influence of the Korean NGOs, however, is so powerful that the Korean Ministry of Gender Equality's home page carries a wartime photo of Korean girls belonging to the Women's Labour Volunteer Corps (*Chongshindae*) incorrectly identifying them as comfort women.[33] Although the mixing up of the volunteer corps with the comfort women is historically inaccurate, it reflects the nationalist narrative of victimization to which the majority of the Korean population subscribes today.

The most likely scenario is that unscrupulous wartime recruiters of the *ianfu* spun tales of "a job at a factory in Japan" as a means to lull their victims and their gullible rural relatives into thinking that their daughters would be taken to Japan as members of the volunteer corps. Another reason why the *ianfu* have become conflated with the *Chongshindae* in the Korean consciousness may be because the most active period of recruitment for both took place at the same time, in the latter stages of the war. Research by Takasaki Sôji raises serious doubts about any members of *Chongshindae* being recruited by the colonial government for duty as *ianfu* although Takasaki concedes that a very small number of the girls could have been diverted to comfort stations after the factories they were assigned to had been bombed. One survivor states that this is what happened to her. However, as the *Chongshindae* were to be assigned to work at factories where Japanese language literacy was required, they had to have had a fairly high level of education. In 1942, according to official figures, high school enrolment for girls in Korea stood at 30,000.[34] If one accepts the estimates of numbers of comfort women as "between 50,000 and 200,000", a considerably high proportion of teenage Korean girls attending school would have had to have been deceived into becoming sex slaves for *Chongshindae* to be synonymous with *ianfu*. Since the total number of *Chongshindae* from Korea came to fewer than 4,000 for the entire duration of the war, the numbers do not add up. In his report on the Peninsular Women's Volunteer Labour Corps, Takasaki strongly implies that leaders of the Korean *ianfu* support groups are aware that most of the surviving comfort women were not *Chongshindae*, and yet, the Korean language name of the Korean Council, *Han'guk Chongshindae Munje Taech'aek Hyeopuihoe* (literally, "Korean Council to Tackle the Problems of the Chongshindae") contains this highly problematic word.[35]

That such a perception gap can exist between citizens of Japan, a former colonial power, and those of Korea, a former colony, may be understandable but for this kind of myth to be perpetuated, certain political conditions have to obtain. Every Wednesday, since 8 January 1992, a dwindling number of aging comfort women appears in front of the Japanese Embassy in Seoul, demanding a "sincere apology" for the past. One cannot help wondering if these Wednesday demonstrations might not be part of a nationalist ritual in which the perpetuation of an image of suffering is likely to have greater value for the movement than a compromise solution, even one that might actually bring considerable material benefit to the victims.[36] Indeed, the sight of such anti-Japanese forms of nationalism has triggered a negative reaction from a small but growing group of Korean intellectuals, as can be seen in the response of Park Yu-ha to VAWW's Nishino.

It is an undeniable fact that Korea's politics of grievance is an obstacle to transnational collaboration. While the sufferings of the comfort women cannot be underestimated, nationalism has driven a wedge between Korean civil society groups and potentially influential intellectual allies in Japan. For example, Takasaki, whose work on the *Chongshindae* is referred to above, has been a vocal critic of the Japanese government's handling of negotiations with Korea leading to the 1965 Treaty of Normalization. Another is Uneo Chizuko, professor of sociology at Tokyo University, a prolific writer on feminist issues. Ueno has pointed to the inconsistency of the Korean position of focusing only on non-Japanese comfort women as victims. It is well known that a significant proportion of the *ianfu* were licensed prostitutes from Japan as well as Korea. Possibly in response to the claim by rightwing nationalists in Japan that all *ianfu* were prostitutes, the NGOs ignore the existence of the licensed prostitutes, insisting that all women had been coerced or deceived into becoming "sex slaves". The actual stories that the *ianfu* tell are more complicated and point to a difficult era, when licensed prostitution was legal, when relatives in both Japan and Korea sold their female dependents into debt bondage, and when a Korean woman who escaped a bad marriage or an abusive father stood in great danger of being delivered by unscrupulous associates into the hands of recruiters working for private brothels connected to the military. Ueno has criticized the Korean NGOs and their Japanese supporters for creating an unrealistic "model victim…, a coerced Korean whose purity was sullied".[37] To Ueno, the airbrushing from history of the Japanese licensed prostitute, a victim of the same injustices albeit on a slightly lesser scale than her Korean counterpart, also amounts to an injustice. Ueno has written, "The Korean NGOs have fiercely resisted equating Korean comfort women with Japanese licensed prostitutes but all that this accomplishes is to draw an artificial national boundary dividing one group of victims from another while perpetuating discrimination against prostitutes."[38] The process ends up making it difficult for the "impure victims" (Japanese former comfort women) to come forward. None have.

There is reason to believe that as long as Korean NGOs subscribe to a national narrative in which Japanese are permanently characterized as perpetrators while Koreans embrace victimization, there is little hope for the emergence of the kind of mainstream civil society alliances that made post-war reconciliation in Europe possible among former adversaries. Although narratives stressing national suffering are universal, in the case of Korea the failure of successive governments to promote free discussion of the complex nature of the colonial experience, a time when the country experienced economic development under conditions of national humiliation, has nurtured simplistic black and white visions of noble patriots struggling against venal collaborators.[39] As Sheila Miyoshi Jager has pointed out, in the power shift that took place immediately after the end of the Cold War in Korea, "talk of the past has become a hot button issue."[40] In other words, history has become a convenient tool by which to settle old scores. The laws passed under President Roh to ferret out past collaborators is but one example of the kind of "instrumentalization of history" which is viewed as no longer acceptable in the parts of Europe which have experienced the process of historical reconciliation with neighbours.[41]

Japanese NGOs — Relevant but Marginal

The geopolitical environment of post World War II Europe created conditions in which historical reconciliation could be seen as being in the national interest of each state. During the Cold War, the major European powers faced a common enemy in the form of communism; they received massive encouragement from the United States to coordinate economic policies partly to assure speedy recovery from the ravages of war, and partly so as to put an end to wasteful and dangerous practices of economic nationalism, which had been among the causes of World War II. The Marshall Plan would spawn the OECD, the United States would become a prime mover for the establishment of NATO, and U.S. leaders would provide encouragement to Monnet and Schuman to press forward with the establishment of the European Coal and Steel Community, the first step to the creation of the European Union.[42]

In the Far East, however, American foreign policy during the Cold War would encourage division, not unity. The Cold War demarcation line dividing the communist and capitalist camp in Asia — known back in the 1950s as the "bamboo curtain" — placed Japan and the People's Republic of China in opposing camps, thus making it impossible to carry on constructive dialogues about the past. In the case of Korea, division and war, followed by decades of poverty conspired to delay coming to terms with a complicated relationship with Japan. As for Japan, the Cold War created domestic ideological divisions, which would make certain that Japan would lack the domestic consensus[43] on historical issues necessary to engage former victims and enemies in constructive dialogue.

Contrasting geopolitics meant that in Europe, de-Nazification of Germany became absolutely necessary for the harmonious functioning of NATO. In Japan, however, the Cold War required the mobilization of Japan's pre-war elite — including the rehabilitation of officials who had overseen aggressive expansion and colonial exploitation — in order to turn Japan into a prosperous ally for the United States in the struggle against communism. But, obtaining the help of Japan's pre-war elite came at a high price: the Western alliance would get an efficient, prosperous Japan with an anti-communist government, but dealing with Japan's negative historical legacy would have to be shelved since asking questions about the past careers of U.S.-backed leaders such as Kishi Nobusuke, an architect of the economy of the Japanese puppet state of Manchukuo and a member of the wartime cabinet of General Tôjô

Hideki, would inevitably tarnish the image of post-war Japan as a "new nation" committed to democratic values.

And, because history had become the Achilles heel of every conservative government since the end of World War II, every unresolved issue — from the Rape of Nanking, to Unit 731 (the Imperial Army's bacteriological warfare centre in northern China), payment of compensation to individual victims of Japanese aggression (such as slave labourers from China and Korea) and the description of such excesses in Japanese history textbooks — all became ammunition for the left to discredit the right. For the right, denying the past and casting doubt even on the most cautious scholarly assessments of damage done by Japan on the Asian mainland, became a legitimate form of defence. As for the mass of Japanese citizens, with each passing year of prosperity under conservative rule, the historical issue became less of an immediate cause.[44]

Mass prosperity under conservative rule in Japan has also contributed to the asymmetry between Japanese and Korean civil society organizations active in the history field. In contrast to Korean advocacy NGOs, which are so powerful[45] that they can help shape government policy on history, in Japan advocacy NGOs have failed to attract a mass membership, not only because of legal and financial constraints on the formation of civil society organizations, but also because for ordinary Japanese citizens digging up unpleasant aspects of their nation's past is not a high priority issue. If anything, the outrage expressed by Beijing and Seoul over former Prime Minister Koizumi Junichirô's visits to Yasukuni Shrine, ostensibly because the souls of fourteen Japanese Class-A war criminals are consecrated there, has served to isolate Japanese advocacy NGOs from ordinary citizens, many of whom disapprove of Koizumi's visits but see Chinese and Korean complaints about the visits as interference in Japan's internal affairs.

That is not to say that the Japanese advocacy NGOs are irrelevant or that ordinary Japanese are insensitive to the sufferings caused by their country on its neighbours during and before World War II.[46] As Rikki Kersten points out, in spite of their small numbers, Japan's "progressive intellectuals" have remained remarkably effective adversaries to successive conservative governments:

> The tireless history textbook campaigners (such as Net 21) insist on detailing the facts of Japan's war atrocities in high school textbooks.... Japan's courts are bursting with former victims of wartime Japan demanding compensation, supported by citizen's groups and teams of pro-bono Japanese lawyers.... And they have had some successes. So-

called 'comfort women' were finally acknowledged by the Japanese government in the early 1990s when a progressive thinker, Yoshimi Yoshiaki, exposed documentary evidence of official complicity.[47]

But, as Kersten concedes, "All of these movements... are self-consciously anti-state.... It is an intellectual life on the periphery, far from the bowels of power...."[48] And as Sheldon Garon has argued, most Japanese, even those who work with civil society organizations, are not predisposed to be anti-state. On the contrary, large numbers of Japanese citizens have positive attitudes toward their government and are happy to collaborate with it to help solve a broad array of social problems.[49]

Isolated from political power, prevented from expanding by legal and financial constraints, and driven by a passionate sense of mission, one must ask if Japanese advocacy NGOs can be expected to become the vanguard of the kind of mainstream movement toward international historical rapprochement that we have seen in Western Europe. To see in high relief once more the differences between Northeast Asian and European approaches to similar historical problems, let us revisit the AWF, this time comparing it with the German Future Fund, set up to address the needs of another group of forgotten victims of World War II.

THE AWF *VERSUS* THE GERMAN FUTURE FUND

Although the AWF has been described above, it is worth examining its origins since its debacle offers a textbook case of the obstacles posed by the combination of marginalized advocacy NGOs and a divisive political environment on historical issues. Confronted in 1992 with irrefutable evidence of official complicity in the recruitment of tens of thousands of women to provide sexual services for the Japanese military, the government came under pressure from two sides: from the left, to accept legal responsibility, show sincere contrition, and provide condolence money; and from the right, to stick to the official position that all pending claims against Japan stemming from World War II have been fully settled by the San Francisco Peace Treaty and subsequent international agreements.[50]

Unused to collaborating with non-state actors and confident that officials are best suited to handling international crises, bureaucrats took the lead and encouraged a group of scholars and prominent individuals to act as advisers to a foundation set up with the support of the Foreign Ministry. In spite of its noble purpose, the AWF became a reviled symbol of leftists and nationalists alike. Funding for AWF came mostly from the

Japanese government but also, significantly, from voluntary contributions made by private individuals, who felt sympathy for the aging *ianfu.*

Although the reasons for combining public and private funding were largely legalistic, the AWF did break new ground in being the first Japanese organization that sought to deal with a controversial historical problem as a public-private partnership. Set up in 1995 under Prime Minister Murayama Tomiichi, a former socialist, AWF sailed into controversy the following year, when Hashimoto Ryûtarô, a political conservative who replaced Murayama, reportedly resisted signing individual letters of apology to surviving comfort women. Hashimoto was also said to have opposed the idea of using funds directly from the national budget to make compensation payments on the grounds that doing so would undermine Japan's official position that all claims against Japan had been settled.[51] Although Hashimoto did eventually sign the letters of apology, the news of his hesitation caused one of the early supporters of the fund, the widow of a former prime minister, to resign, thus severely undermining the AWF's reputation.

What the AWF debacle illustrates is that Japanese advocacy NGOs working in the history field bear such strong animosity against their own government that even when political leaders do take steps to compensate survivors, the pursuit of a political struggle against the state appears to the NGOs to be more attractive than compromise on behalf of long-suffering, elderly victims. In stressing the importance of taking a moral stand against the Japanese government, the marginalized Japanese advocacy NGOs and their much larger Korean nationalist counterparts do share a common purpose. It would seem that reconciliation is not part of the vocabulary of either the Japanese or Korean NGOs that have supported former comfort women in their struggles against the Japanese government.[52]

The inability of the AWF to carry out its goals is remarkable since it bears close structural resemblance to the German Future Fund, which by contrast has been a success.[53] Both funds were set up to address unresolved historical issues, initially reluctantly by two former aggressor states.[54] In the case of the German fund, the need was to provide compensation for the approximately one million surviving victims of Nazi forced labour mostly from former communist countries, who, because of the division of Europe during the Cold War could not be parties to previous compensation schemes. Both the Japanese and the German governments chose a formula in which both government and private funds were mobilized. In both Germany and Japan, conservative forces resisted the compensation schemes and in both countries industry was reluctant to contribute to the funds.

But, by 2000, just two years after law suits were brought against German companies in U.S. courts by survivors of Nazi forced labour, the fund "Remembrance, Responsibility and the Future" was set up and fully functioning. By making contributions to the fund tax deductible, former Chancellor Gerhard Schroeder was able to get nearly 3,000 German companies to take part. Other than paying out the equivalent of US$7.5 billion in compensation to nearly one million survivors, the fund has also undertaken programmes such as arranging for traveling photographic exhibitions on Nazi forced labour, the disbursement of scholarships to needy students, and recently even a German speech contest for Polish children in Gdansk (formerly Danzig) where the first shots of World War II were fired.

By way of contrast, the AWF finished compensating individual former comfort women in 2002 and as has been mentioned already, the fund ceased to exist as of 31 March 2007. No plans exist to commemorate the sufferings of the comfort women, to offer scholarships to needy women in lands where the comfort women were recruited, and no Japanese language speech contests are to be sponsored in neighbouring countries. The AWF debacle highlights the inadequacy of Japanese institutions — governmental and NGO — to give voice to the expressed desire of the majority of Japanese to see victims of past aggression properly compensated.[55]

SOME CONCLUSIONS AND PROPOSALS

Examining European examples of TNA activity is helpful in that we can see clearly that the kind of vibrant, mainstream civil society especially in the advocacy field evident in Europe, is virtually absent in Japan. We can also conclude that for various historical and structural reasons state-NGO relations — especially in the advocacy area — are so hostile in Japan that it is unrealistic to expect European-style government-TNA relations to develop quickly in Northeast Asia. In Korea, on the other hand, the relationship is reversed, with civil society setting the agenda. While the positive effects of government-sponsored reconciliation programs such as officially initiated cultural exchanges, the broadcasting of soap operas on television, joint hosting of sports events, and the promotion of "years of citizens' exchanges" ought not to be dismissed wholesale, such top-down campaigns fail to address historical issues and therefore pose the risk of simply postponing divisive debates in which history can be abused by those in power.

The comparison also helps us see that a vibrant civil society — for Korea does have one — is not the only factor that contributes to reconciliation. Favourable geopolitics, popular support for regional integration, and harmonious state-civil society relations are all contributing factors. We can also see that an entrenched political elite with ties to a negative past (as in the case of Japan) and a heightened sense of nationalism fuelled by domestic politics of grievance (Korea) can negate the work of even the most enthusiastic TNAs.

An obvious question for concerned third parties is, if Northeast Asia lacks home-grown TNAs, then should foundations and governments from outside the region make available the services of their own TNAs? The answer is yes. The first round of Franco-German textbook talks held in the early 1930s was underwritten by the Carnegie Corporation, which is still engaged in brokering peace throughout the world. Although the original Franco-German talks broke down in 1935, the recommendations made by participants at the final meeting before World War II were accepted in full when talks resumed in 1950. One outcome of Carnegie's pre-war funding of textbook talks was the Georg Eckert Institute for Textbook Research at Braunschweig, a repository of more than half a century of German experience in textbook negotiations with former enemies and victims, which recently mediated between Israeli and Palestinian educators. A German political foundation might do well to consider extending invitations to Chinese, Korean and Japanese delegations of educators to tour the facilities and perhaps stay long enough to spend time around a negotiating table.

Another area in which the European experience offers a positive example is in the setting up of foundations whose aim is to turn the sufferings of victims into opportunities for reflection and a renewal of a commitment not to repeat the mistakes of the past. As mentioned above, the agreement in 2001 to compensate victims of Nazi forced labour in former Eastern Bloc countries included the establishment of the German Future Fund. By way of contrast, the disbanding of the AWF represents the squandering of eleven years of investment in reconciliation. What a shame that the process of remembering the sufferings of the *ianfu* cannot be utilized positively to overcome the past by, for example, setting up a joint government-industry fund in Japan to underwrite study at Japanese universities by needy but gifted students from Asian countries. Such a project would serve as a permanent act of atonement as well as a commitment to future cooperation. The Chinese and Korean graduates of Japanese universities funded by such a programme, could act as bridges between Japan and China, as well as Japan and Korea in future economic and cultural relations.

Youth exchanges offer another area where foreign foundations could cooperate with local organizations. An integral part of the reconciliation movement in Europe after World War II was the promotion of youth tourism. The Japanese government is at present promoting inbound tourism, but the goal of the "Yôkoso Japan" programme appears to be limited to improving the bottom line of the ailing domestic tourism industry. With a little extra effort — and outside encouragement — the campaign could be turned into an opportunity to promote Japan-Korea and Japan-China dialogues in a friendly atmosphere at a very basic level.[56] Not all examples of tourism as a peace mechanism need come from Europe. South Africa has been a pioneer in the establishment of transnational nature reserves. While there has been talk of turning the Korean Demilitarized Zone into a peace park, a smaller group has proposed a similar idea for parts of the disputed Southern Kuriles, islands occupied by the Soviet Army in 1945 but claimed by Japan.

Placing the Gardner Feldman grid onto Northeast Asia, one can see that activity is concentrated heavily on adversarial state-NGO relations in the history field. What is needed now are TNAs capable of acting not only as competitors and catalysts, but also as complements and conduits. Of course, the emergence of political leaders and government officials in Northeast Asia capable of dealing sensitively with advocacy NGOs will have to be part of any successful plan to forge a regionally shared perception of the past.

NOTES

1. From 1999 to 2005, the author served as the Japan representative of the Asia Foundation, an American non-profit organization whose mandate includes strengthening civil society. In 2005, the author helped found the International Center for the Study of Historical Reconciliation at Tokyo Keizai University.
2. Members of Japan's conservative elite have never accepted the AWF's mission as legitimate. As recently as 28 October 2006, Deputy Chief Cabinet Secretary Shimomura Hakubun requested that the "government review the historical facts" that are the basis of the 1993 statement by then Chief Cabinet Secretary Kôno Yôhei accepting official responsibility for the wartime "direct and indirect involvement" in the "establishment and management" of comfort stations. Shimomura is among several leading members of the ruling Liberal Democratic Party who would like to see the government rescind the statement

and disavow responsibility for forcible recruitment and maltreatment of comfort women.

3. Unless otherwise stated, Korea refers to South Korea.

4. In this text, Japanese names appear in Japanese word order, family name first, given name second; Korean names are spelled to the extent possible in keeping with the spelling preferred by the Korean person quoted or referred to.

5. For a comprehensive treatment of the Asian Women's Fund and its difficulties in providing compensation to *ianfu*, see: Soh, Chunghee Sarah, "Japan's National/Asian Women's Fund for 'Comfort Women' ", *Pacific Affairs* 76, no. 2 (Summer): 209–33.

6. Lily Gardner Feldman. "The Role of Non-State Actors in Germany's Foreign Policy of Reconciliation: Catalysts, Complements, Conduits, or Competitors?", in Anne-Marie Le Gloanec, *Non-State Actors in International Relations: The Case of Germany* (Manchester: Manchester University Press, 2007).

7. Susan Pharr has defined civil society as consisting of "sustained, organized social activity that occurs in groups that are formed outside the state, the market, and the family." Schwartz, Frank J. and Susan J. Pharr, eds., *The State and Civil Society in Japan* (New York: Cambridge University Press, 2003), p. 3

8. "Disagreements over interpretation of past events between Japan and China, and Japan and Korea can trigger regional instability, and as a result may threaten the peace and security of the entire world." Fujisawa Hôei, "Commentary", in *Sharing the Burden of the Past: Legacies of War in Europe, America and Asia*, edited by Andrew Horvat and Gebhard Hielscher (Tokyo: Asia Foundation/Friedrich Ebert Stiftung, 2003) p. 19.

9. For examples of government-initiated programmes aimed at promoting U.S.-Japan reconciliation, see *Philanthropy and Reconciliation — Rebuilding Postwar US-Japan Relations*, edited by Yamamoto Tadashi, Iriye Akira and Iokibe Makoto (Tokyo: Japan Center for International Exchange, 2006), pp. 101–34.

10. In 2001 during the period of diplomatic friction between Japan and Korea as a result of the Japanese Ministry of Education granting approval to the nationalist history textbook for use in public schools, a senior German official, who asked not to be identified by name, stated that the reason history talks between West Germany and Poland (1972–76) had ended in success was because "We officials were not there."

11. Gardner Feldman, p. 3.

12. Wolfgang Hoepken, former director of the Georg Eckert Institute of International Textbook Research writes, "An early goal of the [Georg Eckert] institute was to eliminate, through collaboration with international partners, the hostile images and negative stereotyping of other people and countries,

which early textbooks had promoted, and thereby to come to a consensual narrative of past and contemporary history. Its basic intention was the 'decontamination' of textbooks and historic concepts that had been poisoned by nationalistic misuse of history." Horvat and Hielscher, eds. *Sharing the Burden...*, p. 3.

13. Gardner Feldman, p. 7.

14. Christian groups have political motives in opposing the AWF and demanding that the government clarify its legal responsibility for the recruitment of comfort women. After interviewing members of Christian groups helping illegal foreigners in Japan, Apichai Shipper and Loren King concluded in "Associative Activism and Democratic Transformation in Japan" (unpublished paper, MIT, 18 February 2002): "Assisting foreigners also strengthens their [Japanese Christian groups'] longstanding campaign against the popular deification of the Japanese emperor." Another motive for Japanese Christians could be a feeling of regret or guilt for past collaboration with the government during World War II. Although some Christians did resist militarism during World War II, the majority of Christian groups bent to pressure from the government to support the war effort. Many regretted setting aside their Christian principles and issued statements to that effect after 1945.

15. In 2004 Korean and Japanese newspapers reported that a number of the Korean Buddhist paintings, stolen from a Buddhist temple in the city of Akashi, in western Japan, had turned up in Korea. The thieves, two Koreans, stated at their trial that they felt no remorse since the paintings were originally Korean. These days, no one but a handful of scholars in Korea and Japan recognize that these paintings represent a shared cultural legacy and that they predate the invasions of Korea by Toyotomi Hideyoshi in the late sixteenth century or Japan's colonial domination of Korea in the twentieth century, eras when Japan did in fact plunder Korea of its cultural artifacts.

16. The Washington-based National Endowment for Democracy attempted in 2000 to encourage the creation of a Japanese foundation devoted to advocacy of democracy throughout Asia. As of present writing, no Japanese political foundation with aims and programmes similar to the German *stiftungs* or with transnational capacity has been set up.

17. Amenomori Takayoshi, "Defining the Nonprofit Sector: Japan", in Salamon, Lester M., and Helmut K. Anheier, "Working Papers of The Johns Hopkins Comparative Nonprofit Sector Project, 1993, p. 8 <http://www.jhu.edu/ccss/pubs/pdf/japan.pdf> (last accessed 1 January 2007).

18. Peaceboat's ability to function as a TNA is closely related to the success of its business model. A disproportionately high percentage of the income of Japanese NGOs in the humanitarian and social development field, an area in which Peaceboat is also active, comes from "for profit" activities that are necessitated by the lack of other kinds of support either from government or

private foundations. For a description of the utter poverty of Japanese non-profits working in the advocacy and international relations areas see Kuroda Kaori, "Current Issues Facing the Japanese NGO Sector," in *Informed*, an Internet publication of The International NGO Training and Research Centre, Bulletin no. 8, May 2003 <www.intrac.org>. The need for "earned income" by Japanese NGOs of the kind that might act as TNAs in historical issues becomes clear on p. 29 of Kuroda's article where she states that as of 25 February 2003, "only 12 organizations out of 10,000 non-profit corporations incorporated under the [1998] NPO Law have been approved as qualified non-profit organizations" permitted to receive tax-deductible donations from private individuals and corporations. In other words, while the 1998 NPO law has provided civil society organizations with legal status, it has not made it possible for them to grow into viable organizations capable of acting as TNAs in any of the various roles described by Gardner Feldman.

19. Peaceboat is international in ways that many Japanese NGOs involved in international relations are not: a significant number of its staff are Japanese-speaking foreign nationals. Other than operating cruises, Peaceboat works together with the European Centre for Conflict Prevention to put on conferences and symposiums on peace-building.

20. Piper, Nicola, "Transnational Women's Activism in Japan and Korea: The Unresolved Issue of Military Sexual Slavery", *Global Networks* 1, no. 2 (2001): 155–70 (ISSN 1470-2266), p. 163. Piper makes reference to a suggestion that "many Korean feminist groups draw on a nationalist discourse of the comfort women as embodying foreign domination of Korea". This question has serious implications for future, broad-based transnational activity since the Japanese and Korean NGOs focus on the comfort women issue for totally different reasons: for the officially approved Korean women's groups, the sufferings of the former comfort women are part of a narrative of national humiliation, a shared tragedy with symbolic meaning, the constant retelling of which is part of an exercise in patriotism; for the much smaller Japanese feminist NGOs the sufferings of the comfort women are part of gender politics for which, at least for the time being, there is little broad-based support in Japan. In the context of a Europe-Asia comparison, this rift is highly significant: TNA activity in Europe represented a desire on the part of people of diverse nationalities to forge a shared vision of the past.

21. Thanks to large-scale officially encouraged immigration to the United States and other English-speaking countries, Korea can now rely on a significant group of English-Korean bilingual speakers who act as a bridge not only in business dealings but also in public diplomacy. Japan has no such cadre of competent English speakers capable of dealing easily with counterparts in foreign countries. Their absence is lamented in op-ed pieces such as this: <http://www.iht.com/articles/2006/12/06/opinion/edkumiko.php>.

22. Sister-city ties offer a good barometer of transnational non-state activity. As of 2005, there were 111 relationships between Korean and Japanese cities and prefectures. Between France and Germany, there were more than 2,200.
23. Amenomori, p. 8.
24. *Rekishi kyôkasho kenkyû — Kankoku teian wo Nihon kyohi* [Japan Rejects Korean Invitation to Engage in Joint History Textbook Research], *Hokuriku Chûnichi Shimbun* evening edition, 22 July 1997, p. 1.
25. Kim Inchoon and Hwang Chansoon, "Defining the Nonprofit Sector in South Korea", Working Papers of The Johns Hopkins Comparative Nonprofit Sector Project no. 41, Baltimore, The Johns Hopkins Center for the Study of Civil Society, accessed at <http://www.jhu.edu/ccss/pubs/pdf/skorea.pdf> (last accessed 1 January 2007). Although the transliteration of Korean terms in this paper does not follow either the official Korean government or the McCune-Reischauer systems of romanization, such an expression as "*beyooungri danche*" [non-profit organization] is clearly the Korean pronunciation of the Japanese Chinese character compound "*hieiri dantai*". Likewise "*simin danche*" [literally citizen's group, meaning NGO] is a cognate of the Japanese "*shimin dantai*", pp. 5–6.
26. Kim and Hwang, p. 4.
27. Estimates of numbers of advocacy activists per population derived from figures available at <http://www.jhu.edu/%7Ecnp/pdf/table301.pdf> (last accessed 1 January 2007).
28. Chung Oknim, "The Role of Korean NGOs; the Political Context," in *Paved with Good Intentions — The NGO Experience in North Korea*, edited by Gordon Flake and Scott Snyder (Westport Connecticut: Praeger, 2003), p. 82.
29. Chung Jin-sung, "Alliances and Conflicts of Civic Societies of East Asia for 'Purging the Past History': Centering on the Issue of Japanese Military Sexual Slavery by Japan", [sic] draft of an English translation prepared for presentation at The Academy of Korean Studies, Global Forum on Civilization and Peace, 7 December 2005, p. 4. The origin of the alliance between mostly Christian Japanese women's NGOs and Korean women's groups dates back to the 1970s when members of the two groups cooperated in a campaign to put an end to so-called "*kisaeng* tourism", the travel to Korea mostly by men from Japan for the purpose of purchasing sexual services by Korean women. The word "*kisaeng*" (traditional Korean female entertainer) was applied to all Korean women engaged in selling sex to foreign tourists, while "sex tourism" had been officially condoned since the 1970s because it was a source of valuable foreign currency for the country.
30. Chung, p. 5.
31. For an account of Japan-Korea non-governmental history discussions that ended inconclusively, see Fujisawa Hôei, " 'Nikkan gôdô rekishi kyôkasho

kenkyûkai' (90-93nen) yume no ato" [Remnants of a Dream: "The 90-93 Joint Japan Korea History Textbook Research Commission] in *Chûô Kôron*, August 2001, pp. 126–33.

32. For background on the various forms of recruitment of *ianfu*, see Soh, Chunghee Sarah, "Human Rights and Humanity: The Case of the 'Comfort Women' ", The ICAS Lectures, Institute for Corean-American Studies, Inc. <http://www.icasinc.org/lectures/cssl1998.html> (last accessed, 1 January 2007).

33. The photograph in the centre of the layout captioned in English as "Choson woman, Korean comfort women of Nagoya" actually shows Korean schoolgirls assigned for work at the Mitsubishi Aircraft Company in that city. The Chinese characters on the sign carried by one of the girls refer to the aircraft company <http://www.hermuseum.go.kr/eng/exp/Experience01.asp> (last accessed 1 January 2007).

34. According to figures released 15 January 1942 by the colonial government general, cited by Takasaki, school enrolments in Korea at all levels stood at 1.86 million. Most students, however, were attending primary school since colonial educational policies purposely failed to make available schooling for Koreans at higher levels. As of 1937, just under 94 per cent of school age Koreans were attending primary school. Girls accounted for about one third of enrolments. Girls' education in general was neglected in Korea until well after independence. For 1937 figures, see Lone, Stewart and Gavan McCormack, *Korea Since 1850* (NY: St. Martin's, 1993), p. 67.

35. For a detailed explanation of the reasons for the perception among Koreans that *Chongshindae* were synonymous with *ianfu*, see Takasaki Sôji, " 'Hantô joshi rôdô teishintai' ni tsuite" [About the Korean Women's Volunteer Labour Corps], at <http://www.awf.or.jp/program/pdf/p041_060.pdf>. After going through the records of Korean schools for the latter years of World War II, when most recruiting for the Volunteer Corps took place, Takasaki found that schools attended by middle and upper class girls sent few (some sent not even one) girls to the Volunteer Corps. The colonial government's *Chongshindae* recruitment programme on the Korean Peninsula was remarkably unsuccessful. Compared to the approximately 4,000 girls recruited as *Chongshindae* in Korea, there were just under 473,000 *Teishintai* (Japanese pronunciation of same Chinese characters as *Chongshindae*) volunteers drafted in Japan who were at their jobs at the end of the war. See also, Soh, Sarah C., "Aspiring to Carft Modern Gendered Selves — 'Comfort Women' and chongshindae in Late Colonial Korea", in *Critical Asian Studies* 36, no. 2 (2004): 175–98. Soh writes: "Notably, despite the widespread Korean equation of comfort women with Chongshindae, only four cases — out of more than sixty published testimonials — were identified as having been initially recruited under the guise of Chongshindae to become comfort women....The postcolonial

appropriation of the term Chongshindae for comfort women by the Korean Council, in fact, not only reflects but also has reinforced the depth and strength of lingering suspicions on the part of Koreans about the abuse of Chongshindae as a convenient mechanism to deceptively recruit comfort women." (p. 182).

36. Soh, C.S., "Japan's National/Asian Women's Fund for "Comfort Women", *Pacific Affairs* 76, no. 2 (Summer): 209–33. Soh observes: "Despite the assumed good will of the advocates for the victims they represent, it is necessary for supporters and observers alike to be alert regarding the insidious workings of power relations found in most political movements, the leaders of which are apt to maneuver and disregard the voices of the subaltern (as in the case of dissenting South Korean survivors) even after they have spoken."

37. Ueno Chizuko, "Posuto reisen to 'Nihonban rekishi shuuseishugi' " [Japanese-style Historical Revisionisms in the Post Cold War Era] in *Ronza*, March 1998, p. 67.

38. Ibid.

39. For an excellent treatment of Korea's economic development under colonial rule, see Eckert, Carter J., *Offspring of Empire — The Koch'ang Kims and the Colonial Origins of Korean Capitalism 1876–1945*, University of Washington Press, Seattle, 1991.

40. Jager, Sheila Miyoshi, "Korean Collaborators: South Korea's Truth Committees and the Forging of a New Pan-Korean Nationalism", in *Japan Focus* (e-zine) <http://www.japanfocus.org/products/details/2170> (last accessed 1 January 2007).

41. Wlodzimierz Borodziej, who as a young Polish academic took part in the 1972–76 West German-Polish history dialogues has written: "[S]ince 1989, as Poland once again attained its sovereignty and Germany was unified, history does not play a large role in our relations. It is certainly still in our minds and will always remain so, because our location as neighbours did not begin in 1989, however, it can no longer be exploited for political reasons." From Borodziej, W., "The German-Polish Textbook Dialogue", in Horvat and Hielscher, p. 37. (The word "*instrumentalisiren*" in the original German has been translated as "exploited for political reasons".)

42. Judt, Tony, *Postwar — A History of Europe Since 1945* (New York: The Penguin Press, 2005). Judt writes on p. 156, "On 30 October 1949, [U.S. Secretary of State] Dean Acheson appealed to Schuman for France to take the initiative in incorporating the new West German state into European affairs." The U.S. request is in direct response to the communist coup in Czechoslovakia and the Berlin blockade.

43. "[T]hose who stick to the pacifist constitution — mainly on the Left — will use, as a reason for their position, the fact that the Japanese cannot be trusted with military power. Look what happened in World War II. It was uniquely

atrocious and horrible and should never happen again. The more they make those arguments, those who are interested in changing the constitution and want Japan to regain the sovereign right to wage war will have to minimize the historical facts with comments like 'every country has waged a war like that and besides it was an anti-colonial war.' " Buruma, Ian, "Commentary" in Horvat and Hielscher, p. 140.

44. For a description of how Japanese enterprise unions, which had originally embraced left wing causes in the 1950s including the promotion of good relations with the PRC, by the late 1960s had moved out of the political sphere, see Suzuki Akira, "The Death of Unions' Associational Life? Political and Cultural Aspects of Enterprise Unions", in Schwartz and Pharr, pp. 195–213.

45. Takasaki refers to an article in the Japanese newspaper, *Asahi Shimbun*, which pits membership of the Korean Council for Women Drafted for Military Sexual Slavery by Japan at 300,000. By way of contrast, the largest Japanese advocacy NGO, the Japan Wild Bird Society, has some 120,000 members.

46. Saaler, Sven, *Politics, Memory and Public Opinion — The History Textbook Controversy and Japanese Society* (Munich: Judicium, 2005). Quoting the results of a survey of Japanese public opinion about Japanese war responsibility carried out by NHK, Japan's public broadcasting network in 2000, Saaler concludes, "The results suggest that a clear majority of Japanese believe that Japan still has continuing responsibility for the war [World War II], a belief that follows logically from the perception of the war as a war of aggression." In the survey referred to by Saaler, 51 per cent of respondents agreed with the statement "World War II was a war of aggression by Japan against its neighbors." Just 15 per cent of those surveyed disagreed with that question. Fifty per cent also agreed that "unresolved problems" required the attention of "later generations....", p. 143.

47. Kersten, Rikki, "The lament of progressivisim: voicing war responsibility in postwar Japan", in International Institute of Asian Studies Newsletter, no. 38 (Autumn 2005), Special Issue "The Asia-Pacific War: History & Memory", Leiden, p. 9.

48. Ibid.

49. Garon, Sheldon, "The Evolution of Civil Society: From Meiji to Heisei", in *Civil Society in the Asia Pacific Monograph Series*, Harvard University Program on U.S.-Japan Relations. Garon states that in Japan "new social forces did not necessarily arise in opposition to the state.... Most societal groups preferred to work *with* the state to realize their objectives...." Garon is referring to mainstream civil society which works with the state to "civilize the nation and alleviate poverty", p. 5. For the attitudes toward the state of non-mainstream civil society activists working in politically controversial areas, see Shipper and King in note 51 below.

50. The boiler-plate expression "subsequent international agreements" refers primarily to the 1965 Japan-Korea Treaty of Normalization by which Korea gave up all further demands for reparations from Japan, and the 1972 agreement between Prime Minister Tanaka Kakuei and Chinese leaders that the PRC would not seek compensation from Japan for war damages. In return, however, it was understood that Japan would actively support the PRC's economic development. In the case of both China and Korea, Japan did this by means of soft loans.

51. Bureaucrats did dip into the public purse to make payments to former comfort women by setting up a separate budget item for "medical needs". These funds, which were calculated depending on the costs of medical care in the women's home countries varied between the equivalent of US$12,000 in the case of the Philippines to US$30,000 for Korean, Taiwanese and Dutch women. The official funds, however, were not paid directly to the women but on their behalf to medical and other institutions in their home countries as part of an elaborate arrangement designed to placate hardliners, who felt that any direct payments from government coffers would undermine Japan's official position that it owed no compensation to foreign individuals. (Personal interview with Ms Ise Momoyo, former director of AWF, 8 October 2005.) For a detailed description of the use of both private and government funds, see *"Ianfu" mondai to Ajia josei kikin* ["The 'comfort women' problem and the Asian Women's Fund", AWF September 2004.]

52. In the dispute over the AWF between the government and activist NGOs, it is not too difficult to perceive a political fault-line. Apichai Shipper and Loren King write in "Associative Activism and Democratic Transformation in Japan" (unpublished paper, MIT, 18 February 2002): "…103 of 107 Japanese staff and volunteers of these groups had never voted for the ruling Liberal Democratic Party….", p. 20. Although Shipper and King studied NGOs involved in supporting illegal foreign workers and victims of trafficking, a number of the same organizations have taken anti-government positions on the former comfort women.

53. For accounts of events leading up to the creation of the German Future Fund, please see Otto Graf Lambsdorff, "The Long Road toward the Foundation Remembrance, Responsibility, and the Future", and J.D. Bindenagel, "US-German Negotiations on and Executive Agreement Concerning the Foundation Remembrance, Responsibility, and the Future", in Horvat and Hielscher eds., *Sharing the Burden…*, pp. 152–60, and pp. 161–72 respectively.

54. The German Future Fund (its official name is Fund for Remembrance, Responsibility and the Future) was set up in response to the launching of a number of lawsuits against German companies in the United States by survivors of Nazi forced labour. Chancellor Helmut Kohl, a conservative, had opposed any arrangements to pay former slave labourers <http://www.religioustolerance.org/fin_nazi.htm>, 18 January 2002.

55. See Saaler, op. cit.
56. "Political reconciliation went hand in hand with reconciliation among people.... Every summer since the 1950s, millions of students began touring Europe individually, favored by the various programs set up in all countries in order to promote youth tourism." Mezzetti, Fernando, "Historical Reconciliation in Italy", in Horvat and Hielscher, eds., *Sharing the Burden...*, p. 50.

Chapter Thirteen
World War II Legacies for India

Sunanda K. Datta-Ray

Modern India was born out of the ashes of World War II. For more than a hundred years before the war India had no international personality, or had only a notional one when the British needed another signatory to the Peace of Versailles or an extra vote at the League of Nations. The war changed all that. Though other factors were at work, the timing and manner of India's midnight tryst with destiny — the transfer of power on 14–15 August 1947 — were largely the result of the tectonic shifts that altered the contours of the world after six searing years of conflict.

The India that emerged was hungry, bankrupt and in ferment. It had very little industry because of the "desire to keep India as a market for British manufactured goods after the war", as Lord Mountbatten noted when his wartime request for large-scale parachute production in India was turned down.[1] Sixty years later, India's rulers are still grappling with the residue of some of those problems. Regardless of the political party they might belong to, they find it unacceptable that the global balance of power as reflected in the composition of the United Nations Security Council, the constitution and operations of international economic and financial agencies and the distribution of nuclear weapons should continue to reflect the war's outcome. Ironically, India was technically one of the victorious nations in 1945. But that does not mean that it either enjoys or approves of the spoils of victory.

While the victors of World War I sought to crush their vanquished enemies, the victors of World War II tried to establish their own permanent supremacy, albeit in a polity that institutions like the United Nations and the World Bank tried to make more equitable. It was the creation of a new two-tier world order. The conviction that this order cannot be graven in stone for all time and that global systems and mechanisms must respond to the changes that have taken place since 1945 inspires India's campaigns to reform the United Nations, revamp the Security Council and obtain global recognition of its status as a nuclear weapons power. The abortive attempt to pioneer a New World information order was an expression of the same impatience with the 1945 *status quo*.

The decision of the Western powers to continue World War II by other means and against other adversaries — the Cold War — has left a more significant legacy whose imprint can be seen and felt in many aspects of Indian life. The heavy reliance on public sector enterprises, for instance, with the state even running a bakery until recent years, is a relic of the combined influence of the socialism that Clement Attlee introduced in Britain in 1945 and independent India's close ties with the Soviet Union. Both were reinforced by a determination not to be exploited any longer as a dumping ground for Western manufactures. More ominously, many of the destabilizing forces that afflict the sub-continent today can be traced back to the Cold War's destructive political rivalry and the devastating arms race that sharpened the edge of the main problems that continue to threaten India's economic and political security. It was American strategic interest in the sub-continent, for instance, that helped to convert the former princely state of Jammu and Kashmir into a cockpit of Islamic terrorism long before the trauma of 11 September 2001. Moscow, New York, Bali, Madrid, London and Baghdad, India has known it all. The Mumbai blasts of 11 July 2006 were part of a grim and continuing series of terrorist attacks flowing from the clash of superpower interests that began long before, as reflected in the Kashmir dispute.

India lives in a tough neighbourhood. Pakistan is poised menacingly on its western flank. Bangladesh, which a former United States ambassador to India calls "a growing centre of international terrorism", borders the east.[2] Sri Lanka to the south is ravaged by civil war. China's shadow looms over all of South Asia. But the most significant extension of wartime ambiguity and ambivalence and Cold War complexities is to be found in the love-hate intensity of India's own uneasy honeymoon with the United States, highlighted by Prime Minister Manmohan Singh's state visit to Washington in July 2005, followed by seemingly unending arguments over the nuclear deal that was signed then and confirmed during President George W. Bush's return visit to India.

Cause and effect cannot be reduced to simplistic formulae in the "large and incredibly diverse country, with vastly disparate convictions and widely divergent customs" that is India, to quote Nobel laureate Amartya Sen's tellingly titled book, *The Argumentative Indian*. Officially, India became an Allied belligerent the moment the viceroy, Lord Linlithgow, a dour Scottish nobleman, went on the air on 3 September 1939 to announce hostilities without consulting or even informing a single Indian. "There was something rotten", India's future (and first) prime minister, Jawaharlal Nehru, exploded, "when one man, and a foreigner and representative of a hated system, could plunge 400 million human beings into war without a slightest reference to them." Nehru wanted to be a willing partner and not coerced into belligerence. But untroubled by such sensitivities, Mohammad Ali Jinnah, whose Muslim League claimed to represent 92 million Indian Muslims, rushed to offer support while urging the viceroy that the only solution to India's woes "lay in partition".[3] Jinnah's hope of being rewarded with a separate Muslim homeland carved out of India after the war was not disappointed.

Nehru's dual approach represented India's mixed response to the war. Though the government was in a state of hostilities against Germany, many Indians sympathized with what they regarded as the enemy's enemy. Some of them may have been flattered by Nazi exaltation of an Aryan lineage and use of the Swastika symbol. But hundreds of thousands of others — basically apolitical young men — joined up because they needed jobs, because they belonged to communities with a martial tradition or because they were loyal to the established authority. Most of these voluntary recruits fought with conspicuous valour against Germany, Italy and Japan. Some liberal intellectuals did acknowledge that fascism was evil; others, especially of the Left which has always been a powerful force in Indian life, were persuaded by the Soviet Union's "Great Patriotic War". But the Nazi peril seemed too remote, and too much like the colonialism that Britain, France and other Western Allies practised, for the Indian political classes as a whole to see the war as the black-and-white tussle between good and evil that it was for the West.

Moreover, the Axis Powers supported Subhas Chandra Bose, revered as Netaji or Great Leader, whose Singapore-based Indian National Army (INA) — 35,000 soldiers according to British military intelligence — offered a quick revolutionary alternative to Britain's slow and grudging steps towards limited autonomy. Since the INA and its provisional government included both Hindus and Muslims, Bose's movement was also seen — and not only by the three million Indians in Southeast Asia — as the future guarantor of a communal unity that Jinnah was determined to shatter. Ba Maw, the Burmese patriot and Bose's comrade in arms, ascribes a greater role to Netaji. "The independence he won during the war was the true beginning of the independence which came to India a few years later", Ba Maw writes in *Breakthrough in Burma: Memoirs of a Revolution, 1939–1946.* "Only the usual thing happened: one man sowed and others reaped after him".

Bose is not forgotten, despite the wistful title, *Bose the Forgotten Hero,* of Shyam Benegal's 2005 film, the most recent portrayal of his heroic adventures. In fact, the Netaji legend is so vibrantly alive that no Indian government dare formally acknowledge the wartime air crash death of an Arthurian hero whom a few diehards in his native Bengal still fondly expect to defy mortality and materialize one day as saviour. Indians were not surprised on 15 August 2005, the eve of the fifty-eighth anniversary of independence day, when an Irish historian, Professor Eunan O'Halpin of Trinity College, Dublin, told a Calcutta audience that he had unearthed documents proving that in March 1941, the British Foreign Office had ordered the Special Operations Executive, a wartime organization formed for sabotage, underground propaganda and other clandestine activities, to assassinate Bose. Apparently, London confirmed the finding three months later.

Contrary pulls on almost every question perpetuate the unresolved dichotomies of the war years. "Argumentative" Indians speak in many voices, governments seldom representing more than the largest minority. Geographically, India was peripheral to the theatre of hostilities but, politically, it was central to the Allied defence: the single crucial purpose of the British military chain from Iraq to Singapore was to ensure that India, the brightest jewel in the British crown, was not prised out of its imperial setting. As history was to prove, there could be no empire without India. Constant fears of invasion underlined India's strategic importance as the retreating British burnt bridges, destroyed boats and laid waste paddy fields in a desperate attempt to thwart the then advancing Japanese and

Bose's INA. Domestic mobilization and the movement of 250,000 American and some 30,000 Nationalist Chinese troops brought the war to the ordinary Indian's doorstep. It was a reminder that India must always look East: Southeast Asia is vital for its security.

There was an even grimmer fallout. Indirectly, the war took toll of an additional three million or more lives. They were victims of a famine caused by military demands, official callousness, and the hoarding and black-marketing that wartime shortages encouraged and that, once entrenched, never quite disappeared from economic life. The devastating famine accounts for the importance accorded to agriculture in independent India's search for food self-sufficiency that led, in turn, to two current phenomena. First, it has made the rural lobby a powerful factor in electoral politics. Second, it bestowed a certain primacy on the Punjab whose position as the country's granary was confirmed when the introduction of Mexican dwarf wheat by American Land Grant colleges after independence led to the economic boom of the Green Revolution.

For a long time India refused to recognize the war's two most significant political legacies — globalization and Pax Americana — with results that are now acknowledged as disastrous. Arun Shourie, a minister in former Prime Minister Atal Behari Vajpayee's Bharatiya Janata Party-led coalition, argues that India "fell behind China by 15 to 20 years" because it "clutch(ed) on to the corpse of 'socialism'".[4] China's per capita gross domestic product, on the basis of purchasing power parity, was US$3,600 in 2002 against India's US$2,200.[5] Those figures stood at US$4,980 and US$2,880 the following year when the gross domestic product figures (duly weighted) for the two countries were U$6,090 billion and US$2,908 billion respectively. Life expectancy in 2003 was 63 years in India and 71 years in China, and the respective female adult literacy figures were 45 per cent and 87 per cent. While 16.6 per cent of Chinese survived on less than a dollar a day in 2003, the share of India's population was 34.7 per cent.[6] John Elliott, a conservative British economics writer, took a less pessimistic view than Shourie of comparative statistics. Acknowledging that "while China is ahead of India in foreign direct investment (FDI)", he argued that "the margin is not nearly as large as is generally assumed" when official claims are "re-assessed". According to Elliott, while China's actual FDI rose from US$11.8 billion to US$13 billion between 1993 and 1994, India's rose from US$0.6 billion to US$0.9 billion in the same period.[7] Even after making allowance for official Chinese exaggeration, the comparison is hardly in India's favour.

Foreign investment might have been even lower if P.V. Narasimha Rao who became prime minister in 1991 (with the present prime minister, a Sikh economist trained at Cambridge and Harvard, in charge of finance) had not brought himself to admit that the world could not be shut out, either economically or politically. Narasimha Rao's forgotten predecessor, Chandra Shekhar, had tried to adjust to global realpolitik by allowing American military aircraft overflight, landing and refuelling facilities during the first Gulf War, but was hounded out of office by Rajiv Gandhi and others thundering that he had sold out to American imperialism. After Rajiv Gandhi's murder, Narasimha Rao and his finance minister quietly but decisively turned round foreign and economic policy to come to terms at last with World War II's long-term aftermath: the end of history which meant the triumph of capitalism and the emergence of the United States as the sole superpower. The Rao-Singh team's calibrated response to market economics eventually resulted in reforms that must be counted as drastic by India's conservative standards. India's outsourcing industry would not have earned US$12.5 billion in 2004 without liberalization. More to the point, the sustained growth rate of about 9 per cent (after years of averaging under 3 per cent — the so-called Hindu rate of growth) is entirely due to economic reforms and accounts for the confidence with which India now takes international initiatives. The 739-page Comprehensive Economic Cooperation Agreement (CECA) that Dr Manmohan Singh and Singapore's Prime Minister Lee Hsien Loong signed in June 2005 is another outcome, expected to yield the additional bonus of resuscitated links with Southeast Asia. India's new proactive economic diplomacy has borne fruit in two directions: the South Asia Free Trade Area (SAFTA) was at last born in July 2006, and India is moving towards far closer cooperation with the Association of Southeast Asian Nations (ASEAN) as a whole.

Everything in today's India flows from the war by way of independence. But the forces that were unleashed or aggravated then have not played out as yet. Pakistan's obsession with Kashmir, China's military build-up, and President Bush's now renamed war on terror, impinge on India as it tries to reconcile large pockets of deprivation at home with soaring aspirations abroad, and national priorities with the demands of globalization. Poised at the crossroads of history, South Asia will continue to be unstable until extraneous intervention — chilling reminder of the Cold War — ends, and the region's indigenous geopolitical forces are allowed to find their natural equilibrium without reference to great power politics. Until then we can only identify some of the more significant markers along a continuum that has no cut-off point.

INDEPENDENCE

Victory held the seeds of defeat for the Allies, setting the stage for many of today's dramas. "We have not got enough troops or authority to keep order", wailed George VI, the last British Emperor of India.[8] His government had spent more than £4,000 million on the war, and had to borrow US$3,750 million from the United States. Attempts to bring Bose's soldiers to trial, the demobilization of thousands of Indian troops, the flood of arms throughout India and the massive upheavals of Mohandas Karamchand (Mahatma) Gandhi's Quit India movement in 1942 — "the most serious rebellion since that of 1857" according to Linlithgow — convulsed India. With units of the army, navy, air force and police joining the revolt, India's three defence chiefs — British naturally — warned that Lord Wavell, the military hero who succeeded Linlithgow as viceroy, would need another five British divisions to rescue the Crown's authority. Each soldier under his command then had to control 10,000 civilians.[9]

The civil unrest and economic abuses that put off some Western investors and entrepreneurs even today can both be traced to wartime recklessness. The nationalist upsurge during what many Indians saw as an imperialist war bestowed respectability on the culture of anti-authority protest, epitomized by the catchy slogan, *"Sarkar ki mal, pani me dal!"* [Into the water with government property]. No matter what the cause of discontent, buses and trains have been the targets of demonstrators ever since. India's parallel economy — black money soared from 21 per cent of the gross domestic product in 1991 to 40 per cent by the early years of the twenty-first century[10] — is another reminder of wartime scarcity when hoarding and speculation precipitated the monstrous tragedy of the Bengal famine and "corruption and black-marketing ravaged the land".[11] The indiscipline that was patriotic during the war became a lifestyle; so did the "civil disobedience" that Mahatma Gandhi and others preached.

Those tumultuous times left many painful scars. Independence meant administrative dislocation, uprooted multitudes and horrendous religious killings. Partition destroyed India's social cohesion, split families and devastated the economy. Industries were cut off from raw materials; and communication lines broken. Where there was one country, there are now three, and the tense relations, aggravated by Cold War strategies, that have erupted in three wars between India and Pakistan bode ill for the hope that the South Asian Association for Regional Cooperation (SAARC) will ever match the European Union in burying historic hostilities for common prosperity.

NON-ALIGNMENT AND THE SOVIET UNION

India's most daunting task today is to correct the lingering effects of its own particular response to the war's ravages and the Cold War tensions that succeeded it. That means venturing beyond the non-alignment (John Foster Dulles, Harry S. Truman's Cold War Secretary of State, dismissed it as "immoral"[12]) that Nehru hoped would allow a clear passage between the superpowers as they carved up the post-war world and the socialism that was expected to usher in a "new civilization", to cite Beatrice and Sidney Webb on the infant Soviet Union. The pragmatic rationale for these philosophical positions was that Moscow provided India with the political, military and economic support that Washington refused both during and after the war. Even the peace and friendship treaty that Indira Gandhi signed with the Soviets in 1971 was forced on her by Richard M. Nixon's famous "tilt" towards Pakistan and Henry Kissinger's infamous collusion with China — both Cold War tactics — in the run-up to the Bangladesh war.

Like the astute Narasimha Rao who claimed to be following "the Nehru line" even as he gave the first prime minister's fabian socialism a deep burial, Dr Manmohan Singh cannot afford to altogether repudiate the past. His ruling United Progressive Alliance (UPA) coalition, led by the Congress Party, depends on too many "argumentative" Indians. Some are in his own ranks. Some lead allied parties like Tamil Nadu's ruling Dravida Munnetra Kazhagam which holds the UPA's disinvestment programme to ransom. So do some sixty-two communist parliamentarians whose following in the country includes a chunk of the thirty million workers in the organized sector. Complaining that the Left's ideological mindset and suspicion of capital, especially from the United States, thwarts bold measures to attract investors and improve productivity, the government is trying to demonstrate that free market economics is a more effective instrument of social equity than socialism. "More jobs and higher incomes pave the way for distributional justice," says Finance Minister Palaniappan Chidambaram. "Without growth, we can only distribute the burden of poverty and, more often than not, a disproportionate share falls on those who are already poor."[13]

The end of history has not necessarily meant the end of all Cold War equations. If the United States remains Pakistan's sponsor, the Soviet Union's Russian successor is a major supplier of armaments to India. Unlike the Americans, Russia supports India's claim to full membership of the United Nations Security Council. Since Russia is also China's principal source of missiles and fighters, it is seen as a potential balancing factor in the Asian equation. Therefore, after some initial hesitation probably on account of the likely American reaction, India responded positively to Moscow's proposal for a "strategic alliance" of India, China and Russia, which led to the foreign ministers of the three countries holding their first trilateral conference in Vladivostok in June 2005. It is also largely due to Russia that India enjoys observer status in the six-nation Shanghai Cooperation Organization (SCO) whose summit declaration in Kazakhstan in early July 2005 called for a reduced American military presence in Central Asia. A Russian commentator attributed Manmohan Singh's absence from the June 2006 SCO summit to American reservations about a group that it "views as a counterbalance to its influence in the region" as well as to Iran's inclusion.[14]

So the Cold War lives on. But a shrunken Russia, beset with economic and other difficulties and trying to refurbish its Asian identity, is in no position to embark on an ambitious twenty-first century version of Rudyard Kipling's Great Game. It lacks the awesome image of the empires of either the Czars or Stalin. That makes it a more acceptable power in Asia. Its mediation is less contentious than America's would be. Its aims in respect of China and the United States, best summed up by the phrase "conditional cooperation", are not unlike India's. What restrains the New Delhi-Moscow relationship from further expansion is Russia's limited capacity to provide material help.

ASIA

The Vladivostok alliance and the SCO are not the only Asian groupings in which India is involved. A Japanese proposal for Japan-India-China cooperation is committed to creating "a new Asian era" which Japan and India define as an "arc of advantage and prosperity". And China's Prime Minister Wen Jiabao proposed a "strategic partnership" when he visited India in April 2005. India, in turn, has geared its diplomacy to bringing together Asia's principal producers and consumers of oil and gas in an association that spans the continent, from the Middle East to China.

These moves reflect Narasimha Rao's attempt to break with colonial conditioning with a "Look East" policy that tried to revive the surge of Asian sentiment that emerged during World War II. Successor governments are building on that foundation. Welcoming Prime Minister Junichiro

Koizumi in April 2005, Manmohan Singh recalled that India had refused to attend the San Francisco Peace Conference that the Allies organized in September 1951, waived its claim to reparation for wartime damage and signed a separate peace treaty that did not mention Japan's defeat. He might also have mentioned Justice Radha Benode Pal, the only Indian among the eleven judges at the Tokyo War Crimes Trial (the International Military Tribunal for the Far East), who was not allowed to read out or publish the 1,235-word dissenting verdict in which he dismissed the conviction of twenty-five Japanese defendants as "victor's justice" and drew attention to Allied perpetration of the horrors of Hiroshima and Nagasaki.[15]

Pearl Harbour was an Asian triumph like Admiral Togo's sinking of the Russian fleet in 1905, which excited the adolescent Nehru.[16] Like Bose and Aung San, who commanded the Burmese Independence Army in one stage of a short but meteoric career that was full of twists and turns, radical young Indians also welcomed the Japanese advance. Sympathy for China's suffering at Japan's hands, reinforced when Chiang Kai-shek and his wife visited India and upheld the independence demand, did not affect pride in Japan.

Indian independence set the precedent for Asia's liberation, as Mahatma Gandhi had predicted to Franklin Delano Roosevelt in 1942.[17] Having set one ball rolling, India picked up another by organizing the first Asian Relations Conference in New Delhi within two years of the war ending. A smaller gathering of thirteen nations in January 1949 discussed how to save Indonesia from the clutches of the Dutch who were trying to return with Anglo-American backing. The Bandung conference, in which Nehru played a leading part with Indonesia's Sukarno and Egypt's Gamal Abdul Nasser, followed in 1955.

The civilizational impetus for this interest goes back thousands of years to *Suvarnabhumi* [Golden Land], as Sanskrit chroniclers called Southeast Asia, and to the Sri Vijaya and Majapahit empires of "Further India". It has undoubtedly been reinforced by what a Singaporean analyst calls the "steady accretion in China's economic, diplomatic and military power".[18] Mao Zedong's 1950 "liberation" of Tibet not only destroyed a traditional buffer state but also converted a monastic backwater into a military base for power projection into South Asia, bringing Asia's two most populous nations, now both nuclear-armed, face to face across the Himalayas.

Historically, India needs no reminding that "the logical end result of an apparent Chinese minuet — 'three steps forwards, and two steps back'

— is one of steady and inexorable advance".[19] Though its reports were brushed under the carpet by successive United States administrations, the American Central Intelligence Agency holds that Chinese help for Pakistan's nuclear and missile programme is designed to keep India bogged down in sub-continental wrangling. Commentators like Shourie warn of Chinese activities in neighbouring countries and the surrounding seas. But in spite of uncertainty about China's long-term aims, the UPA government refuses to be stampeded into a paranoiac response. Claiming that the first principles to resolve the dispute that climaxed in the 1962 war have been established, and encouraged by the increasing volume of Sino-Indian trade, Manmohan Singh sees no reason why the two Asian giants should not co-exist in harmony. Following several economic and political fence-building moves, China's Wen reiterated earlier suggestions of cooperation in information technology. The policy of engaging China goes hand-in-hand with India's increasing involvement in ASEAN and an expanded East Asian Community while studiously avoiding any arrangement that might appear to be designed to contain the region's most formidable player. Two potentially significant events occurred almost simultaneously: the Himalayan trade road through Nathu-la (4,390 metres) between India and Tibet was opened after forty-four years of closure as the first Chinese train made its epochal journey across Tibet. "We are not ganging up against China," Manmohan Singh assured India's parliament in August 2005.

UNITED STATES

India and the United States are rediscovering each other. According to one commentator, World War II provided "the first instance when the two nations recognized themselves as 'natural allies'".[20] Another claims that Roosevelt's moral support for independence during those years "considerably helped in laying firm foundations for solid relations".[21] Neither fully explains the complexities of a relationship that is influenced by India's historic memories of the British company that came to trade and stayed to rule, and is well captured by the Vietnam war slogan, "Yankee go home but take me with you". Indians were disappointed at the American refusal during the war to match New Deal and Atlantic Charter rhetoric with deeds because a "Britain fighting for her life" could not be let down.[22] Relations after the war were more often down than up.

American thinking has changed drastically since Nehru's dream of an Asian Century drove Ambassador Loy W. Henderson to accuse him, already suspect on account of non-alignment, of trying to purge Asia of "all Western military power and ... Western political and economic pressures" in order to "lead a global union of coloured peoples".[23] George W. Bush speaks of a "strategic partnership" to help "India achieve its vision of being a world power in the 21st century".[24] Vajpayee called the two countries "natural allies". Both sides acknowledge that shared democracy and the need for investment, energy, technology and trade and to forge a common front against global terrorism should make for a strong alliance. But the suspicions that flared up during World War II die hard.

The UPA's domestic critics fear that American plans to outsource regional duties such as peacekeeping, disaster relief, the protection of shipping and communication lines and operations to spread democracy might drag India into a surrogate role in the lone superpower's imperial adventures. The returns are not thought to be adequate to the labour and risk. Even China — the unforgiven American Cold War ally — enjoys greater access to advanced American dual-use technology. Secretary of State Condoleeza Rice's reiteration that the sale of F-16s to Pakistan, with no limits on either number or configuration, is necessary to maintain South Asia's "military balance", further confirmed that the world might be unipolar but the Cold War continues in South Asia. Whatever the inspiration, the American policy of strengthening Pakistan's offensive capabilities serves exactly the same purpose as China's by tying India down in a debilitating regional confrontation.

PAKISTAN

One-fifth India's size, with one-seventh the population and a gross domestic product that is one-ninth India's, Pakistan punches absurdly above its weight. It is important only as the spearhead of American strategy ever since the end of the war when the United States saw Pakistan as the free world's bastion against world Communism. The reasons that the Americans give for the alliance have shifted many times since then. Pakistan was going to be the base for operations against the Soviet Union that could also be used to control Middle East oil.[25] It was needed as a diplomatic conduit to China, to funnel money and arms to the Afghan mujahedeen and then to destroy the Taliban. Now, it is indispensable in the fight to vanquish al-Qaeda and Islamist terrorism and spread liberal democracy throughout the Muslim *ummah*. The withdrawal of American protection, it is also argued, would lead to Pakistan's disintegration. Indian concern has remained the same through all these twists and turns of foreign policy logic, focusing on three points. First, Pakistan's rulers have always made it clear that irrespective of American targets, their quarrel is with India. Second, though the United States says it arms Pakistan only against a third party who is their common adversary, American weapons are always deployed in wars with India. Third, the joint American-Pakistani hunt for terrorists on Pakistan's western border is absent on Pakistan's eastern frontier where the infrastructure of terrorist incursions into Kashmir remains in place. Bush was given a list of these nurseries of terror — training camps — in Pakistani-controlled Kashmir. Defence Minister Pranab Mukherjee told his hosts when he signed the New Defence Framework in Washington that the proof of Pakistan's commitment to ending cross-border terrorism would lie in undertaking joint operations with India along the border between the two countries.

This is not the place to repeat the tired details of a dispute that began with the invasion of the then sovereign state of Jammu and Kashmir in 1947. But as a British historian whom Indians do not regard as being well disposed notes, Kashmir "has been the dominant force in shaping the foreign policies of both India and Pakistan; and there can be no doubt that it has infected every aspect of the internal political life of the two nations (to which, in 1971, was added a third, Bangladesh)."[26] A footnote to the Cold War compulsions that enlarged a relatively minor territorial dispute into a major international issue says something about how personal predilections can influence great power policies. Nehru's charge that instead of addressing India's complaint of aggression, the United Nations "treat(ed) the thief and the owner of the house as equals" was really a comment on Josef Korbel, the Czech chairman of the United Nations Commission for India and Pakistan (UNCIP) who was then planning to settle down in the United States. Czechoslovakia's Benes regime, which had nominated him to the United Nations, had since been ousted and Korbel faced imminent deportation and short shrift at the hands of his country's new communist rulers. His daughter, Madeleine Albright, President Bill Clinton's secretary of state, records that while he was mediating in Kashmir, Korbel's "main interest was to arrange for political asylum" and that the "timing was critical, because he needed asylum before he lost his Czechoslovak diplomatic status and was forced to leave the United States".[27] It seems logical to assume that as UNCIP chairman, Korbel was unlikely to risk his and his family's future by obstructing the Truman administration in South Asia.

Pakistan's "major non-NATO ally" title is no empty honour. It entails a special security relationship with the United States and significant benefits in foreign aid and defence cooperation. These include priority delivery of defence material, the right to buy depleted uranium anti-tank rounds, stockpile American military hardware, participate in defence research and development programmes and obtain American government guarantees for loans to purchase arms. These privileges ignore the black-market in nuclear material and technology that the father of Pakistan's atomic programme, Abdul Qadeer Khan, operated. Nor are they affected by the finding of the official American commission probing the Twin Tower strikes that Pakistan colluded with Osama bin Laden, whose camps trained and equipped terrorists for Kashmir, and retained its links with the Taliban for as long as it could.

True, Pakistan is unlikely to be granted the nuclear benefits enshrined in India's recent agreements with the United States. But Bush's patronage has elevated the military dictator of a theocratic state who came to power through a coup that toppled the elected prime minister, to the status of leader of an aggressive campaign to spread the fruits of liberal democracy in Asia.

CONCLUSION

World War II might have had a truly bizarre effect if Roosevelt had had his way at a time when the Allies were at their wits' end. A British diplomat reported from Washington in August 1942 that "amongst other thoughts thrown out by the president" was a plan to try to cross-breed and develop "an Indo-Asian or Eurasian or (better) Euroindasian race" as a counterbalance to the Japanese whom he regarded as "nefarious". Apparently, Roosevelt ordered a scientist to study "the effect of racial crossing" at the Smithsonian Institution.[28]

Mercifully, the world was spared an idea that was more than just hare-brained: it was sinister. Of the war's persistent legacies, the most obviously vexing is India's uncertain relations with a United States that still cannot bring itself to apply in South Asia the geographic logic that determines the power equation in the Americas. Questions regarding China, Pakistan or SAARC are part of the bigger prospect of continental differences being subsumed one day in an Asia that can balance Western domination of global affairs. The American foot in the door of sub-continental politics, lingering relic of the Cold War, helps to prolong that domination and frustrate the prospect of a Concert of Asia that World War II made possible. When it will be achieved depends on many factors, not all of which are within India's competence. But two principal developments are necessary before the lingering after-effects of the war can be exorcized and Indo-American relations set on an even keel. First, the UPA government must make a determined effort not to be hamstrung by the "limited mandate" of which Manmohan Singh complains and take the necessary steps to realize the country's economic potential so that prosperity is not confined to certain pockets. No nation with 300 million people still languishing below the poverty line can aspire to be a great power. Second, the United States must readjust its global objectives and allow South Asia to find its natural balance.

Ultimately, both are wishes rather than certainties. To adapt Zhou Enlai's famous comment on the French Revolution, it is far too soon to come to definitive conclusions about the war's final impact.

NOTES

1. Philip Ziegler, *Mountbatten: The official biography* (London: Collins, 1985).
2. Robert D. Blackwill, "A New Deal for New Delhi", *Wall Street Journal*, 21 March 2005.
3. Stanley Wolpert, *Jinnah of Pakistan* (New Delhi: OUP, 1985).
4. Arun Shourie, *Will the Iron fence save a Tree Hollowed by Termites?* (New Delhi: ASA Rupa, 2005).
5. Michael Backman and Charlotte Butler, *Big in Asia: 25 Strategies for Business Success* (New York: Palgrave Macmillan, 2002).
6. Shankar Acharya, Rediff.com, 27 September 2005.
7. John Elliott, *India and China — Asia's New Giants: Stepping Stones to Prosperity* (New Delhi: Rajiv Gandhi Institute for Contemporary Studies, 1995).
8. Peter Townsend, *The Last Emperor: Decline and Fall of the British Empire* (London: Weidenfeld and Nicolson, 1975).
9. Lawrence James, *The Rise and Fall of the British Empire* (London: Abacus, 1995).
10. Sunanda K. Datta-Ray, *Waiting for America: India and the US in the New Millennium* (New Delhi: HarperCollins, 2003).
11. Sarvepalli Gopal, *Jawaharlal Nehru: A Biography, Volume One: 1889–1947* (New Delhi: Oxford, 1975).
12. Dennis Kux, *Estranged Democracies: India and the United States 1941–1991* (New Delhi: Sage, 1993).
13. P. Chidambaram, *Worldly Wise: Globalization Makes India Richer. It must be Made to Make Every Indian Richer too, Hindustan Times*, Calcutta, 24 June 2005).
14. Dmitry Kosyrev, *Reasons to be in China, The Pioneer*, New Delhi, 15 June 2006.

15. Shreyas Jayasimha, *Victor's Justice, Crime of Silence and the Burden of Listening: Judgement of the Tokyo Tribunal 1948*, An electronic journal, 2001.
16. Jawaharlal Nehru, *Autobiography* (London: Bodley Head, 1949).
17. James Morris, *Farewell the Trumpets* (London: Penguin, 1979).
18. Derek da Cunha, "Southeast Asian Perception of China's Future Security Role in its 'background' " in Jonathan D. Pollcok and Richard H. Yang, *In China's Shadow, Regional Perspectives on Chinese Foreign Policy and Military Development* (RAND, 1998).
19. Da Cunha, ibid.
20. Dinyar Patel, "American Involvement in Cripps Mission", *Span*, March/April 2005.
21. United States Information Service, *How Indian Freedom Movement Started in U.S.*, Calcutta, 29 July 1965.
22. Cordell Hull, *Memoirs of Cordell Hull* (New York: Macmillan, 1948).
23. United States State Department, *Foreign Relations of the United States, Volume VI, Part 2, Asia and the Pacific*, Washington D.C., 1951.
24. Laurinda Keys Long, "The Dynamic U.S.-India Relationship", *Span*, New Delhi, March/April 2005.
25. United States State Department, *Foreign Relations of the United States, Volume VI, The Near East, South Asia and Africa*, Washington D.C., 1949.
26. Alastair Lamb, *Kashmir: A Disputed Legacy 1846–1990* (London: Roxford, 1991).
27. Madeleine Albright with Bill Woodward, *Madam Secretary: A Memoir* (London: Macmillan, 2003).
28. Patrick French, *Liberty or Death* (London: HarperCollins, 1997).

Index

www.ingramcontent.com/pod-product-compliance
Lightning Source LLC
Chambersburg PA
CBHW020811100426
42814CB00001B/21

9 789812 304681